4

Diagnoses and
Prescriptions

STYLe

Edited by
Stoddard Malarkey
University of Oregon

Diagnoses and Prescriptions

HARCOURT BRACE JOVANOVICH, INC.
NEW YORK · CHICAGO · SAN FRANCISCO · ATLANTA

ISBN: 0-15-584672-8

Library of Congress Catalog Card Number: 77–174518

Printed in the United States of America

ACKNOWLEDGMENTS

Headnotes for Parts One and Three are from *Four Quartets* by
T. S. Eliot, copyright, 1942, 1943, by T. S. Eliot; renewed, 1970
by Esme Valerie Eliot. Reprinted with permission of Harcourt
Brace Jovanovich, Inc., and Faber & Faber, Ltd.

Headnote for Part Two is from *The Autobiography of Malcolm X*
with the assistance of Alex Haley. Copyright © 1964 by Alex
Haley and Malcolm X. Copyright © 1965 by Alex Haley and
Betty Shabazz. Reprinted with permission of Grove Press, Inc.

Illustrated by Tom Durfee.

CONTENTS

Introduction
to the
Student

MENS SANA IN CORPORE SANO

The Latin phrase above — "a sound mind in a sound body"—comes from the Roman poet Juvenal. Although he wasn't talking about writing, the phrase is a convenient capsule metaphor for the main idea underlying this book, a metaphor that is picked up and developed in the title and part headings. Taken literally, the phrase implies a basic reciprocity between mind and body: if one is sound, it reinforces the other. Taken metaphorically, it implies a basic reciprocity between thought and writing: if one is sound, it reinforces the other. Sound writing and sound thinking go hand in hand.

Further, the phrase recognizes the two levels of existence on which we all operate, the abstract and intangible level of thought and the specific and tangible level of physical reality. Moving again to metaphor, we can say that thought and writing are the same as mind and body, that writing is the embodiment of thought on the tangible level of physical reality. Keeping the terms of the metaphor, it is possible to offer a definition of style as it relates to writing. If writing is the embodiment of thought, then style is the conscious exercise of that body. Style is the *sound body* of thought, with all that that implies—exercise, control, grace, coordination, and all the rest.

As long as we are dealing with definitions of style, let's look at a couple more. The first is that of a Frenchman, Buffon, who said that "the style is the man himself." The other is that of Jonathan Swift, who claimed that "proper words in proper places makes the trüe definition of style." If you will reflect for a moment you will notice that there is quite a difference in emphasis between the two definitions. The first emphasizes the sound mind, and says in effect, "If you think right, you'll write right." Buffon is saying that the "man himself"—what he thinks and feels and is—will somehow be reflected in the way he writes. This idea has the defects of any oversimplification, for it implies that a good style is the automatic by-product of sound thought.

On the other end of the scale is Swift, who emphasizes the sound body, and says in effect, "If you write right, you've probably thought right." Swift is simply turning Buffon around, and is saying that the "proper words in the proper places" somehow appear on the page if a man has already done the right thinking. Also an oversimplification for obvious reasons.

Most discussions of style tend to emphasize one or the other end of the scale. For example, here is H. L. Mencken, a cynical member of the Buffon school, from the essay in this book on page 146: "They [students] write badly simply because they cannot think clearly. They cannot think clearly because they lack the brains." In other words, if the style is the man, and the man is a dolt, then the writing will be doltish. For a spokesman of the Swiftian persuasion, let us turn to George Orwell, from the essay on page 122: "Modern English, especially written English, is full of bad habits . . . If one gets rid of these bad habits one can think more clearly." In other words, if you can learn to stop writing like a dolt, then you will find it easier to stop thinking like a dolt. Of course no theorist of style completely ignores one side for the other, but most of them exhibit a leaning in one or another direction. So does this book.

It is safe to say that the majority of the essay collections used as textbooks in writing classes derive from the Buffonite school. They generally contain essays that are supposed to catch the attention of the student, engage his interest, stimulate his thinking, and elicit a response which emerges as a written theme. The emphasis tends to be on ideas, on stimulating thinking, and giving the student something to write about. While considerations of style are not ignored, either by the text or the instructor, they tend to be slighted in favor of the content of whatever essays appear in the text. The general effect of all this is to give the sound mind more attention, and hope that somehow the body will follow along.

This book leans in the other direction. It assumes—perhaps rashly, if Mencken is right—that you have a sound mind, or at least a potentially sound mind. In all but the worst papers in the average writing class, some sort of thought process can be observed. But those thought processes will seldom develop into vigorous and lucid written expressions of a related sequence of ideas partly because the body of thought—the style—is deformed, diseased, and disabled. You have experienced this crippling debility, and have described the symptoms of a diseased style every time you have said, "I know what I think, but I just can't express it." The standard answer, deriving from Buffon, is, "Nonsense. If you really knew what you thought, you would be able to express it clearly." And'there is some truth in this response. You will probably find as you practice writing that the ideas you thought so clear were really not, and that faulty expression is due to some extent to faulty thinking. But more often than people like Mencken are willing to allow, the thought is potentially sound enough but the style, the ability to write simply and clearly, is crippled. You can't write clearly because you don't know how — and you don't think it matters.

The selections in this book attempt to correct that deficiency. They assume the basic reciprocity between mind and body — between thought and style. But they are drawn mainly from Swift's and Orwell's end of the scale, rather than from Buffon's and Mencken's. Some of them describe and illustrate the more common diseases of style, so that you will learn to recognize them in your own writing. Some of them demonstrate and try to convince you of the very real importance of good writing in the real world. And some of them offer you prescriptions for developing a healthy style.

The way we think, the relationship between thought and language, the relationship between thought and writing, semantics, stylistics — these are all extremely complex areas of study. The selections included here are but the beginning of a scratch of the surface. None of them is technical or scholarly; none is addressed to a professional audience of scholars or rhetoricians. But they should serve as an introduction to some of the questions of style. And, if thoughtfully absorbed, they should help you achieve a goal that is no less desirable or relevant for being traditional: the ability to write clear, rational — perhaps, occasionally, eloquent — standard English prose.

One

THE DISEASE DESCRIBED:
SOME CAUSES
AND SOME SYMPTOMS

The chances are you don't write very well. Most people don't, especially those who are just beginning. The essays in this section touch on some of the most common ills of writing, with occasional speculation on the source of the infection. You will undoubtedly recognize in this catalog of horrors some that occur in your own writing.

This is called teaching by bad example. The reasoning behind this method is the same as that used to justify public executions. Let these horrors act on you as a deterrent.

Willard Thorp

The Well of English, Now Defiled

In this opening essay, Professor Thorp provides an overview of our topic. He gives several samples of what he calls "No-English," the language in which many of his students write. He traces the causes of this disease to the decay of good writing in several influential sections of our society. Some of these sections are examined in more detail in later essays. In his final paragraphs he anticipates the main point of a later chapter of this book, pointing out that words chosen with care and used with force can have a real effect in the practical world.

When Edmund Spenser paused for a moment in the fourth book of his Faerie Queen to refer reverently to an earlier poet, Geoffrey Chaucer, as that "well of English undefiled," he was implying, I gather, that the English of his own day had become poisoned with ink-horn terms and Italianate expressions. This allusion ought to comfort me as I begin my discussion of the evidences of defilement in English prose today, and more particularly as English teachers see them in the writing we receive from our students. But I am not much comforted, because Spenser and fifty other influential writers of Elizabethan England were busy removing the poison from the well. I am not sure we can again accomplish this kind of sanitary engineering. By 1958 the incidence of poison in the well may have passed the safety mark.

I have been red-pencilling student papers for a good many years and I ought by now to have become resigned or cynical. But I am not, and the reason for my present concern is a sinister change in the kind of writing we have lately been getting from our students. It used to be that we could do our duty and even bring about reforms by sprinkling in the margins of themes those cabalistic signs "coh." (for coherence), "sp." (for spelling), and "gr." (for grammar). But these traditional correctives will no longer serve. We are now too often presented with a kind of prose—if that is the name for it—which is inviolable. A red-pencil used against it becomes as impotent as a sword in a folk-tale which has had a spell put on it. Sometimes this prose resembles remotely a bad translation from a foreign language. Sometimes it suggests that the writer has squeezed together under pressure the jagged ends of several assorted ideas. The only name I have for this monstrosity is NO-ENGLISH.

The writer of No-English is unconscious of the fact that his pages resemble nothing else under the sun. If you say to him, "This is not English. You must tear this up and try again," he will answer plaintively: "But you know what I *mean*, don't you?" He will be indignant if you reply, "I can *guess*, but only because I know what you are supposed to mean."

Let me read you a few choice samples of No-English. These come, alas, from examination papers in my sophomore course in American literature. I shall save the honor of the writers, though not of Princeton, by withholding the names of the perpetrators.

A change from the optimastic view of the individual man as put forth in trancendentic philosophy to the pessimistic view of man kind frought with invalide morals living a superficial life with no direction such as T. S. Eliot flitting bug-eyed from Antwerp to Brussels to London.

He was a man who had dispared to the nature of man and although he had these tendencies of subjection he soon gained aspirations and broke away from the school of disparants and strove on his own beliefs.

When Twain was writing Huckleberry Finn *he decided to implement the voyage as a cohesive catalyst. Twain used a general local. Faulkner has a restrictive local, and Thoreau wrote for everybody in the universal.*

Huck Finn sets out in a cimilar direction, away from society. He also floats on the sea of life and has periodic relations with the surrounding society. The Grangerfords put Huck up, for instance, and promptly acquaint him with social disorganization and bitterness.

The American ideal seemed to hang void in the twenties, a shameful thing because Americans must forage ahead. Eliot was not the gung-ho American as Whitman. Whitman was one of the best examples of this "nature into thought" angle.

To one who cares about the well-forged instrument by which those who use English communicate with one another there are, I submit, some very alarming symptoms of decay and defilement in these passages of No-English. Listened to with half an ear they sound impressive, authoritative, and even powerful. Though their authors were composing complete nonsense, they put down these jumbled words with the self-assurance of an advertising copy-writer or an editor of *Time*.

Why is the tide of No-English flooding in with such power that we cannot stand against it? I think I know some of the reasons.

First in importance is the influence of officialese. This is the age of the official statement from government, of communiqués, of press releases from public relations officers. All writing of this sort must sound impressive and authoritative, for it is composed to be believed in without dissent.

I have here a prime example of officialese which originated, I am happy to say, not in America but England.

It will be apparent that the draining away of senior experienced men will be of such proportions for some years to come as to constitute a serious factor to be contended with in providing for the adequate staffing of State departments. The difficulty in this respect is aggravated by the expansion of governmental activities which has been a feature during the last few years, and which seems likely to persist for some time. This expansion has already imposed considerable strain upon the personnel of the public service and; coupled with the progressive wastage in the ranks of the senior officers to which reference has been made, tends to produce conditions which, on occasion, border on the acute. The Commission is giving its particular attention to the problems contained in and engendered by the circumstances already present and those which it is anticipated will develop in future.

These fourteen lines of "twisted, pretentious, long-winded and down-at-heel" officialese, can, with a little labor, be shortened to five lines.[1] You can always condense officialese by about two-thirds. This is one of the ways you recognize it.

So many senior and experienced officers will leave the service during the next few years that State departments will be short of staff; and the difficulties this will cause will be aggravated if, as seems possible, the State's activities continue to expand. The Commission is giving this matter attention.

My long-suffering ear tells me that my students are more often than not trying to write officialese. And why not? This is the way very important people in our society "reveal" or "announce" what are supposed to be matters of life-or-death. This is the interminable voice of the age—or one of its voices.

The evident desire of the writers of No-English to pack power into their prose I think I can trace to another defiler of the well of English. Almost every magazine an undergraduate picks up is likely to be written in a hot-rod style which bursts with energy in every sentence. Authors who wish to sell their wares to *Time, Look,* and *Life* must write in a 500-horse-power style. And their editors, as well, seem to live in constant fear that if they take the foot off the accelerator the reader will drop off to sleep between sentences or, bored and indifferent, turn on the television set.

---

[1] This example of officialese and the condensation of it I have borrowed from Eric Partridge and John W. Clark, *British and American English Since 1900* (1951), p. 44.

Two qualities of *Time*-style exert an especially subtle influence. The supercharged *Time*- or *Newsweek*-sentence teaches the student that his prose should never be quiet. It must always shock with the hot-foot. You cannot imagine, for instance, *Time*'s printing one of the calm and witty essays of E. B. White. It would be as much out of place as a preacher at a jitterbug contest.

The souped-up article also teaches the student-reader that certain words are absolute as definitions of attributes of mind and body. No variations or gradations are possible and so none need be sought. Take, for instance, one of *Time*'s pet words—paunchy. As one whose paunchiness is increasingly distressful to him, I resent this word's invariability. There was a time when I had a little professorial pot; later I was "stout" (as we used to say, in a politer era); then I became, I suppose, definitely pot-bellied. But in *Time*'s view I have always been paunchy and there is no need for other words to describe my long struggle with the flesh, my triumphs and my eventual defeat. That is what I have been—paunchy—from graduation day until this moment. Consider another of *Time*'s favorites—bug-eyed. Gone are the possibilities of playing with such fine old words as startled, afeared, aghast, agog, spell-bound, open-mouthed, thunder-struck. And neither is there any way of knowing whether the man affected with bug-eyedness inherited his condition or is a hyperthyroid case or is exophthalmic. He is just bug-eyed—that's all.

Much more to be feared than the poison-vials of officialese or of *Time* is the expensively distilled poison of advertising-style. Students cannot escape it—nor can we. Though we have our mental blinders in place, as we try to read down the river of text in the middle of the page, a glowing specimen of cheesecake lures us to the left-hand column and the depilatory she is applying, all unconcerned to be in so public a place with almost no clothes on. The poet Karl Shapiro has characterized the alarming magnetic pull of advertising in five lines of his satiric poem "Drug Store."

> *And every nook and cranny of the flesh*
> *Is spoken to by packages with wiles.*
> *"Buy me, buy me," they whimper and cajole;*
> *The hectic range of lipsticks pouts,*
> *Revealing the wicked and the simple mouth.*

Everywhere we go we are assaulted by the ad-man. We cannot escape him by taking to the highways or diving into a subway station. He pursues us even in our dreams. His latest horror—subliminal-perception on TV—has just come upon us.

One of the most insidious things about advertising-style is that it burns up the language at a furious rate because there is so much oxygen in it. The new Plymouth, the ad-man says, is *newest, most modern* of the low-price three. Also *biggest*. Its Power-Flow 117 motor is *brilliant*. Its Power-Flite no-clutch transmission is the *finest made*. The next ad-writer for Plymouth is going to find ashes all over his cubicle. What can he dig out of the dictionary which is newer than "newest," bigger than "biggest," higher than "highest horsepower in the field"?

In the next place, consider the consumption of debased advertising metaphors which goes on in one issue of *Look* or *Life*. We note that "a new day has dawned for the car owners of America." Can this startling statement mean that the atomic-powered automobile has arrived? Not at all. Firestone is merely marketing a new tire. And how are we to "open the door on tomorrow"? By such exciting experiences as getting married? having a baby? a plane trip to Europe? Certainly not. That "door on tomorrow" will open if you make an itsy-bitsy deposit on a Dodge. And what is this on the next page?—"Like all great ideas, this one's slightly marvelous—yet so simple." Can it be we are about to hear something of the order of magnitude of the second law of thermodynamics or Leibnitz's theory of the monads? We are not so easily fooled. We know instinctively, after years of indoctrination, that this great idea will prove, alas, to be only Sta-Flat's creation of a new girdle, with extra strength where you need it most ("midriff, waist, tummy").

I hope I shall live long enough to watch the ad-men run out of metaphors. It will be a happy day. Writers of strong but simple prose may then have a chance again. When there are no more metaphors for

> *Kleenex, Kotex, Gleem, and Lux,*
> *Schick and Mosco, and Coldeen,*
> *Zemo, Scripto, Schlitz, and Duz,*
> *Cutex, Crispies and Bactine*

the ad-men will have to go back to their old-fashioned unmetaphorical, harmless style, still used, I'm happy to report, by Sergeant's *Sure-Shot* Capsules: "Stop Worms! Don't neglect worms in your dog!. . .75¢ at any pet counter."

There is another defiler of modern prose whose poisoning is carried out under the cover of darkness. Consequently I should find it difficult to identify him in a police-court line-up. Professor John Clark of the University of Minnesota declares that the culprit is the second-rate newspaper reporter. I am not sure he is the chief offender, but I am certain that some person or persons unknown have put over on us lately a most peculiar, very limited vocabulary which serves, unfortunately, to cover every situation in modern life. In listing these words—about forty in number—Professor Clark notes that "if an historical novelist of fifty or a hundred years from now should wish to give his readers a fairly realistic illusion of the flavor of everyday American English of the 1950's, he could adopt no more economical means than to sprinkle his dialogue with these expressions."

To prove to myself how constantly these pesky words (and a few others) turn up and how unthinkingly we ourselves resort to them, I tried to see if I could use every one of them in a little descriptive scene from campus life. I can report that it took me less than ten minutes to write this vivid and highly dramatic scene, so easily did these words fall into place. I read it to you, not with pride but with shame of authorship.

> *A teen-ager dropped into my office today, much worried about his inferiority complex and anxious to adjust. He seemed to think I was a sincere-type professor and had some know-how in interpersonal relations. He said there was a campus-inspired rumor that I am good at human engineering and so thought he'd contact me and get a few constructive angles. First I tried to fit him into some frame of reference and then I processed him by screening him with some questions, and so got the overall picture. (I discovered, by the way, that his mother is a low-grade homemaker.) I then briefed him on the need for grasping our most unique set-up here and seeing how we are geared for modern living. Next I made him the proposition that he be less negative, more relaxed, and mix with a few of the outstanding youth at the top-flight level of our student body. He would be sure, I said, to find them like-minded, percentagewise. When we finished off, he thanked me for our little stream-lined get-together and said he would try to integrate better. I found the experience so educational that I think I'll author an article about it after I've researched the matter further.*

I hope my little parable horrifies you as much as it does me. I shall try to restrain my disgust while I point out a number of things to be learned from it.

Some of the offensive expressions are hand-me-downs from pseudo-scientific writing; some derive from the writing of sociologists and psychologists; some emanate from the sales-conference and the business convention. Several reveal the codified anxieties of modern life, while others are the slogans of "positive thinking" which are supposed to cure these anxieties. Because these expressions make up an important part of the vocabulary of his time, the modern student is compelled to use them. But what appalls one most is that these elected words of ours—as is always the case—reveal the preoccupations and the state of mind of the age in which we live. And what they reveal is disturbing. While this fictional professor was having his cozy little stream-lined interview with this hypothetical student, neither of them was a human being—a person, as Shakespeare once said, with hands, organs, dimensions, senses, affections, passions; fed with food, subject to diseases, warmed and cooled with winter and summer. The student was an intelligence test to be taken and scored; the professor was a machine to grind out medians, percentiles, and normal distribution curves.

I come finally to chief defiler of undergraduate writing. And I regret to say we professors are certainly the culprits. And what we are doing we do in all innocence and with the most laudable of motives. This is a serious accusation, and I must justify it or shut up.

There is one predicament in our present kind of collegiate education which, I am convinced, confuses the student who desires to write good English, which may, indeed, lead him to believe that there is no necessity for trying to write in the great tradition of English prose. What I am referring to is the tremendous specialization which the subjects in our curriculum have undergone in this century. Because the fields of learning now share very little common ground, they (and we) no longer possess a common language. The historian cannot understand the equations of the physicist and the physicist cannot understand the new vocabulary developed by the sociologist. The professor of literature who lectures about "levels of meaning," the "texture and tension of poetry," the wonderful "ambiguities" in Melville's prose, and the "personal symbolism" in the poetry of Robert Frost, opens the eyes but not the ears of his colleague in chemistry who had no idea literature was *that* difficult. This impenetrability of our particular subjects to the uninitiated does not worry us—as professors—to any great extent. We go our separate ways, happy in our isolation. We rejoice in our own jargon. We suppose, rightly of course, that our colleagues in other fields understand the strange stuff they deliver from the lecture platform.

But I have begun to notice lately that our better students take an unholy pride in the specialized vocabularies they encounter as they move through their academic day. Suppose we imagine what the impact of specialized subjects and the vocabularies by which they are presented may be on a conscientious sophomore who really wishes to comprehend what his lecturers, hour after hour, are telling him. At 8:30 in his physics class he hears this:

Barrier Design

At atmospheric pressure the mean free path of a molecule is of the order of a ten-thousandth of a millimeter or one tenth of a micron. To insure true "diffusive" flow of the gas, the diameter of the myriad holes in the barrier must be less than one tenth the mean free path. Therefore the barrier material must have almost no holes which are appreciably larger than 0.01 micron (4×10^{-7} inch), but must have billions of holes of this size or smaller. These holes must not enlarge or plug up as the result of direct corrosion or dust coming from corrosion elsewhere in the system. The barrier must be able to withstand a pressure "head" of one atmosphere.

At 9:30 our sophomore is in his place in his music class in Elementary Harmony. His professor, whom the student likes very much because he hopes to be a composer, also, some day, has been talking about triads in minor keys. After the late-comers have got to their seats he begins:

When the dominant and sub-mediant triads (V and V.I) are connected in the minor mode, the voices have to move along certain fixed lines in order to avoid consecutive 5ths and octaves and the augmented 2nd. The leading-tone always ascends to the tonic (or descends from it). Two of the upper voices must move in contrary motion to the bass, and the 3rd is always to be doubled in the triad on the sixth degree, in four-part writing.

Our earnest sophomore has a much-needed coke in the Student Center at 10:30 but at 11:30 he is in the Psychology building, eager to hear Professor Jungfreud talk on "Hedonic Summation." The professor begins:

When two simple stimuli are combined in some total perception, the hedonic tone of the resultant depends upon the sum of the hedonic tones of the two stimuli. We must, however, limit this principle in two ways. (a) It holds only when it can operate without interference by some of the other hedonic laws [I have explained] . (b) It holds only when the relative importances of the different constituents in the sum are determined and taken into account.

After a breather at lunch and fifteen minutes at the pool-table, sopho-more Sandy is back in place at 1:30, listening to the Professor of Religion who is talking today on the relations between mysticism and magic. Here is what Sandy gets down—correctly, believe it or not—in his notebook.

> *To the two dogmas of the "Astral Light" or universal agent and the "power of the will" there is to be added a third: the doctrine of Analogy, or implicit correspondence between appearance and reality, the microcosm of man and the macrocosm of the universe, the seen and the unseen worlds. In this, occultism finds the basis of all its transcendental speculations. Quod superius sicut quod inferius—the first words of that Emerald Table which was once attributed to Hermes Trismegistus himself—is an axiom which must be agree-able to all Platonists.* [2]

Finally, at 2:30, comes Sandy the seeker's last lecture of the day. The course is American Literature and the professor is talking about the pam-phleteers of the American Revolution. He does up Tom Paine neatly in the last ten minutes of the hour and concludes by saying: "The opening para-graph of Paine's great propaganda pamphlet, 'The Crisis,' which put heart into Washington's ragged little army in December, 1776 and turned the fortunes of war in our favor, contains one of the most eloquent passages of prose written in the eighteenth century." He quotes Paine's words:

> *These are the times that try men's souls. The summer soldier and the sunshine patriot will, in this crisis, shrink from the service of their country; but he that stands it now, deserves the love and thanks of man and woman. Tyranny, like hell, is not easily conquered; yet we have this consolation with us, that the harder the conflict, the more glorious the triumph. What we obtain too cheap, we esteem too lightly; it is dearness only that gives every thing its value. Heaven knows how to put a proper price upon its goods; and it would be strange indeed if so celestial an article as FREEDOM should not be highly rated.*

What does Sandy, the sophomore, think, if he can think at all, after the day's barrage of special terms and concepts; and with the weather

---

[2] The knowing reader will recognize these four quotations. These learned professors have cribbed, verbatim, from: Henry DeWolf Smyth, *Atomic Energy for Military Purposes*, Princeton University Press, 1945, p. 177; Arthur Foote and Walter R. Spalding, *Modern Harmony*, Arthur P. Schmidt Co., 1924, p. 41; Baring, Langfeld, and Weld, *Psychology, A Factual Textbook*, John Wiley and Sons, 1935, pp. 376-377; and Evelyn Underhill, *Mysticism*, E. P. Dutton, 1926, p. 191 — Ed.

warm outside and the crack of ball against bat coming in the window? I very much fear that this is what he thinks: "Why does the old boy ask me to listen to such stuff? What does it *tell* me for sure? I've learned important things today, a lot of them. I know how to control dominant and submediant triads in the minor mode. I've got the real poop on Hedonic Summation, and Professor Underhill certainly came through on the doctrine of analogy in mysticism. What did this jerk Tom Paine say back there that's worth listening to now? It's eloquent, is it; so what?"

Who among Sandy's faculty friends will tell him that although it is important to know all he has learned during the day, and that the beginning of wisdom is the certitude of fact, nevertheless there is something beyond fact which is of the utmost importance for him. If, in his pride of knowledge, he refuses to learn how to communicate his knowledge, his ideas and his aspirations, in language that is simple, sensuous, passionate, direct, honest, precise, varied, strong though quiet, *and* eloquent, he will never bring men to his way of thinking. He will have condemned himself to the prison of the public relations officer or the life of the Madison Avenue adman or to the drudgery, without the final reward, of the narrow specialist-scholar. Sandy deserves to win a better fate. He might become a member of the company of those who have moved men to laudable action. He might, through his skill with words, join, in time, John Milton whose *Areopagitica* still defines the rules of free enquiry, and Jonathan Swift who spoke for the oppressed in Ireland and so for enslaved men everywhere, and Thomas Jefferson, and John Stuart Mill, *and* Tom Paine whose words, Sandy does not realize, were more useful to Washington than ten thousand fighting men.

Who among us is ready to speak sternly to Sandy, our pride and our hope, though he still writes No-English.

2

Stuart Chase

Gobbledygook

In his book, The Power of Words, *Mr. Chase popularized a word coined by Congressman Maury Maverick and now generally applied to inflated and obscure writing. It is a landmark in the identification and attack on bad writing. You will remember that Professor Thorp also singled out gobbledygook as one of the sources of infection in student prose. It, and its near relative, jargon, are among the most common defects of beginning writers. They try to hide their lack of ideas behind a cloud of needless words and pseudo-scientific phrases.*

In passing, Mr. Chase touches on a couple of points you will want to keep in mind. The first is the problem of knowing where to draw the line between obscure jargon and necessary technical or scientific terminology. The second is the necessity of keeping clearly in mind who your reader is. Both of these points are dealt with more fully later on.

$\mathcal{S}$aid Franklin Roosevelt, in one of his early presidential speeches: "I see one-third of a nation ill-housed, ill-clad, ill-nourished." Translated into standard bureaucratic prose his statement would read:

> It is evident that a substantial number of persons within the Continental boundaries of the United States have inadequate financial resources with which to purchase the products of agricultural communities and industrial establishments. It would appear that for a considerable segment of the population, possibly as much as 33.333* of the total, there are inadequate housing facilities, and an equally significant proportion is deprived of the proper types of clothing and nutriment.

> *Not carried beyond four places.

This rousing satire on gobbledygook—or talk among the bureaucrats—is adapted from a report prepared by the Federal Security Agency in an attempt to break out of the verbal squirrel cage. "Gobbledygook" was coined by an exasperated Congressman, Maury Maverick of Texas, and means using two, or three, or ten words in the place of one, or using a five-syllable word where a single syllable would suffice. Maverick was censuring the forbidding prose of executive departments in Washington, but the term has now spread to windy and pretentious language in general.

"Gobbledygook" itself is a good example of the way a language grows. There was no word for the event before Maverick's invention; one had to say: "You know, that terrible, involved, polysyllabic language those government people use down in Washington." Now one word takes the place of a dozen.

A British member of Parliament, A. P. Herbert, also exasperated with bureaucratic jargon, translated Nelson's immortal phrase, "England expects every man to do his duty":

> England anticipates that, as regards the current emergency, personnel will face up to the issues, and exercise appropriately the functions allocated to their respective occupational groups.

A New Zealand official made the following report after surveying a plot of ground for an athletic field:

> It is obvious from the difference in elevation with relation to the short depth of the property that the contour is such as to preclude any reasonable developmental potential for active recreation.

Seems the plot was too steep.

An office manager sent this memo to his chief:

> Verbal contact with Mr. Blank regarding the attached notification of promotion has elicited the attached representation intimating that he prefers to decline the assignment.

Seems Mr. Blank didn't want the job.

> A doctor testified at an English trial that one of the parties was suffering from "circumorbital haematoma."

Seems the party had a black eye.

> In August 1952 the U.S. Department of Agriculture put out a pamphlet entitled: "Cultural and Pathogenic Variability in Single-Condial and Hyphaltip Isolates of Hemlin-Thosporium Turcicum Pass."

Seems it was about corn leaf disease.

On reaching the top of the Finsteraarhorn in 1845, M. Dollfus-Ausset, when he got his breath, exclaimed:

> The soul communes in the infinite with those icy peaks which seem to have their roots in the bowels of eternity.

Seems he enjoyed the view.

A government department announced:

> Voucherable expenditures necessary to provide adequate dental treatment required as adjunct to medical treatment being rendered a pay patient in in-patient status may be incurred as required at the expense of the Public Health Service.

Seems you can charge your dentist bill to the Public Health Service. Or can you?

Legal talk. Gobbledygook not only flourishes in government bureaus but grows wild and lush in the law, the universities, and sometimes among the literati. Mr. Micawber was a master of gobbledygook, which he hoped would improve his fortunes. It is almost always found in offices too big for face-to-face talk. Gobbledygook can be defined as squandering words, packing a message with excess baggage and so introducing semantic "noise." Or it can be scrambling words in a message so that meaning does not come through. The directions on cans, bottles, and packages for putting the contents to use are often a good illustration. Gobbledygook must not be confused with double talk, however, for the intentions of the sender are usually honest.

I offer you a round fruit and say, "Have an orange." Not so an expert in legal phraseology, as parodied by editors of *Labor:*

> *I hereby give and convey to you, all and singular, my estate and interests, right, title, claim and advantages of and in said orange, together with all rind, juice, pulp and pits, and all rights and advantages therein . . . anything hereinbefore or hereinafter or in any other deed or deeds, instrument or instruments of whatever nature or kind whatsoever, to the contrary, in any wise, notwithstanding.*

The state of Ohio, after five years of work, has redrafted its legal code in modern English, eliminating 4,500 sections and doubtless a blizzard of "whereases" and "hereinafters." Legal terms of necessity must be closely tied to their referents, but the early solons tried to do this the hard way, by adding synonyms. They hoped to trap the physical event in a net of words, but instead they created a mumbo-jumbo beyond the power of the layman, and even many a lawyer, to translate. Legal talk is studded with tautologies, such as "cease and desist," "give and convey," "irrelevant, incompetent, and immaterial." Furthermore, legal jargon is a dead language; it is not spoken and it is not growing. An official of one of the big insurance companies calls their branch of it "bafflegab." Here is a sample from his collection:

> *One-half to his mother, if living, if not to his father, and one-half to his mother-in-law, if living, if not to his mother, if living, if not to his father. Thereafter payment is to be made in a single sum to his brothers. On the one-half payable to his mother, if living, if not to his father, he does not bring in his mother-in-law as the next payee to receive, although on the one-half to his mother-in-law, he does bring in the mother or father.*

You apply for an insurance policy, pass the tests, and instead of a straightforward "here is your policy," you receive something like this:

> *This policy is issued in consideration of the application therefor, copy of which application is attached hereto and made part hereof, and of the payment for said insurance on the life of the above-named insured.*

Academic talk. The pedagogues may be less repetitious than the lawyers, but many use even longer words. It is a symbol of their calling to prefer Greek and Latin derivatives to Anglo-Saxon. Thus instead of saying: "I like short clear words," many a professor would think it more seemly to say: "I prefer an abbreviated phraseology, distinguished for its lucidity." Your professor is sometimes right, the longer word may carry the meaning better—but not because it is long. Allen Upward in his book *The New Word* warmly advocates Anglo-Saxon English as against what he calls "Mediterranean" English, with its polysyllables built up like a skyscraper.

Professional pedagogy, still alternating between the Middle Ages and modern science, can produce what Henshaw Ward once called the most repellent prose known to man. It takes an iron will to read as much as a page of it. Here is a sample of what is known in some quarters as "pedageese":

> *Realization has grown that the curriculum or the experiences of learners change and improve only as those who are most directly involved examine their goals, improve their understandings and increase their skill in performing the tasks necessary to reach newly defined goals. This places the focus upon teacher, lay citizen and learner as partners in curricular improvement and as the individuals who must change, if there is to be curriculum change.*

I think there is an idea concealed here somewhere. I think it means: "If we are going to change the curriculum, teacher, parent, and student must all help." The reader is invited to get out his semantic decoder and check on my translation. Observe there is no technical language in this gem of pedageese, beyond possibly the word "curriculum." It is just a simple idea heavily oververbalized.

In another kind of academic talk the author may display his learning to conceal a lack of ideas. A bright instructor, for instance, in need of prestige may select a common sense proposition for the subject of a learned monograph—say, "Modern cities are hard to live in" and adorn it with imposing polysyllables: "Urban existence in the perpendicular declivities of megalopolis . . ." et cetera. He coins some new terms to transfix the reader—"mega-decibel" or "strato-cosmopolis"—and works them vigorously. He is careful to add a page or two of differential equations to show the "scatter." And then he publishes, with 147 footnotes and a bibliography to knock your eye out. If the authorities are dozing, it can be worth an associate professorship.

While we are on the campus, however, we must not forget that the technical language of the natural sciences and some terms in the social sciences, forbidding as they may sound to the layman, are quite necessary. Without them, specialists could not communicate what they find. Trouble arises when experts expect the uninitiated to understand the words; when they tell the jury, for instance, that the defendant is suffering from "circumorbital haematoma."

Here are two authentic quotations. Which was written by a distinguished modern author, and which by a patient in a mental hospital? You will find the answer at the end of the chapter.

> *(1) Have just been to supper. Did not knowing what the woodchuck sent me here. How when the blue blue blue on the said anyone can do it that tries. Such is the presidential candidate.*

> *(2) No history of a family to close with those and close. Never shall he be alone to be alone to be alone to be alone to be alone to lend a hand and leave it left and wasted.*

REDUCING THE GOBBLE

As government and business offices grow larger, the need for doing something about gobbledygook increases. Fortunately the biggest office in the world is working hard to reduce it. The Federal Security Agency in Washington, with nearly 100 million clients on its books, began analyzing its communication lines some years ago, with gratifying results. Surveys find trouble in three main areas: correspondence with clients about their social security problems, office memos, official reports.

Clarity and brevity, as well as common humanity, are urgently needed in this vast establishment which deals with disability, old age, and unemployment. The surveys found instead many cases of long-windedness, foggy meanings, clichés, and singsong phrases, and gross neglect of the reader's point of view. Rather than talking to a real person, the writer was talking to himself. "We often write like a man walking on stilts."

Here is a typical case of long-windedness:

Gobbledygook as found: *"We are wondering if sufficient time has passed so that you are in a position to indicate whether favorable action may now be taken on our recommendation for the reclassification of Mrs. Blank, junior clerk-stenographer, CAF 2 , to assistant clerk-stenographer, CAF 3 ?"*

Suggested improvement: *"Have you yet been able to act on our recommendation to reclassify Mrs. Blank?"*

Another case:

Although the Central Efficiency Rating Committee recognizes that there are many desirable changes that could be made in the present efficiency rating system in order to make it more realistic and more workable than it now is, this committee is of the opinion that no further change should be made in the present system during the current year. Because of conditions prevailing throughout the country and the resultant turnover in personnel, and difficulty in administering the Federal programs, further mechanical improvement in the present rating system would require staff retraining and other administrative expense which would seem best withheld until the official termination of hostilities, and until restoration of regular operations.

The F.S.A. invites us to squeeze the gobbledygook out of this statement. Here is my attempt:

The Central Efficiency Rating Committee recognizes that desirable changes could be made in the present system. We believe, however, that no change should be attempted until the war is over.

This cuts the statement from 111 to 30 words, about one-quarter of the original, but perhaps the reader can still do better. What of importance have I left out?

Sometimes in a book which I am reading for information—not for literary pleasure—I run a pencil through the surplus words. Often I can cut a section to half its length with an improvement in clarity. Magazines like the *Reader's Digest* have reduced this process to an art. Are long-windedness and obscurity a cultural lag from the days when writing was reserved for priests and cloistered scholars? The more words and the deeper the mystery, the greater their prestige and the firmer the hold on their jobs. And the better the candidate's chance today to have his doctoral thesis accepted.

The F.S.A. surveys found that a great deal of writing was obscure although not necessarily prolix. Here is a letter sent to more than 100,000 inquirers, a classic example of murky prose. To clarify it, one needs to *add* words, not cut them:

> *In order to be fully insured, an individual must have earned $50 or more in covered employment for as many quarters of coverage as half the calendar quarters elapsing between 1936 and the quarter in which he reaches age 65 or dies, whichever first occurs.*

Probably no one without the technical jargon of the office could translate this: nevertheless, it was sent out to drive clients mad for seven years. One poor fellow wrote back: "I am no longer in covered employment. I have an outside job now."

Many words and phrases in officialese seem to come out automatically, as if from lower centers of the brain. In this standardized prose people never *get jobs*, they "secure employment"; *before* and *after* become "prior to" and "subsequent to"; one does not *do*, one "performs"; nobody *knows* a thing, he is "fully cognizant"; one never *says*, he "indicates." A great favorite at present is "implement."

Some charming boners occur in this talking-in-one's-sleep. For instance:

> *The problem of extending coverage to all employees, regardless of size, is not as simple as surface appearances indicate.*
>
> *Though the proportions of all males and females in ages 16-45 are essentially the same...*
>
> *Dairy cattle, usually and commonly embraced in dairying...*

In its manual to employees, the F.S.A. suggests the following:

Instead of	Use
give consideration to	*consider*
make inquiry regarding	*inquire*
is of the opinion	*believes*
comes into conflict with	*conflicts*
information which is of a confidential nature	*confidential information*

Professional or office gobbledygook often arises from using the passive rather than the active voice. Instead of looking you in the eye, as it were, and writing "This act requires . . ." the office worker looks out of the window and writes: "It is required by this statute that . . ." When the bureau chief says, "We expect Congress to cut your budget," the message is only too clear; but usually he says, "It is expected that the departmental budget estimates will be reduced by Congress."

Gobbled: *"All letters prepared for the signature of the Administrator will be single spaced."*

Ungobbled: *"Single space all letters for the Administrator." (Thus cutting 13 words to 7.)*

Only people can read. The F.S.A. surveys pick up the point that human communication involves a listener as well as a speaker. Only people can read, though a lot of writing seems to be addressed to beings in outer space. To whom are you talking? The sender of the officialese message often forgets the chap on the other end of the line.

A woman with two small children wrote the F.S.A. asking what she should do about payments, as her husband had lost his memory. "If he never gets able to work," she said, "and stays in an institution would I be able to draw any benefits? . . . I don't know how I am going to live and raise my children since he is disable to work. Please give me some information. . . ."

To this human appeal, she received a shattering blast of gobbledygook, beginning, "State unemployment compensation laws do not provide any benefits for sick or disabled individuals . . . in order to qualify an individual must have a certain number of quarters of coverage . . ." et cetera, et cetera. Certainly if the writer had been thinking about the poor woman he would not have dragged in unessential material about old-age insurance. If he had pictured a mother without means to care for her children, he would have told her where she might get help—from the local office which handles aid to dependent children, for instance.

Gobbledygook of this kind would largely evaporate if we thought of our messages as two way—in the above case, if we pictured ourselves talking on the doorstep of a shabby house to a woman with two children tugging at her skirts, who in her distress does not know which way to turn.

Results of the survey. The F.S.A. survey showed that office documents could be cut 20 to 50 per cent, with an improvement in clarity and a great saving to taxpayers in paper and payrolls.

A handbook was prepared and distributed to key officials. They read it, thought about it, and presently began calling section meetings to discuss gobbledygook. More booklets were ordered, and the local output of documents began to improve. A Correspondence Review Section was established as a kind of laboratory to test murky messages. A supervisor could send up samples for analysis and suggestions. The handbook is now used for training new members; and many employees keep it on their desks along with the dictionary. Outside the Bureau some 25,000 copies have been sold (at 20 cents each) to individuals, governments, business firms, all over the world. It is now used officially in the Veterans Administration and in the Department of Agriculture.

The handbook makes clear the enormous amount of gobbledygook which automatically spreads in any large office, together with ways and means to keep it under control. I would guess that at least half of all the words circulating around the bureaus of the world are "irrelevant, incompetent, and immaterial"—to use a favorite legalism; or are just plain "unnecessary"—to ungobble it.

My favorite story of removing the gobble from gobbledygook concerns the Bureau of Standards at Washington. I have told it before but perhaps the reader will forgive the repetition. A New York plumber wrote the Bureau that he had found hydrochloric acid fine for cleaning drains, and was it harmless? Washington replied: "The efficacy of hydrochloric acid is indisputable, but the chlorine residue is incompatible with metallic permanence."

The plumber wrote back that he was mighty glad the Bureau agreed with him. The Bureau replied with a note of alarm: "We cannot assume responsibility for the production of toxic and noxious residues with hydrochloric acid, and suggest that you use an alternate procedure." The plumber was happy to learn that the Bureau still agreed with him.

Whereupon Washington exploded: "Don't use hydrochloric acid; it eats hell out of the pipes!"

Note: The second quotation on page 19 comes from Gertrude Stein's *Lucy Church Amiably.*

3

Malcolm Cowley

Sociological Habit Patterns in Linguistic Transmogrification

*Mr. Cowley deals with a problem mentioned earlier—
the distinction between jargon and necessary technical language. Sociology and other disciplines in the same general
area — psychology, political science, education, anthro-
pology — are particularly subject to criticism for the pro-
liferation of gobbledygook. It is a pity that such is the case,
for it is just those disciplines that attract and impress many
students. So the beginning writer compounds his danger of
being infected by habituating those areas in which the
plague is particularly virulent.*

*A long word is not necessarily better than a short one;
two words are not necessarily as good as one.*

J have a friend who started as a poet and then decided to take a postgraduate degree in sociology. For his doctoral dissertation he combined his two interests by writing on the social psychology of poets. He had visited poets by the dozen, asking each of them a graded series of questions, and his conclusions from the interviews were modest and useful, though reported in what seemed to me a barbarous jargon. After reading the dissertation I wrote and scolded him. "You have such a fine sense of the poet's craft," I said, "that you shouldn't have allowed the sociologists to seduce you into writing their professional slang —or at least that's my judgmental response to your role selection."

My friend didn't write to defend himself; he waited until we met again. Then dropping his voice, he said: "I knew my dissertation was badly written, but I had to get my degree. If I had written it in English, Professor Blank"—he mentioned a rather distinguished name—"would have rejected it. He would have said it was merely belletristic."

From that time I began to study the verbal folkways of the sociologists. I read what they call "the literature." A few sociologists write the best English they are capable of writing, and I suspect that they are the best men in the field. There is no mystery about them. If they go wrong, their mistakes can be seen and corrected. Others, however—and a vast majority—write in a language that has to be learned almost like Esperanto. It has a private vocabulary which, in addition to strictly sociological terms, includes new words for the commonest actions, feelings, and circumstances. It has the beginnings of a new grammar and syntax, much inferior to English grammar in force and precision. So far as it has an effect on standard English, the effect is largely pernicious.

Sometimes it misleads the sociologists themselves, by making them think they are profoundly scientific at points where they are merely being verbose. I can illustrate by trying a simple exercise in translation, that is, by expressing an idea first in English and then seeing what it looks like in the language of sociology.

An example that comes to hand is the central idea of an article by Norman E. Green, printed in the February, 1956, issue of the *American Sociological Review*. In English his argument might read as follows:

"Sociological Habit Patterns in Linguistic Transmogrification" from the *Reporter*, Vol. 15, No. 4, September 20, 1956, Copyright 1956 by Malcolm Cowley. Reprinted with permission of the author.

Rich people live in big houses set farther apart than those of poor people. By looking at an aerial photograph of any American city, we can distinguish the richer from the poorer neighborhoods.

I won't have to labor over a sociological expression of the same idea, because Mr. Green has saved me the trouble. Here is part of his contribution to comparative linguistics. "In effect, it was hypothesized," he says—a sociologist must never say "I assumed," much less "I guessed"—"that certain physical data categories including housing types and densities, land use characteristics, and ecological location"—not just "location," mind you, but "ecological location," which is almost equivalent to locational location —"constitute a scalable content area. This could be called a continuum of residential desirability. Likewise, it was hypothesized that several social data categories, describing the same census tracts, and referring generally to the social stratification system of the city, would also be scalable. This scale could be called a continuum of socio-economic status. Thirdly, it was hypothesized that there would be a high positive correlation between the scale types on each continuum."

Here, after ninety-four words, Mr. Green is stating, or concealing, an assumption with which most laymen would have started, that rich people live in good neighborhoods. He is now almost ready for his deduction, or snapper:

This relationship would define certain linkages between the social and physical structure of the city. It would also provide a precise definition of the commonalities among several spatial distributions. By the same token, the correlation between the residential desirability scale and the continuum of socio-economic status would provide an estimate of the predictive value of aerial photographic data relative to the social ecology of the city.

Mr. Green has used 160 words—counting "socio-economic" as only one—to express an idea that a layman would have stated in thirty-three. As a matter of fact, he has used many more than 160 words, since the whole article is an elaboration of this one thesis. Whatever may be the virtues of the sociological style—or Socspeak, as George Orwell might have called it—it is not specifically designed to save ink and paper. Let us briefly examine some of its other characteristics.

Fuzzing up the obvious. A layman's first impression of sociological prose, as compared with English prose, is that it contains a very large proportion of abstract words, most of them built on Greek or Latin roots. Often

—as in the example just quoted—they are used to inflate or transmogrify a meaning that could be clearly expressed in shorter words surviving from King Alfred's time.

These Old English or Anglo-Saxon words are in number less than one-tenth of the entries in the largest dictionaries. But they are the names of everyday objects, attributes, and actions, and they are also the pronouns, the auxiliary verbs, and most of the prepositions and conjunctions, so that they form the grammatical structure of the language. The result is that most novelists use six Anglo-Saxon words for every one derived from French, Latin, or Greek, and that is probably close to the percentage that would be found in spoken English.

For comparison or contrast, I counted derivations in the passage quoted from the *American Sociological Review,* which is a typical example of "the literature." No less than forty-nine per cent of Mr. Green's prose consists of words from foreign or classical languages. By this standard of measurement, his article is more abstruse than most textbooks of advanced chemistry and higher mathematics, which are said to contain only forty per cent of such words.

In addition to being abstruse, the language of the sociologists is also rich in neologisms. Apparently they like nothing better than inventing a word, deforming a word, or using a technical word in a strange context. Among their favorite nouns are "ambit," "extensity" (for "extent"), "scape-goating," "socializee," "ethnicity," "directionality," "cathexis," "affect" (for "feeling"), "maturation" (for both "maturing" and "maturity"), and "com-monalities" (for "points in common"). Among their favorite adjectives are "processual," "prestigeful," and "insightful"—which last is insightful to murder—and perhaps their favorite adverb is "minimally," which seems to mean "in some measure." Their maximal pleasure seems to lie in making new combinations of nouns and adjectives and nouns used as adjectives, until the reader feels that he is picking his way through a field of huge boulders, lost among "universalistic-specific achievement patterns" and "complementary role-expectation-sanction systems," as he struggles vainly toward "ego-integrative action orientation," guided only by "orientation to improvement of the gratification-deprivation balance of the actor"—which last is Professor Talcott Parsons' rather involved way of saying "the pleas-ure principle."

But Professor Parsons, head of the Sociology Department at Harvard, is not the only delinquent recidivist, convicted time and again of corrupting the language. Among sociologists in general there is a criminal fondness for using complicated terms when there are simple ones available. A child says "Do it again," a teacher says "Repeat the exercise," but the sociologist says "It was determined to replicate the investigation." Instead of saying two things are alike or similar, as a layman would do, the sociologist describes them in being either isomorphic or homologous. Instead of saying that they are different, he calls them allotropic. Every form of leadership or influence is called a hegemony.

A sociologist never cuts anything in half or divides it in two like a layman. Instead he dichotomizes it, bifurcates it, subjects it to a process of binary fission, or restructures it in a dyadic conformation—around polar foci.

THE NEW GRAMMAR

So far I have been dealing with the vocabulary of sociologists, but their private language has a grammar too, and one that should be the subject of intensive research by the staff of a very well-endowed foundation. I have space to mention only a few of its more striking features.

The first of these is the preponderance of nouns over all the other parts of speech. Nouns are used in hyphenated pairs or dyads, and sometimes in triads, tetrads, and pentads. Nouns are used as adjectives without change of form, and they are often used as verbs, with or without the suffix "ize." The sociological language is gritty with nouns, like sanded sugar.

On the other hand, it is poor in pronouns. The singular pronoun of the first person has entirely disappeared, except in case histories, for the sociologist never comes forward as "I." Sometimes he refers to himself as "the author" or "the investigator," or as "many sociologists," or even as "the best sociologists," when he is advancing a debatable opinion. On rare occasions he calls himself "we," like Queen Elizabeth speaking from the throne, but he usually avoids any personal form and writes as if he were a force of nature.

The second-personal pronoun has also disappeared, for the sociologist pretends to be speaking not to living persons but merely for the record. Masculine and feminine pronouns of the third person are used with parsimony, and most sociologists prefer to say "the subject," or "X. . . . ," or "the interviewee," where a layman would use the simple "he" or "she." As for the neuter pronoun of the third person, it survives chiefly as the impersonal subject of a passive verb. "It was hypothesized," we read, or "It was found to be the case." Found by *whom?*

The neglect and debasement of the verb is another striking feature of "the literature." The sociologist likes to reduce a transitive verb to an intransitive, so that he speaks of people's adapting, adjusting, transferring, relating, and identifying, with no more of a grammatical object than if they were coming or going. He seldom uses transitive verbs of action, like "break," "injure," "help," and "adore." Instead he uses verbs of relation, verbs which imply that one series of nouns and adjectives, used as the compound subject of a sentence, is larger or smaller than, dominant over, subordinate to, causative of, or resultant from another series of nouns and adjectives.

Considering this degradation of the verb, I have wondered how one of Julius Caesar's boasts could be translated into Socspeak. What Caesar wrote was *"Veni, vidi, vici"*—only three words, all of them verbs. The English translation is in six words: "I came, I saw, I conquered," and three of the words are first-personal pronouns, which the sociologist is taught to avoid. I suspect that he would have to write: "Upon the advent of the investigator, his hegemony became minimally coextensive with the areal unit rendered visible by his successive displacements in space."

The whole sad situation leads me to dream of a vast allegorical painting called "The Triumph of the Nouns." It would depict a chariot of victory drawn by the other conquered parts of speech—the adverbs and adjectives still robust, if yoked and harnessed; the prepositions bloated and pale; the conjunctions tortured; the pronouns reduced to sexless skeletons; the verbs dichotomized and feebly tottering—while behind them, arrogant, overfed, roseate, spilling over the triumphal car, would be the company of nouns in Roman togas and Greek chitons, adorned with laurel branches and flowering hegemonies.

4

Ralph Schoenstein

This Is Our Goodest Hour

Another plague spot mentioned by Professor Thorp was advertising. With some sideswipes at governmental gobbledygook, Mr. Schoenstein elaborates on that theme. There is a relationship between Professor Thorp's "No-English" and what Schoenstein calls "dung-tongue."

The point he raises is an important one. Deviation from standard English usage as a means of attracting attention and selling your product is legitimate, and can occasionally be witty and amusing. For a writer to offer such deviations as standard usage *in a formal essay is a symptom of the contagion.*

The Army may have recalled me this morning, but I can't be sure. I received a six-page directive from the headquarters of the Army Security Agency. The first sentence says: "Dissemination of the contents of this directive will be restricted to key personnel who are directly concerned with the implementation thereof." A friend of mine who knows a little English says this sentence means that the directive applies only to the people it applies to; but I don't think this translation catches the full meaning. For example, what about "the implementation thereof"? I think the directive applies only to men with shovels.

Fortunately, the next paragraph clarifies everything. It explains: "Policies and procedures prescribed herein are sufficiently flexible to permit latitude in implementation. Detailed guidance is provided only when uniformity is required." So it turns out that the men with shovels are allowed to dig wherever they want, while the non-shovelers will be told what to do only when the Army wants them all to do it the same way. Otherwise, improvised chaos is permissible.

Of course, the directive has its definitions. One section says: "Significant terms used herein are defined as follows: (a) AS-USAR Personnel— Includes both male and female; (b) Spouse—A husband or wife." By making it clear that the directive applies only to the Army's men and women, the Security Agency has freed all active reserve dogs, commissioned children, and National Guard cows to operate on their own. Moreover, note the splendid camouflage in the definition of spouse. This is to mislead the Russians, who'll never suspect that a spouse is really a bourbon-powered rocket carrying a chimpanzee with perfect pitch.

This military prose made me and my wife start reminiscing about the English language. You remember the English language. You can still contact it in documentaries about Winston Churchill. In fact, it's still taught at several colleges that aren't implementing the mass production of scientists. My wife and I were wondering exactly when English became a dead language. She felt it took a mortal wound on the day a man picked up his crayon to write "tastes good like a cigarette should." This inspired conjunction opened the floodgates: it made English suspect. During the peak of its popularity, I was reckless enough to tell a friend, "This hair tonic tastes good as hair tonic should." He looked at me as if I'd just kicked my mother —sorry, *like* I'd just kicked my mother.

"You pedants think I don't know that like isn't a conjunction," he said. "Well, my wisdom goes far beyond archaic grammar. A language must be a living, growing thing. In colloquial speech, what's correct often sounds stilted. Like I know I really should say 'tastes good *insomuch as* a cigarette should.' But like *sounds* better. Of course, there are times when it doesn't. Take the man who said, 'Don't know what to call her but she's mighty like a rose.' Imagine the *strength* this line would have gained had he been colloquially hep enough to say, 'Don't know what to call her but she's mighty *as* a rose.' His beloved not only would have had beauty but stamina, too."

My friend had sounded the battle cry for the Colloquial Revolution. Soon ads were telling me about a stocking with "a marvelously young heel," not to be confused with a stocking that had a senile heel, or even one wearily middle-aged. No longer was a marvelously young heel an old rat who'd taken hormones. Usagewise, from Madison Avenue to the Pentagon, English was getting spoke better like "The Scarlet Letter." It was a fun time for all.

The revolution won a major victory when a soft drink made people as young as their socks. This drink was advertised for those who "think young." Though I'd always loved this drink, I had to stop taking it, for something that made you think young would surely be poison for a reminiscing fool like me who spent most of his time thinking old and blue. The first time I heard this ad on my radio, I thought it was a line from a play about the early education of a great psychologist. I thought I'd tuned in just when a teacher scolds his brilliant but lazy pupil by saying, "Think, Jung!"

Soon, one could reach nirvana merely by sipping this drink in a room heated by the gas that advertised, "Think clean." All over America, people made childish by the drink were now taking the gas for a chaser; for what good was it to be young and *dirty?* Booksellers pushing Henry Miller wanted to fight back by advertising "Think low"; but they realized that since cleanliness was next to godliness, to fight against minds purified by gas would be to fight on the side of Satan.

This living, growing language, this drive to in the near future effectuate something better than English, received a federal blessing when Pentagon officials military secretwise finalized a quite unique problem of implementing the release of photographic-type pictures to press and air media by saying, "Not classified but not publishable." Local officials joined the crusade. Throughout New York, I saw posters about a government pamphlet that told "the true facts about inflation." These were not to be confused with the *false* facts about inflation, which were in a different and much grimmer pamphlet. As part of the city's safety campaign, other posters showed a cat that said, "I've got nine lives. Do you?" Do *I've* got nine lives? Of course I've don't.

The true facts about inflation are part of a trend toward reinforced language that was started by Hollywood, where a naked noun is indecent, where artists already are dreaming about something "even' greater than ' The Greatest Story Ever Told.'" "She's very dead," says the private eye in a movie that's "Strictly for Adults Only." (Movies that are merely "For Adults Only" admit children who shave.) "Tough break," says his secretary. "She was slightly pregnant." Soon, very dead won't be strong enough. Our deadest people will have to be very much dead, or perhaps colossally dead. Then being merely dead will be a condition of health. I wonder if the teen-ager who's slightly pregnant has an easier time breaking the news to mother than one who's pregnant without modification. Of course, the girl who's very pregnant has already taken gas. Let's hope it was the brand that took her out thinking clean.

The colloquial crusade has been so successful that I just heard a televised jingle in which a little girl sings that a certain cereal "is gooder than all the rest." Finding this eloquent child was an expensive search. She had to be stolen from a soft drink that she'd been calling "the deliciousest." Then she had to be trained to correct a speech defect, for she kept saying that the cereal was "the best." For a long time, the best—sorry, the goodest—she could do was to call the cereal "the most good," which was hardly goodest enough for a sponsor spending that kind of money.

In addition to training a backward child, this sponsor was also spending thousands of dollars to find out what was the goodest slogan to make people eat his cereal. He hired top motivational research experts who spent months probing the ·psychology of non-Asiatic-oriented consumer group response to visual inducements evidenced as video stimuli. After definitizing extensive research into consumered products, these experts concluded that most people are morons, brainwise. This surely was useful knowledge for the sponsor, but he had to know much more. Were these morons also *hungry?*

He and his advertising agency then considered the most poetic slogans: (1) Crummies is gooder than all the rest; (2) Crummies has deliciousness; (3) Crummies is the eatingest cereal; and a few colloquial ones. Number two was eliminated because it was too close to English; one account executive swore it *was* English. Some of the men liked number three, but it was too similar to the slogan for a toothpaste that called itself "the

33

cleaningest." One man wanted "Crummies nutritions you up." His colleagues said this was pure Keats but people weren't ready for it. Ironically, the next day a tea manufacturer advertised that his bag "psyches you up." Now the Crummies people realized that they'd underrated the intelligence of their consumers. "We've got to stop writing down to morons," said a media man.

"Well, that's water over the flagpole," said another. "What about 'Crummies libidos you up'?"

"It swings good," said the account executive, "but it's a bad image to orientate the kids with, sexwise. 'Crummies libidos you *down*' would be more wider accepted, parentwise."

"I'm frankly afraid of libido up *or* down," said the sponsor. "I'd rather not use foreign words. Let's skip the Italian and finalize with simple English: 'Crummies is gooder.'"

In his next ad, the tea manufacturer said that tea not only psyches you up but is also "the most cheerful stuff in the world" (and therefore even more euphoric than the soft drink with "laughing bubbles"). I was delighted to read this because I hate sullen tea, though I don't mind if my coffee is a little depressed. Of course, coffee no longer has to be blue now that a certain instant is advertising "a wake-up flavor." This brand isn't to be confused with "the coffee-er coffee," which doesn't have to wake you up because it doesn't let you go to sleep in the first place.

If English is dying, what is taking its place? A new language I call dung-tongue, which is often so close to English that nine out of ten independent doctors can't tell the difference. "Have a *real* cigarette!" cries the man who's telling you that his brand actually contains tobacco and not sawdust or chow mein like a cigarette shouldn't. This man wants you to try a cigarette that's too virile to "air-soften every puff" or "travel and gentle the smoke," a cigarette that may not be "friendly to your taste" but at least is ruggedly cordial.

The bards of dung-tongue may have poisoned English, but our health does concern them. Yesterday while riding a bus, depressed by tired blood, old heels, and dirty thoughts, I suddenly saw an ad that said, "Stops useless coughing!" How heartened I was by this news! How exhilarated I felt to know that at least one medicine on this sick planet lets you do only *useful* coughing. Lord knows there's little enough of it.

So perhaps there's still hope for a people that's fighting air pollution by smoking "twice as refreshed," a people growing softer each day from "sponge-ability" (which I'd always thought meant a talent for freeloading). Perhaps the time is near when we'll also have the pill that will stop useless hemorrhage. It would be the ideal sponsor for the quiz show called "Who Do You Trust?"

5

Russell Lynes

Dirty Words

In Four Quartets, *T. S. Eliot speaks of words that "decay with imprecision." In another place he speaks of words as "shabby equipment always deteriorating in the general mess of imprecision." It is this decay of words, usually through overuse in imprecise contexts, that Lynes attacks. You will have noticed this phenomenon. A word becomes popular, occupies every other sentence you hear or read for a couple of years, and finally becomes almost completely meaningless. They are called "vogue words." If you use vogue words in your writing, make sure you use them precisely. They may lend a meretricious gloss to your essay, but they are no substitute for clarity.*

In the middle of his essay, Lynes makes a point elaborated later by Malcolm Bradbury, that the definition of words changes depending on who uses them. Again the issue is clarity: if you use a word in other than its standard meaning, be sure your audience knows what you're about.

Possibly it is a reaction against the prevalence of four-letter words in literature today, but there is a kind of dirty language that has become part of common parlance that seems to me far more pernicious than just plain ----! Four-letter words, whatever one may think of their general use in fiction (where they mostly occur), at least have very specific meanings and convey images or ideas or situations that are at once graphic and precise, and often emphatic. The dirty words to which I object are befouling conversation and nonfiction and most especially the conversation and prose of what is presumed to be the educated community. They are substitutes for thought, most of them, or, to put it another way, they exude a mist which rises between a speaker and his listener so that all that can be perceived through it is a kind of fuzz. Some of the words to which I refer unquestionably meant something once, but they are now used to create an aura of sense, not sense itself.

But let me be meaningful.

If you know what I mean by *meaningful*, you know more than I do. It is one of those words that sounds as though it were loaded and when you fire it the noise is impressive but the blood it draws is none. A "meaningful" conversation in my experience is one from which both parties withdraw, each convinced that the other said nothing but that he himself said something profound. A "meaningful" experience sometimes seems to be one in which the emotions have been stirred but the precise meaning of the situation escapes one. If the word serves any useful function at all it is as a cover-up for indecision. To some persons, for example, looking at a sculpture of a goat by Picasso is a pleasure, to others it is a joke or disgusting; to those who don't know what they think it is a "meaningful experience." One never has to make up one's mind about what is meaningful; the word does it for one.

Some of the dirty words come in pairs like *creative* and *constructive*, both of which are examples of what happens to perfectly nice words when they fall into bad company. "Creative people" are not what you would think; they are not painters, sculptors, choreographers, poets, novelists, or composers, all of whom are artists. Creative people do "constructive" thinking in advertising agencies and in editorial offices and let somebody else worry about the costs. "Creative" people, indeed, do "constructive" thinking which, at its very best, is "meaningful."

One of the ways of promoting creative thinking in both business and bureaucracy today is a method analogous to getting blood from a stone known in the gutter slang of our time as *brainstorming*. It involves another dirty word which I think it necessary to define at once because it is impossible to talk the argot of today without using it. The word is *dialogue*. Private individuals may still have conversations or they may talk things over, but scholars, public servants, foundation executives, radio and television commentators (if you'll excuse the expression), and "generations" indulge in what is usually referred to in the singular as a "dialogue." A dialogue rarely happens between two persons. A dialogue is an attempt to relieve a situation defined by another cliché known as *lack of communication*. But before we consider "communication," which has a special darkness of its own, let us dispose of "brainstorming," which is the miscellaneous use of untrained and undisciplined brains engaged in a dialogue hoping to produce something that is meaningful. It assumes that even the lamest brain under pressure—perhaps because it is a nerve (or *nerve center*, a phrase now commonly used in the communications business and other industries to indicate the office where the public-relations department keeps management from making a public fool of itself)—can produce a *sensitive response*.

Recently there appeared in the *New York Times* a report of a young lady who had got in trouble with the authorities at Barnard College because she was discovered to be living off-campus with a Columbia College junior. She said she had gone to the office of Barnard's president, but declared, "I just couldn't communicate with her. She seemed insensitive."

There in a single statement is the nub of the problem commonly referred to as "the failure of communication between generations," which is a newly devised verbal weapon used by the young when they do not wish to admit that they know what their elders are talking about but in fact know quite well, and used by the old to shield themselves from having to bother. Almost the simplest definition of "communication" is that it is something that doesn't happen between generations because of the *generation gap*. (See below for a study of the importance of the "gap" in modern society and politics.) Lack of communication between generators, however, is not communication's only kind of lack. It is the lack of communication between those who are sensitive and those who are insensitive which keeps the generations from being unified.

I can remember back to the time when *sensitive* was frequently used to mean touchy, chip-on-shoulder, easily wounded, and when *insensitive* meant thick-skinned, Philistine, boorish, and was frequently applied by nonathletes to athletes and by English professors to scientists. Now a sensitive person is one who sees things as I do, and an insensitive person is one who doesn't like the things I like and sees no reason to struggle to like them. This is especially true in relation to the arts, but it also applies, as in the case of the Barnard girl, to mores. There is, however, another use of the word which cannot be overlooked by anyone who reads book reviews. It is the equivalent of inertia, in the sense that the sensitive novel is one in which almost nothing happens but in which the characters (and most especially the one who represents the novelist him- or herself) vibrates with reaction to a situation which is essentially static and which nobody can do anything to change.

People who make a great many other people feel sensitive in the current (and I contend bawdy) use of the word are, as I do not need to remind you, *charismatic.* I sometimes wonder as I listen to my acquaintances, read the press, and hear wise men explain the world on television, how we managed to communicate meaningfully at all until someone a few years ago propelled the ancient word "charisma" into current slang. Now if you haven't charisma you haven't spiritual or political *it,* which was a simpler word in use in the 'twenties to mean much the same thing, except that "it" had the added attraction of *sex appeal,* another phrase that is all but extinct. It is as necessary for the political analyst to use "charisma" today as it is for the political aspirant to incorporate it in his (here's another) *ambience.** If you can project your charisma in the right ambience you have achieved a position so invulnerable as to leave no room for dialogue, a situation for which we have invented another meaningful phrase, *credibility gap.*

I said we would come to the importance of "gap" to our society. Gap is a three-letter word, though it has the impertinence of a four-letter word. (Gap certainly sounds like ----, for example.) Used with the word credibility, it once may have had some meaning, but it has come to be an epithet and a slogan. Presumably it means the difference between the truth as "they" see it and the truth as "we" see it. There used to be a word "prevarication" which is no more cumbersome than "credibility gap" and suggests much the same thing. Prevarication, a minor kind of camouflage, has always been a part of daily life . . . a state of nature, you might say. Women lie about their age, men about their incomes, children about their marks in school, politicians about their intentions, and girls about their virginity. This is

---

* The French spell it *ambiance.*

merely prevarication. I would call the distance between the knees and the hem of a miniskirt a genuine credibility gap.

Outside the ambience of political affairs, and the *ambivalence* (now *there's* one!) of political pundits there are some phrases so benighted that I hesitate to mention them in this family magazine. Look upon the phrase "environmental management," for example, and blush for your native tongue. I am told that putting background music in an art gallery (or a dairy barn) is "e------------ m---------." There is no language so slovenly as that which is invented to make trades seem like professions. There is, indeed, a low expression for this process—to *upgrade*. "Upgrading" is frequently a matter of concealing a plain fact with a fancy phrase. I remember a tooth powder that used to carry on its container the legend, "also efficacious for cleansing artificial dentures."

Words like *empathize* and *ecumenism,* which we got along without perfectly well a few years ago, now fall like showers of commas into the most innocent conversations. I am not sure that to "empathize with" somebody is much worse than to "identify with" him, except for the sound reason that "to identify" is a respectable verb and "to empathize" is a noun that has lost its moorings. "Ecumenism," which used to have a certain theological standing, is rapidly becoming a synonym for "cool it, boys, let's get together." Even so, these two bits of intellectualistic slang are preferable to certain other clichés so commonly heard as to be allowed to befoul the language almost unnoticed. No study today is worth its salt unless it is *in depth*; no memorandum can be taken seriously unless it is a *position paper*; and everyone is at sea until he is *orientated*. No man takes a stand any more; he *assumes a posture* or a *stance*, soft words for soft convictions. I have even heard it said that no head of a family deserves the dignity of that position unless he *nest-eggs!*

I have left to the last the word of all words that seems to me the most offensive nine-letter word in common usage among the educated classes. The word is *dichotomy*.

As for dichotomy, I'm of two minds about it.

Frank Sullivan

The Cliché Expert Testifies

When vogue words or vogue phrases fail to die a natural death from overexposure, but stay in use forever, they tend to become clichés. So, too, with stock phrases that once were vivid, but are now worn with use. (Ideas, attitudes, and situations can also become clichés, but that's another matter.) Clichés are hard to avoid. A sample: "On a day now lost in the mists of time (cliché) a sports-writer who must have had a touch of poetry in him (cliché) was reporting a football game. Looking down at the parallel white lines, and probably thinking of the heat of battle (cliché), in an inspired moment (cliché) a vivid metaphor (cliché) struck him, and one of the most venerable clichés (cliché) was born: the 'gridiron.' Clichés should be avoided like the plague (cliché)."

But let us turn the stage over (cliché) to the cliché expert, Mr. Arbuthnot.

The Cliché Expert
Testifies on Baseball

Q — Mr. Arbuthnot, you state that your grandmother has passed away and you would like to have the afternoon off to go to her funeral.

A — That is correct.

Q — You are an expert in the clichés of baseball—right?

A — I pride myself on being well versed in the stereotypes of our national pastime.

Q — Well, we'll test you. Who plays baseball?

A — Big-league baseball is customarily played by brilliant out-fielders, veteran hurlers, powerful sluggers, knuckle-ball artists, towering first basemen, key moundsmen, fleet base runners, ace southpaws, scrappy little shortstops, sensational war vets, ex-college stars, relief artists, rifle-armed twirlers, dependable mainstays, doughty right-handers, streamlined backstops, power-hitting batsmen, redoubtable infielders, erstwhile Dodgers, veteran sparkplugs, sterling moundsmen, aging twirlers, and rookie sensations.

Q — What other names are rookie sensations known by?

A — They are also known as aspiring rookies, sensational new-comers, promising freshmen, ex-sandlotters, highly touted striplings, and youngsters who will bear watching.

Q — What's the manager of a baseball team called?

A — A veteran pilot. Or youthful pilot. But he doesn't manage the team.

Q — No? What does he do?

A — He guides its destinies.

Q — How?

A — By the use of managerial strategy.

Q — Mr. Arbuthnot, please describe the average major-league-baseball athlete.

A — Well, he comes in three sizes, or types. The first type is tall, slim, lean, towering, rangy, huge, husky, big, strapping, sturdy, handsome, powerful, lanky, rawboned, and rugged.

Q — Quite a hunk of athlete.

A — Well, those are the adjectives usage requires for the description of the Type One, or Ted Williams, ballplayer.

Q — What is Type Two like?

A — He is chunky or stocky—that is to say, Yogi Berra.

Q — And the third?

A — The third type is elongated and does not walk. He is Ol' Satchmo, or Satchel Paige.

Q — What do you mean Satchmo doesn't walk?

A — Not in the sports pages, he doesn't. He ambles.

Q — You mentioned a hurler, Mr. Arbuthnot. What is a hurler?

A — A hurler is a twirler.

Q — Well, what is a twirler?

A — A twirler is a flinger, a tosser, He's a moundsman.

Q — Moundsman?

A — Yes. He officiates on the mound. When the veteran pilot tells a hurler he is to twirl on a given day, that is a mound assignment, and the hurler who has been told to twirl is the mound nominee for that game.

Q — You mean he pitches?

A — That is right. You have cut the Gordian knot.

Q — What's the pitcher for the other team called?

A — He is the mound adversary, or mound opponent, of the mound nominee. That makes them rival hurlers, or twirlers. They face each other and have a mound duel, or pitchers' battle.

Q — Who wins?

A — The mound victor wins, and as a result he is a mound ace, or ace moundsman. He excels on the mound, or stars on it. He and the other moundsmen on his team are the mound corps.

Q — What happens to the mound nominee who loses the mound duel?

A — He is driven off the mound.

Q — What do you mean by that?

A — He's yanked. He's knocked out of the box.

Q — What's the box?

A — The box is the mound.

Q — I see. Why does the losing moundsman lose?

A — Because he issues, grants, yields, allows, or permits too many hits or walks, or both.

Q — A bit on the freehanded side, eh? Where does the mound victor go if he pitches the entire game?

A — He goes all the way.

Q — And how does the mound adversary who has been knocked out of the box explain his being driven off the mound?

A — He says, "I had trouble with my control," or "My curve wasn't working," or "I just didn't have anything today."

Q — What happens if a mound ace issues, grants, yields, allows, or permits too many hits and walks?

A — In that case, sooner or later, rumors are rife. Either that or they are rampant.

Q — Rife where?

A — In the front office.

Q — What's that?

A — That's the place where baseball's biggies—also known as baseball moguls—do their asking.

Q — What do they ask for?

A — Waivers on erratic southpaw.

Q — What are these baseball biggies further known as?

A — They are known as the Shrewd Mahatma or as Horace Stoneham, but if they wear their shirt open at the neck they are known as Bill Veeck.

Q — What do baseball biggies do when they are not asking for waivers?

A — They count the gate receipts, buy promising rookies, sell aging twirlers, and stand loyally by Manager Durocher.

Q — And what does Manager Durocher do?

A — He guides the destinies of the Giants and precipitates arguments with the men in blue.

Q — What men in blue?

A — The umpires, or arbiters.

Q — What kind of arguments does Durocher precipitate?

A — Heated arguments.

Q — And the men in blue do what to him and other players who precipitate heated arguments?

A — They send, relegate, banish, or thumb them to the showers.

Q — Mr. Arbuthnot, how do you, as a cliché expert, refer to first base?

A — First base is the initial sack.

Q — And second base?

A — The keystone sack.

Q — What's third base called?

A — The hot corner. The first inning is the initial frame, and an inning without runs is a scoreless stanza.

Q — What is one run known as?

A — A lone run, but four runs are known as a quartet of tallies.

Q — What is a baseball?

A — The pill, the horsehide, the old apple, or the sphere.

Q — And what's a bat?

A — The bat is the willow, or the wagon tongue, or the piece of lumber. In the hands of a mighty batsman, it is the mighty bludgeon.

Q — What does a mighty batsman do?

A — He amasses runs. He connects with the old apple. He raps 'em out and he pounds 'em out. He belts 'em and he clouts 'em.

Q — Clouts what?

A — Circuit clouts.

Q — What are they?

A — Home runs. Know what the mighty batsman does to the mighty bludgeon?

Q — No. What?

A — He wields it. Know what kind of orgies he fancies?

Q — What kind?

A — Batting orgies. Slugfests. That's why his team pins.

Q — Pins what?

A — All its hopes on him.

Q — Mr. Arbuthnot, what is a runner guilty of when he steals home?

A — A plate theft.

Q — And how many kinds of baseball games are there?

A — Five main classifications: scheduled tussles, crucial contests, pivotal games, drab frays, and arc-light tussles.

Q — And what does the team that wins—

A — Sir, a baseball team never wins. It scores a victory, or gains one, or chalks one up. Or it snatches.

Q — Snatches what?

A — Victory from the jaws of defeat.

Q — How?

47

A — By a ninth-inning rally.

Q — I see. Well, what do the teams that chalk up victories do to the teams that lose?

A — They nip, top, wallop, trounce, rout, down, subdue, smash, drub, paste, trip, crush, curb, whitewash, erase, bop, slam, batter, check, hammer, pop, wham, clout, and blank the visitors. Or they zero them.

Q — Gracious sakes! Now I know why ballplayers are old at thirty-five.

A — Oh, that isn't the half of it. They do other things to the visitors.

Q — Is it possible?

A — Certainly. They jolt them, or deal them a jolt. They also halt, sock, thump, larrup, vanquish, flatten, scalp, shellac, blast, slaughter, K.O., mow down, topple, whack, pound, rap, sink, baffle, thwart, foil, maul, and nick.

Q — Do the losers do anything at all to the victors?

A — Yes. They bow to the victors. And they taste.

Q — Taste what?

A — Defeat. They trail. They take a drubbing, pasting, or shellacking. They are in the cellar.

Q — What about the victors?

A — They loom as flag contenders. They're in the first division.

Q — Mr. Arbuthnot, what is the first sign of spring?

A — Well, a robin, of course.

Q — Yes, but I'm thinking of our subject here. How about when the ballplayers go south for spring training?

A — Ballplayers don't go south for spring training.

Q — Why, they do!

A — They do *not*. They wend their way southward.

Q — Oh, I see. Well, do all ballplayers wend their way southward?

A — No. One remains at home.

Q — Who is he?

A — The lone holdout.

Q — Why does the lone holdout remain at home?

A — He refuses to ink pact.

Q — What do you mean by that?

A — He won't affix his Hancock to his contract.

Q — Why not?

A — He demands a pay hike, or salary boost.

Q — From whom?

A — From baseball's biggies.

Q — And what do baseball's biggies do to the lone holdout?

A — They attempt to lure him back into the fold.

Q — How?

A — By offering him new contract.

Q — What does lone holdout do then?

A — He weighs offer. If he doesn't like it, he balks at terms. If he does like it, he inks pact and gets pay hike.

Q — How much pay hike?

A — An undisclosed amount in excess of.

Q — That makes him what?

A — One of the highest-paid baseball stars in the annals of the game, barring Ruth.

Q — What if baseball's biggies won't give lone holdout pay hike?

A — In that case, lone holdout takes pay cut, old salary, or job in filling station in home town.

Q — Now, when baseball players reach the spring training camp and put on their uniforms—

A — May I correct you again, sir? Baseball players do not put on uniforms. They don them.

Q — I see. What for?

A — For a practice session or strenuous workout.

Q — And why must they have a strenuous workout?

A — Because they must shed the winter's accumulation of excess avoirdupois.

Q — You mean they must lose weight?

A — You put it in a nutshell. They must be streamlined, so they plunge.

Q — Plunge into what?

A — Into serious training.

Q — Can't get into serious training except by plunging, eh?

A — No. Protocol requires that they plunge. Training season gets under way in Grapefruit and Citrus Leagues. Casey Stengel bars night life.

Q — Mr. Arbuthnot, what is the opening game of the season called?

A — Let me see-e-e. It's on the tip of my tongue. Isn't that aggravating? Ah, I have it—the opener! At the opener, fifty-two thousand two hundred and ninety-three fans watch Giants bow to Dodgers.

Q — What do those fifty-two thousand two hundred and ninety-three fans constitute?

A — They constitute fandom.

Q — And how do they get into the ballpark?

A — They click through the turnstiles.

Q — Now then, Mr. Arbuthnot, the climax of the baseball season is the World Series, is it not?

A — That's right.

Q — And what is the World Series called?

A — It's the fall classic, or crucial contest, also known as the fray, the epic struggle, and the Homeric struggle. It is part of the American scene, like ham and eggs or pumpkin pie. It's a colorful event.

Q — What is it packed with?

A — Thrills. Drama.

Q — What kind of drama?

A — Sheer or tense.

Q — Why does it have to be packed with thrills and drama?

A — Because if it isn't, it becomes drab fray.

Q — Where does the fall classic take place?

A — In a vast municipal stadium or huge ballpark.

Q — And the city in which the fall classic is held is what?

A — The city is baseball mad.

Q — And the hotels?

A — The hotels are jammed. Rooms are at a premium.

Q — Tickets, also, I presume.

A — Tickets? If you mean the cards of admission to the fall classic, they are referred to as elusive Series ducats, and they *are* at a premium, though I would prefer to say that they are scarcer than the proverbial hen's teeth.

Q — Who attends the Series?

A — A milling throng, or great outpouring of fans.

Q — What does the great outpouring of fans do?

A — It storms the portals and, of course, clicks through the turnstiles.

Q — Causing what?

A — Causing attendance records to go by the board. Stands fill early.

Q — What else does the crowd do?

A — It yells itself hoarse. Pent-up emotions are released. It rides the men in blue.

Q — What makes a baseball biggie unhappy on the morning of a Series tussle?

A — Leaden skies.

Q — Who is to blame for leaden skies?

A — A character known to the scribes as Jupiter Pluvius, or Jupe.

Q — What does rain dampen?

A — The ardor of the fans.

Q — If the weather clears, who gets credit for that?

A — Another character, known as Old Sol.

Q — Now, the team that wins the Series—

A — Again, I'm sorry to correct you, sir. A team does not win a Series. It wraps it up. It clinches it.

Q — Well, then what?

A — Then the newly crowned champions repair to their locker room.

Q — What reigns in that locker room?

A — Pandemonium, bedlam, and joy.

Q — Expressed how?

A — By lifting youthful pilot, or his equivalent, to the shoulders of his teammates.

Q — In the locker room of the losers, what is as thick as a day in —I mean so thick you could cut it with a knife?

A — Gloom. The losers are devoid.

Q — Devoid of what?

A — Animation.

Q — Why?

A — Because they came apart at the seams in the pivotal tussle.

Q — What happens to the newly crowned champions later?

A — They are hailed, acclaimed, and fêted. They receive mighty ovations, boisterous demonstrations, and thunderous welcomes.

Q — And when those are over?

A — They split the Series purse and go hunting.

Q — Mr. Arbuthnot, if a powerful slugger or mighty batsman wields a mighty bludgeon to such effect that he piles up a record number of circuit clouts, what does that make him?

A — That is very apt to make him most valuable player of the year.

Q — And that?

A — That makes the kids of America look up to him as their hero.

Q — If most valuable player of the year continues the batting orgies that make the kids of America worship him, what then?

A — Then he becomes one of Baseball's Immortals. He is enshrined in Baseball's Hall of Fame.

Q — And after that?

A — Someday he retires and becomes veteran scout, or veteran coach, or veteran pilot. Or sports broadcaster.

Q — And then?

A — Well, eventually a memorial plaque is unveiled to him at the opener.

Q — Thank you, Mr. Arbuthnot. You have been most helpful. I won't detain you any longer, and I hope your grandmother's funeral this afternoon is a tense drama packed with thrills.

A — Thanks a lot. Goodbye now.

Q — Hold on a moment, Mr. Arbuthnot. Just for my own curiosity —couldn't you have said "thanks" and "goodbye" and let it go at that, without adding that "lot" and "now" malarkey?

A — I could have, but it would have cost me my title as a cliché expert.

The Cliché Expert Testifies on Politics

— Mr. Arbuthnot, I hear you've become a campaign orator.

A — Fellow American, you have heard correctly. I've been on the stump all fall.

Q — In that case you ought to be up on your campaign-oratory clichés.

A — Well, sir, it is not my wont to brag, but I believe I may say with all due modesty that I can point with pride and view with alarm as sententiously and bombastically as any senator who ever thrust one arm in his frock coat and with the other called upon high heaven to witness the perfidy of the Other Party.

Q — Describe your candidate, Mr. Arbuthnot.

A — My candidate is a man four-square, a true representative of the people, a leader worthy of the trust which has been placed in him, and a standard-bearer who will carry the banner of our ga-reat and ga-lorious party to victory.

Q — Is he a man of prophetic vision?

A — He is indeed. He is also a man of sterling character and a champion of the rights of the people.

Q — What kind of champion?

A — A stalwart champion.

Q — What is he close to?

A — The soil.

Q — Is his name Jones?

"The Cliché Expert Testifies on Politics" from *A Rock in Every Snowball* by Frank Sullivan. Copyright 1938, 1940, 1941, 1942, 1943, 1944, 1945, 1946 by Frank Sullivan. Reprinted with permission of Little, Brown and Co.

A — It is not. I have nothing against Mr. Jones personally, but I can't see where he's fitted to be President.

Q — Why not?

A — He may be a first-rate businessman, but what does he know about government?

Q — Then your candidate's name is Brown.

A — Not at all. I'm a lifelong Democrat and I've always voted the straight Democratic ticket, but this year I'm taking a walk.

Q — Why?

A — Because old party lines are disappearing. What this country needs is a *businessman* in the White House.

Q — Then your man is Jones, after all.

A — Jones is all right personally, but I don't like the crowd he's tied up with.

Q — What crowd?

A — Oh, the public utilities, the Old Guard, and so on. Besides, what does he know about foreign affairs?

Q — Mr. Arbuthnot, I can't figure out *where* you stand. Let's get back to your campaign-oratory clichés. What kind of questions have you been discussing?

A — Burning questions. Great, underlying problems.

Q — What have you arrayed yourself against?

A — The forces of reaction. There must be no compromise with the forces of reaction.

Q — And now, Mr. Arbuthnot, may I ask you to characterize these times?

A — These are troubled times, sir. We are met here today in an hour of grave national crisis.

Q — What do you, as a campaign orator, propose to do in this grave hour?

A — I shall demand, and denounce, and dedicate. I shall take stock. I shall challenge, pledge, stress, fulfill, indict, exercise, accuse, call upon, affirm, and reaffirm.

Q — Reaffirm what?

A — My undying faith in the principles laid down by the Founding Fathers. And I shall exercise eternal vigilance that our priceless heritage may be safeguarded.

Q — Admirable, Mr. Arbuthnot. And that reminds me: What is it you campaign orators rise above?

A — Narrow partisanship. We must place the welfare of our country above all other considerations, including our desire to win.

Q — Mr. Arbuthnot, how do you campaign orators dedicate yourselves?

A — We dedicate ourselves anew to the task that lies before us.

Q — How does your party approach this task?

A — With a solemn realization of the awful responsibility that rests upon us in this hour of unprecedented national stress.

Q — When our country is—

A — Sore beset by economic ills.

Q — How else do you approach the task?

A — With supreme confidence that our ga-reat party will prove worthy of its ga-lorious tradition.

Q — And if your party failed to approach the task in that spirit, Mr. Arbuthnot, would you say that—

A — It would indeed be recreant to its sacred trust.

Q — Ah. But you feel that it won't be recreant?

A — No, my fellow American, a tha-a-o-u-sand times no! The ga-reat party of Washington, and Jefferson, and Lincoln, and Wilson, and Roosevelt, and Cleveland, and Grant, Garfield, Hayes, and Arthur will not fail our country in this, her hour of need.

Q — Hurrah for Jones!

A — The candidate of Big Business?

Q — Then hurray for Brown!

A — He wants to be a dictator.

Q — Then three rousing cheers for Green!

A — If elected, he couldn't even control his own party.

Q — Then hurray for Smith!

A — Elect him and you'll *never* get rid of him.

Q — I'm afraid there's no pleasing you today, Mr. Arbuthnot. Would you mind telling me who's to blame for our country's hour of need?

A — The Other Party.

Q — What has the Other Party proved?

A — Its utter incapacity to govern. Its record is an unbroken record of failure, of forgotten campaign pledges, of callous disregard for the welfare of the country.

Q — What is the Other Party undermining?

A — The American way of life. It is spending vast sums of the taxpayers' money.

Q — For what?

A — To build up a huge political machine. It has aroused class hatred. Fellow American, in this solemn hour, when the sacred institutions of democracy are challenged on every side and the world is rent by strife, I charge the Other Party with having betrayed the pee-pul of these Yew-nited States.

Q — What must the pee-pul do?

A — They must rise in their wrath and elect my candidate.

Q — Mr. Arbuthnot, perhaps you'll tell us just what kind of leader the hour calls for?

A — A leader who will lead this country out of the wilderness, eliminate waste and extravagance in government, do away with red tape and bureaucratic inefficiency, solve the problem of unemployment, improve living conditions, develop purchasing power, raise the standard of living, provide better housing, and insure national defense by building a navy and air force second to none.

Q — What about the farmer?

A — The farmer must have relief.

Q — What kind of relief?

A — Farm relief. Labor must have the right to organize. Economy must be the watchword. Mounting deficits must cease; so must these raids on the public treasury. I view with alarm the huge and unwarranted increase in our national debt. Generations yet unborn! Those who would undermine our sacred institutions! Bore from within! Freedom of speech! Monroe doctrine! I call upon every patriotic American—

Q — Regardless of race or creed?

A — Be quiet!... regardless of race or creed, from the snow-capped peaks of the Rockies—

Q — To the pine-clad shores of Maine?

A — Shut *up!*...to the pine-clad shores of Maine to have faith in the American way of life. Subversive doctrines! Undesirable aliens! Lincoln!

Q — What kind of Lincoln?

A — The Immortal Lincoln! The Immortal Washington! The Immortal Jefferson! The time for evasions has passed. We must face the facts, put our shoulders to the wheel, put our house in order, meet the challenge of the dictators, carry aloft the torch of liberty, fulfill our high destiny, face the future with confidence, and march forward to victory at the polls in November.

7

Morris Freedman

The Seven Sins
of Technical Writing

*There is little in Freedman's essay that has not been
said before in earlier selections. We include it here, however, lest you should say to yourself that because you are
going to be a scientist or a technician the problems of style
are of no concern to you. Notice that the same diseases —
jargon, wordiness, clichés, indifference to the reader, and
the rest — crop up just as much in technical writing as
they do elsewhere.*

Let me start by saying at once that I do not come to you tonight just as a professor of English, for, frankly, I do not think that I would have very much to say to you only as someone expert in the history of the use—and misuse—of the language. And any remarks on literature might be confusing, at least without extensive elaboration, for the values and objectives of literature seem so very different at first from those of technical writing—although fundamentally many of these values and objectives coincide. And I am sure that you are more than familiar with such things as clichés, comma splices, fragmentary sentences, and the other abominations we deal with in freshman composition. These obviously have nothing to do specifically with technical writing.

But I want to say, before anyone thinks that I class technical writing entirely by itself, immune from rules and requirements of communication that govern other kinds of writing, that technical writing calls for the same kind of attention and must be judged by the same standards as any other kind of writing; *indeed, it calls for a greater attention and for higher standards*. And I say this as a former science and medical writer for the popular press; as a former writer of procedure manuals and directives for the government; as a former editor of technical studies in sociology, statistics, law, and psychology; as a former general magazine editor; as a writer of fiction, essays, and scholarly articles; and, not least, as a professor of English. We can see at once why technical writing must be measured by higher standards, or, at least, by different ones, if anyone will not grant me that they are higher. Technical writing is so immediately functional. Confusing directions accompanying an essential device in a jet plane may result in disaster; bad writing elsewhere can have as its most extreme effect merely boredom.

Yet, while technical writing implicitly calls for great care, it differs from other kinds of writing in that its practitioners are, by and large, first technicians and only incidentally writers. And principally because of this arrangement, I think, technical writing has become characterized by a collection of sins peculiar to this discipline alone. I say the *collection* is peculiar to technical writing, not any one of the sins alone. Any newspaper, weekly magazine, encyclopedia, textbook, any piece of writing you might name, will contain one or another of these sins, in greater or lesser profusion. But I know of no kind of writing that contains as many different sins in such great

"The Seven Sins of Technical Writing" from *College Composition and Communication,* February 1958. Copyright © 1958 by the National Council of Teachers of English. Reprinted with permission of the publisher and Morris Freedman.

number as technical writing, and with such great potential for danger. To repeat, the sins in the world at large—at least, of the sort I'm talking about —often don't matter much. And sometimes, too, they don't matter in technical writing. As my students argue when I correct them in informative writing: "You got the meaning, didn't you?" Yes, I did, and so do we all get the meaning when a newspaper, a magazine, a set of directions stammers out its message. And I suppose, too, we could travel by ox-cart, or dress in burlap, or drive around with rattling fenders, and still get through a day.

But technical writing in this age can no more afford widespread sloppiness of expression, confusion of meaning, rattletrap construction than a supersonic missile can afford to be made of the wrong materials, or be put together haphazardly with screws jutting out here and there, or have wiring circuits that may go off any way at all, or—have a self-destructive system that fails because of some fault along the way in construction. Technical writing today—as I need hardly reiterate to this audience—if it is much less than perfect in its streamlining and design may well result in machines that are less than trim, and in operation that is not exactly neat. This is at worst; at best, poor technical writing, when its effect is minimized by careful reading, hinders efficiency, wastes time. Let me remark, too, that the commission of any one of these sins, and of any one of many, many lesser ones, is really not likely alone to be fatal, just as one loose screw by itself is not likely to destroy a machine; but always, we know, sins come in bunches, the sin of avarice often links hands with the sin of gluttony, one loose screw may mean others, and, anyway, the ideal of no sins at all— especially in something like technical writing, where the pain of self-denial should be minimal—is always to be strived for.

A final word before I launch into the sins (whose parade, so long delayed, will prove, I hope, so much more edifying—like a medieval tableau). The seven I list might be described as cardinal ones, and as such they are broad and overlapping, perhaps, rather than specific and very clearly distinguished from one another. They all contribute to making technical writing less clear, concise, coherent, and correct than it should be.

Sin 1, then, might be described as that of INDIFFERENCE, neglecting the reader. I do not mean anything so simple as writing down to an engineer or physicist, although this is all too common and may be considered part of this sin. This writing down—elaborating the obvious—is one reason the abstract or summary has become so indispensable a part of technical reports; very often, it is all the expert needs to read of the whole report, the rest being a matter of all too obvious detailing. Nor do I mean writing above the heads of your audience either, which is a defect likely to be taken care of by a thoughtful editor. Both writing over or under the heads of your reader, or to the side, are really matters of careless aiming and, as such, of indifference, too. But what I mean here by indifference are short-cuts of expression, elliptical diction, sloppy organization, bringing up points and letting them hang unresolved, improper or inadequate labelling of graphic material, and the like. This is communication by gutturals, grunts, shrugs, as though it were not worth the trouble to articulate carefully, as though the reader didn't matter—or didn't exist. This is basically an atti-tude of disrespect: *Caveat lector*—let the reader beware. Let the reader do his own work; the writer isn't going to help him.

Here is the concluding sentence from a quite respectable report, one most carefully edited and indeed presented as a model in a handbook for technical writers used by a great chemical firm. The sentence is relatively good, for it takes only a second reading to work out its meaning (perhaps only a slow first one for someone trained in reading this kind of writing):

> *When it is assumed that all of the cellulose is converted to ethyl cellulose, reaction conversion of cellulose to ethyl cellulose, per cent of cellulose reacted, and reaction yield of ethyl cellulose based on cellulose are each equal to 100%.*

This is admittedly a tough sentence to get across simply, considering that "cellulose" is repeated in several different contexts. Yet two guiding principles would have made it much clearer: (1) always put for your reader first things first (here, the meaning hangs on the final phrase, "each equal to 100%," which comes at the end of a complicated series); and (2) clearly separate items in a series. (The second rules seems to me one of the most important in technical writing where so many things have to be listed so often.) Here is the recast sentence:

> *If all the cellulose is converted to ethyl cellulose, each of the fol-lowing factors is then equal to 100%:*
> 1. *reaction conversion of cellulose to ethyl cellulose.*
> 2. *proportion of cellulose reacted.*
> 3. *reaction yield of ethyl cellulose based on cellulose.*

The changes are not great, certainly, but in the process we have eliminated the indisputable notion of a percent being equal to a percent, and have ar-ranged the series so that both the eye and the mind together can grasp the information immediately. Sin 1 then can be handled, one way, by cutting out indirect Rube Goldbergish contraptions and hitting your points directly on their heads, one, two, three.

The remaining sins I shall discuss are extensions of this primal one, disregard for the reader. Sin 2 may be designated as FUZZINESS , that is, a general fuzziness of communication—vague words, meaningless words, wrong ones. The reader uses his own experience to supply the meaning in such writing; the writing itself acts only as a collection of clues. The military specializes in this sort of thing. I recall an eerie warning in an air force mess hall: "Anyone smoking in or around this mess hall will be dealt with accordingly." It still haunts me. Here is a caution in a handbook of technical writing with which you may be familiar: "Flowery, euphemistic protestations of gratitude are inappropriate." We know what this means, of course, but we ourselves supply the exact meaning. It happens that a "euphemism" is "the substitution of an inoffensive or mild expression for one that may offend or suggest something unpleasant." At least, that's what *Webster's Collegiate* says it is.

Here are some other examples: "The intrinsic labyrinth of wires must be first disentangled." The writer meant "network," not "labyrinth"; and I think he meant "internal" for "intrinsic" and "untangled" for "disentangled." Item: "The liquid contents of the container should then be disgorged via the spout by the operator." Translation: "The operator should then empty the container." Here is a final long one:

> *When the element numbered one is brought into tactual contact with the element numbered two, when the appropriate conditions of temperature have been met above the previously determined safety point, then there will be exhibited a tendency for the appropriate circuit to be closed and consequently to serve the purpose of activating an audible warning device.*

Translation:

> *When the heat rises above the set safety point, element one touches element two, closing a circuit and setting off a bell.*

Prescription to avoid Sin 2: use, concrete, specific words and phrases whenever you can, and use only those words whose meaning you are sure of. (A dictionary, by the way, is only a partial help in determining the correct and *idiomatic* use of a word.) English is perhaps the richest of languages in offering a variety of alternatives for saying the same thing.

Sin 3 might be called the sin of EMPTINESS . It is the use of jargon and big words, pretentious ones, where perfectly appropriate and acceptable small and normal words are available. (There is nothing wrong with big words in themselves, provided they are the best ones for the job. A steam shovel is right for moving a boulder, ridiculous for picking up a handkerchief.) We may want to connect this sin with the larger, more universal one of pride, the general desire to seem important and impressive. During World War II a high government official devoted much time to composing an effective warning for a sticker to be put above light switches. He emerged with "Illumination is required to be extinguished on these premises on the termination of daily activities," or something of the sort. He meant "Put the lights out when you go home."

The jargon I'm talking about is not the technical language you use normally and necessarily for efficient communication. I have in mind only the use of a big word or a jumble of words for something that can be said more efficiently with familiar words and straightforward expressions. I have in mind also a kind of code language used to show that you're an insider, somewhere or other: "Production-wise, that's a high-type machine that can be used to finalize procedure. The organization is enthused." There is rarely any functional justification for saying "utilize" or "utilization" for "use," "prior to" for "before," "the answer is in the affirmative or negative" for "yes or no," or for using any of the "operators, or false verbal limbs," as George Orwell called them, like "render inoperative," "prove unacceptable," "exhibit a tendency to," "serve the purpose of," and so on and on.

Again, one can handle this sin simply by overcoming a reluctance to saying things directly; the most complex things in the world can be said in simple words, often of one syllable. Consider propositions in higher math or logic, the Supreme Court decisions of men like Brandeis and Holmes, the poetry of Shakespeare. I cannot resist quoting here Sir Arthur Quiller-Couch's rendition in jargon of Hamlet's "To be or not to be, that is the question." I am sure you all know the full jargon rendition of the soliloquy. "To be, or the contrary? Whether the former or the latter be preferable would seem to admit of some difference of opinion."

Sin 4 is an extension of 3: just plain WORDINESS. The principle here is that if you can say anything with more words than necessary for the job, then by all means do so. I've already cited examples of this sin above, but compounded with other sins. Here is a purer example, the opening of a sentence in a technical writing handbook: "Material to be contained on the cover of the technical report includes ..." This can be reduced to "The cover of the technical report should include ..." Another example, less pure: "The front-mounted blade of the bulldozer is employed for earth moving operations on road construction jobs." Translation: "The bulldozer's front blade moves earth in road building." Item: "There is another way of accomplishing this purpose, and that is by evaporation." Translation: "Evaporation is another way of doing this." Instead of saying simply that "the bulldozer's front blade moves earth," you say it "is employed for earth moving operations," throwing in "employed" and "operations," as though "moves" alone is too weak to do this tremendous job. The cure for this sin? Simply reverse the mechanism: say what you have to in the fewest words.

Sin 5, once again an extension of the immediately preceding sin, is a matter of BAD HABITS , the use of pat phrases, awkward expressions, confusing sentence structure, that have, unfortunately, become second nature. Again, I'm not alluding to the perfectly natural use of familiar technical expressions, which may literally be called clichés, but which are not efficiently replaceable. Sin 5 is a matter of just not paying attention to what you say, with the result that when you do suddenly pay attention, you see the pointlessness or even humor of what you have set down. Perhaps the most common example of this sin is what has been called "deadwood," or what may be called "writing for the simple minded." Examples: "red in color," "three in number," "square in shape," "the month of January," "the year 1956," "ten miles in distance," and the like. What else is red but a color, three but a number, square but a shape, January but a month, 1956 but a year, ten miles but a distance? To say that something is "two inches wide and three inches long" is to assume that your reader can't figure out length and width from the simple dimensions "two inches by three inches." I once read that a certain machine was 18 feet high, "vertically," the writer made sure to add; and another time that a certain knob should be turned "right, in direction."

A caution is needed here. There are many obvious instances when qualification is necessary. To say that something is "light," for example, is plainly mysterious unless you add "in color" or "in weight" or, perhaps, "in density" (unless the context makes such addition "deadwood").

I would include under Sin 5 the locutions "as far as that is concerned" (lately shortened to "as far as that"), "as regards," "with regard to," "in the case of" ("In the case of the case enclosing the instrument, the case is being studied"). These are all too often just lazy ways of making transitions (and, thus, incidentally, quite justifiable when speed of writing is a factor).

Sin 6 is the DEADLY PASSIVE , or, better, deadening passive; it takes the life out of writing, making everything impersonal, eternal, remote and dead. The deadly passive is guaranteed to make any reading matter more difficult to understand, to get through, and to retain. Textbook writers in certain fields have long ago learned to use the deadly passive to create difficulties where none exist; this makes their subject seem weightier, and their accomplishment more impressive. (And, of course, if this is ever what you have in mind on an assignment, then by all means use the deadly passive.) Sin 6 is rarely found alone; it is almost indispensable for fully carrying out the sins of wordiness and jargon. Frequently, of course, the passive is not a sin and not deadly, for there simply is no active agent and the material must be put impersonally.

Examples of this sin are so easy to come by, it is difficult to find one better than another. Here is a relatively mild example of Sin 6:

> The standardization of procedure in print finishing can be a very important factor in the efficient production of service pictures. In so far as possible, the smallest number of types and sizes of paper should be employed, and the recommended processing followed. The fewer paper grades and processing procedures used, the fewer errors and make-overs that are likely. Make-overs are time-consuming and costly.

Here it is with the deadly passive out and some other changes made:

> To produce service pictures efficiently, a standard way of finishing prints can be very important. You should use as few types and sizes of paper as possible, and you should follow the recommended procedure for processing. In this way, you will make fewer errors, and have to re-do less work. You will save time and money.

Associated with the deadly passive, as you might see from the two passages above, is the use of abstract nouns and adjectives for verbs. Verbs always live; nouns and adjectives just sit there, and abstract nouns aren't even there. Of course, there are a number of other ways of undoing the passivity of the passage I quoted, and of making other improvements, just as there were other ways of handling any of the specimens I have cited in the train of horrors accompanying my pageant of sins.

Finally we come to Sin 7, the one considered the deadliest by many, and not only by teachers of English but by technical writers and technologists of various sorts: MECHANICAL ERRORS I don't think this sin the deadliest of all. It does happen to be the easiest one to recognize, the one easiest to deal with "quantitatively," so to speak, and the easiest one to resist. I suppose it is considered deadliest because then those who avoid it can so quickly feel virtuous. It can promptly be handled by good works alone. Actually most technical writing happens to be mechanically impeccable; not one of the examples I have used tonight had very much mechanically wrong with it. If anything, technical people tend to make too much of formal mechanics. I remember working with a physicist who had much trouble saying anything in writing. While his general incapacity to write was almost total, one thing he did know, and know firmly, and that was that a split infinitive was to be abhorred. That, and using a preposition to end a sentence with. He could never communicate the simplest notion coherently, but he never split an infinitive or left a preposition at the end of a sentence. If Nobel Prizes were to be awarded for never splitting infinitives or for encapsulating prepositions within sentences, he would be a leading candidate.

There are a handful of mechanical errors which are relevant to technical writing, and these are important because they are so common, especially in combination with other sins. (Split infinitives or sentence-ending prepositions, need I say, are not among them.) These are dangling participles and other types of poorly placed modifiers, and ambiguous references. There are others, a good number of others, but the ones I mention creep in most insidiously and most often.

Here are some examples stripped down to emphasize the errors:

Raising the temperature, the thermostat failed to function.

Who or what raised the temperature? Not the thermostat, I presume; and if it did somehow, as the result of current flowing in its wiring, then this ought to be said quite plainly.

The apparatus is inappropriately situated in the corner since it is too small.

What is too small? Apparatus or corner?

Every element in the device must not be considered to be subject to abnormal stress.

What is meant here is that "Not every element in the apparatus must be considered subject to abnormal stress," almost the opposite of the original taken literally.

I should like to conclude by emphasizing something I glanced at in my introduction, that the seven sins of technical writing are to be avoided not so much by a specific awareness of each, accompanied by specific penance for each, as by a much more general awareness, by an attitude toward subject matter, writing process, and reader that can best be described only as "respectful." You will not help yourself very much if you rely on such purely mechanical aids as Rudolph Flesch's formulas for "readable writing," or on slide rules measuring readability, much as you may be tempted to do so.

These can be devil's snares, ways to make you think you are avoiding sin. There are no general texts, either, at present that will help you in more than very minor ways. The only aids you can safely depend on are the good book itself, that is, a good dictionary (there are many poor ones), any of the several volumes by H. W. Fowler, and occasional essays, here and there, by George Orwell, Jacques Barzun, Herbert Read, Somerset. Maugham, and others. And these, I stress, can only be *aids*. What is most important in eliminating sin in technical writing is general attitude—as it may well be in eliminating sin anywhere.

I repeat that technical writing must be as rationally shaped as a technical object. A piece of technical writing, after all, is something that is shaped into being for a special purpose, much as a technical object. The design engineer should be guided in his work by the requirements of function almost alone. (Of course, if he happens to have a boss who likes to embellish the object with useless doo-dads, why then he may have to modify his work accordingly to keep his job—as automobile designers do every day; but we try never to have in mind unreasonable situations of this sort.) It is as pointless for the design engineer to use three bolts where one would do (both for safety and function), to make an object square when its use dictates it should be round, to take the long way through a process when there is a short way, as it is for the technical writer to commit any of the sins I have mentioned. Technical writing—informative writing of any sort—should be as clean, as functional, as inevitable as any modern machine designed to do a job well. If I will not be misunderstood in throwing out this thought, I should like to suggest to you that good technical writing should be like good poetry—every word in its exact place for maximum effect, no word readily replaceable by another, not a word too many or too few, and the whole combination, so to speak, invisible, not calling attention to its structure, seemingly effortless, perfectly adapted to its subject.

If one takes this general approach to the shaping of a piece of technical writing, and there really can't be much excuse for any other, then there is no need to worry about any of the sins I mention. Virtue may not come at once or automatically, for good writing never comes without effort, however fine one's intentions, but it will certainly come, and perhaps even bring with it that same satisfaction the creative engineer experiences. Technical writing cleansed of its sins is no less worthy, no less impressive, an enterprise than good engineering itself. Like mathematics to physics, technical writing is a handmaid to technology, but like mathematics, too, it can be a helpmate, that is, an equal partner. But it can achieve this reward of virtue only by emphasizing the virtues of writing equally with those of technology.

Wallace Stegner

Good-bye to All T--t

Stegner deals with a problem that has become more and more acute in recent years. To what extent do you include in your writing words that may be considered obscene or offensive by some readers?

Stegner's answer to the question is basically an appeal to decorum — not the genteel and hypocritical decorum of "polite society," but literary decorum, a sense of the literary fitness of things, of the feeling for the right word in the right spot. In other words, he is suggesting that the use of such words be governed by the writer's sense of style. He mentions restraint, by which he means a writer's control of tone and emphasis and purpose. "Under the right circumstances, any word is proper." The force of the sentence lies in the qualifying phrase.

ot everyone who laments what contemporary novelists have done to the sex act objects to the act itself, or to its mention. Some want it valued higher than fiction seems to value it; they want the word "climax" to retain some of its literary meaning. Likewise, not everyone who has come to doubt the contemporary freedom of language objects to strong language in itself. Some of us object precisely because we value it.

I acknowledge that I have used four-letter words familiarly all my life, and have put them into books with some sense that I was insisting on the proper freedom of the artist. I have applauded the extinction of those d----d emasculations of the Genteel Tradition and the intrusion into serious fiction of honest words with honest meanings and emphasis. I have wished, with D. H. Lawrence, for the courage to say shit before a lady, and have sometimes had my wish.

Words are not obscene: naming things is a legitimate verbal act. And "frank" does not mean "vulgar," any more than "improper" means "dirty." What vulgar does mean is "common"; what improper means is "unsuitable." Under the right circumstances, any word is proper. But when any sort of word, especially a word hitherto taboo and therefore noticeable, is scattered across a page like chocolate chips through a tollhouse cookie, a real impropriety occurs. The sin is not the use of an "obscene" word; it is the use of a loaded word in the wrong place or in the wrong quantity. It is the sin of false emphasis, which is not a moral but a literary lapse, related to sentimentality. It is the sin of advertisers who so plaster a highway with neon signs that you can't find the bar or liquor store you're looking for. Like any excess, it quickly becomes comic.

If I habitually say shit before a lady, what do I say before a flat tire at the rush hour in Times Square or on the San Francisco Bay Bridge? What do I say before a revelation of the inequity of the universe? And what if the lady takes the bit in her teeth and says shit before *me?*

I have been a teacher of writing for many years and have watched this problem since it was no bigger than a man's hand. It used to be that with some Howellsian notion of the young-girl audience one tried to protect tender female members of a mixed class from the coarse language of males trying to show off. Some years ago Frank O'Connor and I agreed on a system. Since we had no intention whatever of restricting students' choice of subject or language, and no desire to expurgate or bowdlerize while reading their stuff aloud for discussion, but at the same time had to deal with these young girls of an age our daughters might have been, we announced that any stuff so strong that it would embarrass us to read it aloud could be read by its own author.

It was no deterrent at all, but an invitation, and not only to coarse males. For clinical sexual observation, for full acceptance of the natural functions, for discrimination in the selection of graffiti, for boldness in the use of words that it should take courage to say before a lady, give me a sophomore girl every time. Her strength is as the strength of ten, for she assumes that if one shocker out of her pretty mouth is piquant, fifty will be literature. And so do a lot of her literary idols.

Some acts, like some words, were never meant to be casual. That is why houses contain bedrooms and bathrooms. Profanity and so-called obscenities are literary resources, verbal ways of rendering strong emotion. They are not meant to occur every ten seconds, any more than—Norman Mailer to the contrary notwithstanding—orgasms are.

So I am not going to say shit before any more ladies. I am going to hunt words that have not lost their sting, and it may be I shall have to go back to gentility to find them. Pleasant though it is to know that finally a writer can make use of any word that fits his occasion, I am going to investigate the possibilities latent in restraint.

I remember my uncle, a farmer who had used four-letter words ten to the sentence ever since he learned to talk. One day he came too near the circular saw and cut half his fingers off. While we stared in horror, he stood watching the bright arterial blood pump from his ruined hand. Then he spoke, and he did not speak loud. "Aw, the dickens," he said.

I think he understood, better than some sophomore girls and better than some novelists, the nature of emphasis.

9

William H. Whyte, Jr.

You, Too, Can Write the Casual Style

One of the characteristics of a good personal essay is the sense the reader gets of a definite personality expressing itself in its distinctive voice. But this does not mean that a writer should allow himself to be coy, cute, or affected. Affectation in writing is as offensive as it is in the flesh.

In this essay, Mr. Whyte publicly executes several well-known writers who have popularized the affectations he calls the "Casual Style." There are other stylistic poses besides the Casual. They should probably be avoided. Unless you are adopting a mask or a pose for a particular rhetorical effect, the best thing to do is be yourself as honestly as you can.

A revolution has taken place in American prose. No longer the short huffs and puffs, the unqualified word, the crude gusto of the declarative sentence. Today the fashion is to write casually.

The Casual Style is not exactly new. Originated in the early Twenties, it has been refined and improved and refined again by a relatively small band of writers, principally for the *New Yorker,* until now their mannerisms have become standards of sophistication. Everybody is trying to join the club. Newspaper columnists have forsaken the beloved metaphors of the sports page for the Casual Style, and one of the quickest ways for an ad man to snag an award from other ad men is to give his copy the low-key, casual pitch; the copy shouldn't sing these days—it should whisper. Even Dr. Rudolf Flesch, who has been doing to much to teach people how to write like other people, is counseling his followers to use the Casual Style. Everywhere the ideal seems the same: be casual.

But how? There is very little down-to-earth advice. We hear about the rapier-like handling of the bromide, the keen eye for sham and pretension, the exquisite sense of nuance, the unerring ear for the vulgate. But not much about actual technique. The layman, as a consequence, is apt to look on the Casual Style as a mandarin dialect which he fears he could never master.

Nonsense. The Casual Style is within everyone's grasp. It has now become so perfected by constant polishing that its devices may readily be identified, and they change so little that their use need be no more difficult for the novice than for the expert. (That's not quite all there is to it, of course. Some apparently casual writers, Thurber and E. B. White, among others, rarely use the devices.)

The subject matter, in the first place, is not to be ignored. Generally speaking, the more uneventful it is, or the more pallid the writer's reaction to it, the better do form and content marry. Take, for example, the cocktail party at which the writer can show how bored everyone is with everyone else, and how utterly fatuous they all are anyhow. Since a non-casual statement—e.g., "The party was a bore"—would destroy the reason for writing about it at all, the Casual Style here is not only desirable but mandatory.

Whatever the subject, however, twelve devices are the rock on which all else is built. I will present them one by one, illustrating them with examples from such leading casual stylists as Wolcott Gibbs, John Crosby, John McCarten, and (on occasion) this magazine's "Mr. Harper." If the reader will digest what follows, he should be able to dash off a paragraph indistinguishable from the best casual writing being done today.

(1) *Heightened Understatement.*   Where the old-style writer would say, "I don't like it," "It is not good," or something equally banal, the casual writer says it is *"something less than* good." He avoids direct statement and strong words—except, as we will note where he is setting them up to have something to knock down. In any event, he qualifies. "Somewhat" and "rather," the bread-and-butter words of the casual writer, should become habitual with you; similarly with such phrases as "I suppose," "it seems to me," "I guess," or "I'm afraid." "Elusive" or "elude" are good, too, and if you see the word "charm" in a casual sentence you can be pretty sure that "eludes me," or "I find elusive," will not be far behind.

(2) *The Multiple Hedge.*   Set up an ostensibly strong statement, and then, with your qualifiers, shoot a series of alternately negative and positive charges into the sentence until finally you neutralize the whole thing. Let's take, for example, the clause, "certain names have a guaranteed nostalgic magic." Challenge enough here; the names not only have magic, they have guaranteed magic. A double hedge reverses the charge. "Names which have, *I suppose* [hedge 1], a guaranteed nostalgic magic, *though there are times that I doubt it* [hedge 2]...."

We didn't have to say they were guaranteed in the first place, of course, but without such straw phrases we wouldn't have anything to construct a hedge on and, frequently, nothing to write at all. The virtue of the hedge is that by its very negating effect it makes any sentence infinitely expansible. Even if you have so torn down your original statement with one or two hedges that you seem to have come to the end of the line, you have only to slip in an anti-hedge, a strengthening word (e.g., "definitely," "unqualified," etc.), and begin the process all over again. Witness the following quadruple hedge: "I found Mr. Home entertaining *from time to time* [hedge 1] on the ground, *I guess* [hedge 2], that the singular idiom and unearthly detachment of the British upper classes have *always* [anti-hedge] seemed *reasonably* [hedge 3] droll to me, *at least in moderation* [hedge 4]." The art of plain talk, as has been pointed out, does not entail undue brevity.

If you've pulled hedge on hedge and the effect still remains too vigorous, simply wipe the slate clean with a cancellation clause at the end. "It was all exactly as foolish as it sounds," says Wolcott Gibbs, winding up some 570 casual words on a subject, "and I wouldn't give it another thought."

(3) *Narcissizing Your Prose.* The casual style is nothing if not personal; indeed, you will usually find in it as many references to the writer as to what he's supposed to be talking about. For you do not talk about the subject; you talk about its impact on you. With the reader peering over your shoulder, you look into the mirror and observe your own responses as you run the entire range of the casual writer's emotions. You may reveal yourself as, in turn, listless ("The audience seemed not to share my boredom"); insouciant ("I was really quite happy with it"); irritated ("The whole thing left me tired and cross"); comparatively gracious ("Being in a comparatively gracious mood, I won't go into the details I didn't like"); or hesitant ("I wish I could say that I could accept his hypothesis").

(4) *Preparation for the Witticism.* When the casual writer hits upon a clever turn of phrase or a nice conceit, he uses this device to insure that his conceit will not pass unnoticed. Suppose, for example, you have thought of something to say that is pretty damn good if you say so yourself. The device, in effect, is to say so yourself. If you want to devastate a certain work as "a study of vulgarity in high places," don't say this flat out. Earlier in the sentence prepare the reader for the drollery ahead with something like "what I am tempted to call" or "what could best be described as" or "If it had to be defined in a sentence, it might well be called...."

Every writer his own claque.

(5) *Deciphered Notes Device; or Cute-Things-I-Have-Said.* In this one you are your own stooge as well. You feed yourself lines. By means of the slender fiction that you have written something on the back of an envelope or the margin of a program, you catch yourself good-humoredly trying to decipher these shrewd, if cryptic, little jottings. Viz.: "Their diagnoses are not nearly as crisp as those I find in my notes"; "...sounds like an inadequate description, but it's all I have on my notes, and it may conceivably be a very high compliment."

(6) *The Kicker.* An echo effect. "My reactions [included] an irritable feeling that eleven o'clock was past Miss Keim's bedtime,"—and now the Kicker—"*not to mention my own.*" This type of thing practically writes itself. "She returns home. She should never have left home in the first place. --- ------- ------ - ''*

---

* "And neither should I."

(7) *Wit of Omission.* By calling attention to the fact that you are not going to say it, you suggest that there is something very funny you could say if only you wanted to. "A thought occurred to me at this point," you may say, when otherwise stymied, "but I think we had better not go into *that.*"

(8) *The Planned Colloquialism.* The casual writer savors colloquialisms. This is not ordinary colloquial talk—nobody is more quickly provoked than the casual writer by ordinary usage. It is, rather, a playful descent into the vulgate. Phrases like "darn," "awfully," "as all getout," "mighty," and other folksy idioms are ideal. The less you would be likely to use the word normally yourself the more pointed the effect. Contrast is what you are after, for it is the facetious interplay of language levels—a blending, as it were, of the East Fifties and the Sticks—that gives the Casual Style its offhand charm.

(9) *Feigned Forgetfulness.* Conversation gropes; it is full of "what I really meant was" and "maybe I should have added," backings and fillings and second thoughts of one kind or another. Writing is different; theoretically, ironing out second thoughts beforehand is one of the things writers are paid to do. In the Casual Style, however, it is exactly this exposure of the writer composing in public that makes it so casual. For the professional touch, then, ramble, rebuke yourself in print ("what I really meant, I guess"), and if you have something you feel you should have said earlier, don't say it earlier, but say later that you guess you should have said it earlier.

(10) *The Subject-Apologizer, or Pardon-Me-for-Living.* The Casual Stylist must always allow for the possibility that his subject is just as boring to the reader as it is to him. He may forestall this by seeming to have stumbled on it by accident, or by using phrases like: "If this is as much news to you as it is to me," or "This, in case you've been living in a cave lately, is. . . ."

(11) *The Omitted Word.* This all began modestly enough the day a *New Yorker* writer dropped the articles "the" and "a" from the initial sentence of an anecdote (e.g., "Man we know told us"; "Fellow name of Brown"). Now even such resolutely lowbrow writers as Robert Ruark affect it, and they are applying it to any part of speech anywhere in the sentence. You can drop a pronoun ("Says they're shaped like pyramids"); verb ("You been away from soap opera the last couple of weeks?"); or preposition ("Far as glamour goes...").

(12) *The Right Word.* In the lexicon of the casual writer there are a dozen or so adjectives which in any context have, to borrow a phrase, a

guaranteed charm. Attrition is high—"brittle," "febrile," "confected," for example, are at the end of the run. Ten, however, defy obsolescence: *antic, arch, blurred, chaste, chill, crisp, churlish, disheveled, dim, disembodied.*

They are good singly, but they are even better when used in tandem; cf., "In an arch, antic sort of way"; "In an arch, blurred sort of way"; "In an arch, crisp sort of way." And so on.

Finally, the most multi-purpose word of them all: "altogether." Frequently it is the companion of "charming" and "delightful," and in this coupling is indispensable to any kind of drama criticism. It can also modify the writer himself (e.g., "Altogether, I think ..."). Used best, however, it just floats, unbeholden to any other part of the sentence.

Once you have mastered these twelve devices, you too should be able to write as casually as all getout. At least it seems to me, though I may be wrong, that they convey an elusive archness which the crisp literary craftsman, in his own dim sort of way, should altogether cultivate these days. Come to think of it, the charm of the Casual Style is something less than clear to me, but we needn't go into *that.* Fellow I know from another magazine says this point of view best described as churlish. Not, of course, that it matters.

10

Joseph C. Pattison

How to Write an 'F' Paper: Fresh Advice for Students of Freshman English

We close this section with a handy list of reminders. Mr. Pattison touches most of the points covered earlier. Notice that he discusses ideas as well as sentences and paragraphs, thus reaffirming the mutual relationship between sound mind and sound body we spoke of earlier.

Writing an "F" paper is admittedly not an easy task, but one can learn to do it by grasp of the principles to use. The thirteen below, if practiced at all diligently, should lead any student to that fortune in his writing.

Obscure the ideas:

1. Select a topic that is big enough to let you wander around the main idea without ever being forced to state it precisely. If an assigned topic has been limited for you, take a detour that will allow you to amble away from it for a while.

2. Pad! Pad! Pad! Do not develop your ideas. Simply restate them in safe, spongy generalizations to avoid the need to find evidence to support what you say. Always point out repetition with the phrase, "As previously noted. . . ." Better yet, repeat word-for-word at least one or two of your statements.

3. Disorganize your discussion. For example, if you are using the time order to present your material, keep the reader alert by making a jump from the past to the present only to spring back into the past preparatory to a leap into the future preceding a return hop into the present just before the finish of the point about the past. Devise comparable stratagems to use with such other principles for organizing a discussion as space, contrast, cause-effect, and climax.

4. Begin a new paragraph every sentence or two.

By generous use of white space, make the reader aware that he is looking at a page blank of sustained thought.

Like this.

Mangle the sentences:

5. Fill all the areas of your sentences with deadwood. Incidentally, "the area of" will deaden almost any sentence, and it is particularly flat when displayed prominently at the beginning of a sentence.

6. Using fragments and run-on or comma-spliced sentences. Do not use a main subject and a main verb, for the reader will get the complete

"How to Write an 'F' Paper: Fresh Advice for Students of Freshman English" from *College English,* October 1963. Copyright © 1963 by the National Council of Teachers of English. Reprinted with permission of the publisher and Joseph C. Pattison.

thought too easily. Just toss him part of the idea at a time, as in "Using fragments. . . ." To gain sentence variety, throw in an occasional run-on sentence thus the reader will have to read slowly and carefully to get the idea.

7. Your sentence order invert for statement of the least important matters. That will force the reader to be attentive to understand even the simplest points you make.

8. You, in the introduction, body, and conclusion of your paper, to show that you can contrive ornate, graceful sentences, should use involution. Frequent separation of subjects from verbs by insertion of involved phrases and clauses will prove that you know what can be done to a sentence.

Slovenize the diction:

9. Add the popular "-wise" and "-ize" endings to words. Say, "Timewise, it is fastest to go by U.S. 40," rather than simply, "It is fastest to go by U.S. 40." Choose "circularize" in preference to "circulate." Practice will smartenize your style.

10. Use vague words in place of precise ones. From the start, establish vagueness of tone by saying, "The thing is . . ." instead of, "The issue is . . ." Make the reader be imaginative throughout his reading of your paper.

11. Employ lengthy Latinate locutions wherever possible. Shun the simplicity of style that comes from apt use of short, old, familiar words, especially those of Anglo-Saxon origin. Show that you can get the *maximum* (L.), not merely the *most* (AS.), from every word choice you make.

12. Inject humor into your writing by using the wrong word occasionally. Write "then" when you mean "than" or "to" when you mean "too." Every reader likes a laugh.

13. Find a "tried and true" phrase to use to clinch a point. It will have a comfortingly folksy sound for the reader. Best of all, since you want to end in a conversational and friendly way, sprinkle your conclusion with clichés. "Put a little frosting on the cake," as the saying goes.

Well, too ensconce this whole business in a nutshell, you, above all, an erudite discourse on nothing in the field of your topic should pen. Thereby gaining the reader's credence in what you say.

Suggestion-wise, one last thing: file-ize this list for handy reference the next time you a paper write.

Two

THE RESULTS OF CONTAGION: STYLE AND "THE REAL WORLD"

> I became increasingly frustrated at not being able to express what I wanted to convey in letters that I wrote, especially those to Mr. Elijah Muhammad. In the street, I had been the most articulate hustler out there — I had commanded attention when I said something. But now, trying to write simple English, I not only wasn't articulate, I wasn't even functional. How would I sound writing in slang, the way I would say it, something such as, "Look, daddy, let me pull your coat about a cat, Elijah Muhammad—"
>
> —*The Autobiography of Malcolm X*

The previous section should have made you aware of the more pustulant excrescences that mar your style. But so what? Are not these the cranky cavils of professional nit-pickers? If these people didn't make a profession out of knocking writing, they'd have to go out and earn an honest living. This is all well and good for the classroom, but it doesn't really matter outside.

Not so. As Malcolm X's eloquent testimony shows, it does matter. Without a command of language, without a clear and forceful style, he would have remained a mute prisoner in that jail, filled with inarticulate and ineffective rage. Years of copying the dictionary and reading for hours a day made him a powerful force in the real world. The section of his autobiography from which the above passage comes is entitled "Saved."

The way you say something does matter. Words do have an impact on the real world of men and events. There are people outside the classroom who do care about your style. What we're talking about here is general semantics, but most of the selections that follow were written by men more concerned with practical semantics—i.e., style—than with theory. Note in some of them the complaints about the same old flaws dealt with in Part One.

1

Malcolm Bradbury

The New Language of Morals

We mentioned earlier the problem of people using the same word with different meanings. Bradbury discusses this phenomenon and uses it to suggest that such shifts reflect a change in the fundamental moral outlook of our society. De Tocqueville in a later essay will touch on this same topic again.

Since we think and write in words, their meaning is essential, not only to communication but to our entire consciousness. By implication, Bradbury's essay is an argument for clarity and responsibility in the use of words.

From time to time, the moral vocabulary of a society seems to alter substantially, in response to social changes and the conscious or unconscious election of new leaders of thought and opinion. In these times it is easy to tell what side of the fence people are on, not so much by the opinions they express as by the words they use to express them. There grows up an Elect of discourse, using words in a new, a special, a group way, and using a language with its own honorific words and concepts. One interesting example of such a word is *Puritan*, which is used in many quarters to denote a suspicious and repressive attitude towards pleasurable indulgence, but which is esteemed in other quarters as meaning almost the exact opposite. The two groups encountered each other, with perceptible raising of eyebrows, at the *Lady Chatterley's Lover* trial, when Prosecuting Counsel, speaking with the voice of conventional educated culture, confronted Professor Hoggart, speaking with the voice of modern literary culture, and confusion ensued.

Another similar key-word, conveniently separating Elect from Mass, is *Life*. To most people, Life is what we get up and go to every day, however unwillingly; and it is hard to see how Being on the Side of Life is the property of some persons more than others. But this formulation, taken over apparently from the artists of the Decadence, has now a substantial vogue. The Life Enhancers and the Life Diminishers are seen as two contrary parties in society—seen, of course, by the self-confessed Life Enhancers. The characteristic of moral vocabularies is that they have a way of praising those who use them. There is a modern formulation which divides people into Hips and Squares, but of course it is really only those who are, or think themselves, Hip that use it. The American formulation of Far In and Far Out is a distinction made by the Far Out. It is true that the word *bourgeois* is largely a formulation of the bourgeois, but only because they had sufficient urbanity to see themselves from outside, which meant that they ceased in fact to be bourgeois, in their own view at least. So it is with the Side of Lifers; it is rare to find anyone describing himself, or his friends, as being on the Side of Death.

There is nothing more dangerous than for a young man in our society to appear in public with the wrong mode of discourse. The honorific words of one group are the condemnatory words of another; hence the difficulty experienced by candidates for certain rather advanced departments in universities when they have the misfortune to be praised by their headmas-

"The New Language of Morals" reprinted with permission of the author.

ters as *loyal*. One man's praise is another man's stigma. In a recent *Observer* series on *Patriotism,* a number of eminent people presented themselves before us in poses of acute embarrassment, rather as a bishop might in being found in a brothel in the old days. Here they were, modern men, most of them, being asked to discourse in a traditional vocabulary which was hardly likely to be current among readers who had doubtless sucked in *A Farewell to Arms* with mother's milk:

> *I was always embarrassed by the words sacred, glorious, and sacrifice and the expression in vain. We had heard them, sometimes standing in the rain almost out of earshot, so that only the shouted words came through, and had read them, on proclamations that were slapped up by billposters over other proclamations, now for a long time, and I had seen nothing sacred, and things that were glorious had no glory and the sacrifices were like the stockyards at Chicago if nothing was done with the meat except bury it. There were many words you could not stand to hear and finally only the names of places had dignity.... Abstract words such as glory, honour, courage, or hallow were obscene....*

The fact of the matter is that the traditional discourse associated with the public virtues, made up of words like *patriotism, loyalty, courage* and *public spirit,* has tended to lapse, and indeed instead of attributing high motives to people who manifest them many of us are more than ready to be cynical about them. There used once to be a whole pattern of honorific words which described a happy correlation between a man's values and the aims and intentions of his society; but these are as unfashionable as the invocations to *thrift* and *self-help* that were current in Victorian society and have now disappeared in a time when we require people to spend rather than save, consume rather than produce. Most of the words that describe bridging motions between man and society have tended to vanish from the discourse of the moderns, though they remain solidly in the speech of those for whom a degree of social engagement seems impressive and worthy. Similarly many of the words that stigmatized those who made a bad bridge between self and society have lost their force. There used once to be a wealth of words which manifested a general sense of the low repute in which evil and antisocial conduct was held. Nowadays, when we regard evil as a moral preference different from our own, we tend to turn to the neutral discourse of sociology or psychology. We likewise tend to suspect hierarchical words, like *superior, refined* and so on. The preference today seems to be for apparently neutral and seemingly unhierarchical words without a public moral content. In this sense, the power of moral assertion in discourse would appear to be declining. In fact, of course, it is being re-formed. New hierarchies and moral inferences emerge.

Words asserting a public standard of morality, roughly agreed on as a general direction for human aspiration, tend to be replaced by words as-serting a relativistic and private conception. Linked with this is the discard-ing, in the newer vocabulary, of words seeming to imply a preference for fathers over sons. *Paternalism* is a case of a word now demoted and used pejoratively—linguistically the fraternal society is already with us—and *educational* has suffered a similar fate. The word *mature*, on the other hand, has undergone an interesting process of adaptation and reclamation, for it is now regarded as a moral quality almost exclusively the property of the young. This particular corrective process has struck particularly hard at Western religion, which has both a sense of the value of public moral con-sensus and a strong paternalistic symbolism. In consequence those aspects of religion which tend towards the fatherly, the authoritative or the social have been demoted, while those to do with the youthful and the private have been stressed of late. As more than one vicar has observed, Christi-anity is really a teenage religion; as others have suggested, it should never have become an institution at all, for this has set an organization in-tervening between man and his creator; as yet others have indicated, it never intended to become morally assertive, to take up that most unattrac-tive of properties, a high moral tone. Religion thus tends to be de-moral-ized, and many of the clergy are at pains to point out that there is little moral consensus in the Church; it is the need to worship they are agreed on, though there are theologians without the clergy's degree of personal interest who hardly see the need for that. Thus in recent months we have heard a great deal about "religionless Christianity," which is, to put the matter crudely, Christianity divested of all the social apparatus which has enabled it to survive and be powerful. The new religionists—who, as a friend of mine once put it, believe in at the most one God and pray To Whom It May Concern—pay little attention to the superb sociology of the Church in the past. How cleverly, by means of great effectiveness and fre-quent undesirability, it kept alive the power of religion over the community! But for the new religionists it is the individual rather than the social impli-cations of faith that matter; and the whole tone of their discourse reflects this fact, their pronouncements emphasizing contacts between man and creator, their words being personal, unabstract, tentative. As with the new philosophers the point of enquiry is the seeing eye and the thinking mind; and a logical consequence, already being reached in philosophy, is that dis-course will in fact totally cease, other people lying beyond the self in a fear-some universe in whose reality one cannot for a moment trust.

Let me not suggest, however, that the Church is the stronghold of the new moral discourse—this is, on the whole, not so. Generally it is on the side of moral consensus and the moral assertion, offering its positions almost as if they had some external authority. And thus it is the Church's words that are most suspect. In his Reith Lectures Professor Carstairs stigmatized Saint Paul as "an authoritarian character," a man who attempted to insist on a sexual morality remote from that of the Trobriand Islanders, and the tendency towards this sort of insistence is to be found extensively in the history of the Church. In his recent book on *The Family* the sociologist Ronald Fletcher collects together a veritable courtesy-book of old-style moral usages, most of them using the word *moral* itself. Many of the spokesmen he selects were Methodists who espoused a strict and traditional idea of public morality; they are here to be found complaining that the modern family has gone downhill, and in support of their impression they did not quote statistics but spoke rhetorically of the nation's "dire moral peril," of the "seedy dingy moral apathy of our time," "the moral failure of the home" and so on. Mr. Fletcher counters with the new mode of discourse, against moral decline he offers different behaviour. His tone is evidently more permissive but the interesting thing is that it is not without its prophetic note. He expresses "irritation" with the old manner (anger plays a substantial part in the new moral tone) and demands forward-looking thinking, better statistics, other words. So the point is not that the new prophets are without morality but that they have a different and a flatter style of moral speech to distinguish them. (In fact the word *moral* is central to the new discourse; but it means something rather different.)

What, then, we may perceive in the quiet linguistic changes that are taking place in our society at the moment is a tendency towards the heightening of private values at the expense of public ones, of the energization of words that tend to express this, and an opprobrious weighting to certain traditional words which have been of evident value to public men of the past. The very overtones of the word *establishment* (i.e., that which is established is automatically to be suspected) suggests the fund of resources behind the new-style speakers, while the Conservative Party have long ceased defending the existence of anything on the grounds that it is traditional, though the test of time and the test of existence are as good tests as any. The gradual spreading of the new discourse naturally spreads the implied attitudes behind it (for one of the ways in which we acquire values is through acquiring an organized vocabulary—this is why vocabulary has power). And spreading it is, so that most of us now find that we straddle two linguistic worlds. The new language has extending currency. The ready acceptance of what it is conventional to call "satire" is the acceptance of the tone of voice, quizzical, demanding, informal, vernacular, often faintly offensive and doctrinaire, which is appropriate to the new language, and which many writers have been exploring. The group of new-style speakers is thus spreading, and is leading to some gradual alienation of those who use the older tone of voice. One may examine this process in a number of conscious users of language, such as journalists or broadcasters. The formality of B.B.C. official speech used to be one of our great reassurances; it spoke for order, like guards on trains. Now, in a wave of informality, even the news is changing. The names of contributors to newsreels are frequently mentioned (personal), announcers cough regularly and carefully do not, as they easily can, switch the cough out (informal), the opinions of people in the street are canvassed, though they frequently have none (democratic), and interviewers are aggressive and sometimes even offensive (vernacular). So, personal, informal, democratic and vernacular, comes the new common speech for all things.

However, the co-existence of the two modes of language can lead to confusion in these intermediate times, and it is not surprising that many people, caught between the two camps, feel now and then that a little assistance is needed. For most of us borrow our speech from all that is available, and these are hard days. One might take again the already mentioned instance of the word *moral*. In the old style of discourse (hereafter designated as OS) the word describes the obligation to choose between right and wrong; in new style (NS) it refers to the *difficulty* of choosing between right and wrong. It should be noted then that many words have diametrically opposite meanings or intonations, and a short glossary here would not come amiss:

Youth = a person not yet fully mature (OS); a person fully mature (NS).

Mature = wise, responsible, capable of holding positions of power (OS); wise, conscious of difficulty, incapable of holding positions of power (NS).

Rebellious = out of touch with cultural experience (OS); in touch with cultural experience (NS).

Spontaneous = ill-considered, hasty (OS); imaginatively perceptive (NS).

Apathy = not being interested in taking on social duties and obligations (OS); being interested in taking on social duties and obligations (NS).

Paternal = taking an intelligent and encouraging interest in the young (OS); imposing upon and destroying the young (NS).

Culture = reading books, pursuing the arts (OS); doing anything (NS).

91

Commitment = an unfortunate obligation to a cause (OS); a necessary obligation to a cause (NS).

Hypocrisy = pretending to believe in what is self-evident (OS); believing in what pretends to be self-evident (NS).

Sinful = doing what everyone knows to be wrong (OS); knowing what everyone does to be wrong (NS).

Tradition = the proper preoccupation of the living with the dead (OS); the morbid preoccupation of the dead with the living (NS).

The list of course can be extended indefinitely.

A further problem emerges, however, when we find not the same word for different concepts, but different words for the same concept. Here, once again, a short list might give some guidance:

Guilt (OS) = *shame* (NS).

Puritan (OS) = *censor* (NS).

Libertine (OS) = *puritan* (NS).

Father (OS) = *brother* (NS).

Righteous indignation (OS) = *anger* or *hate* (NS).

Vulgar (OS) = *phoney* (NS).

Us (OS) = *them* (NS).

Them (OS) = *us* (NS).

There are many deductions that can be made from these slim and summary lists; it is outside my purpose here to make them. Studies are needed of the frequency with which each of these groups uses certain central words, and of particular interest are those words that appear frequently in the discourse of one group and never in the discourse of the other. In some cases they indicate the vanishing of certain concepts (*virginity* might for instance be one among NS-speakers) and the invention of others (*commitment* perhaps, totally irrelevant to OS-speakers). My purpose here is simply to point out, to those who aspire to enter the arena of social discussion, that one's alliances may be determined by the very discourse one has acquired or chooses to espouse. The importance of a common language in establishing the freemasonry of the Elect has been the theme of many modern novels, which frequently show private languages triumphing over public ones, the vernacular defeating the literary, the words of youth defeating the words of the aged. The idea of such an Elect, a central group of moral sophisticates who either triumph over or plunge more deeply into experience, whose private vision is higher than any public one, recurs frequently in fiction; it is present in Hemingway and Salinger, Lawrence and Sillitoe. It is present for that matter in Jane Austen. The logical development of the situation is to be found in the Beat Generation, an out group that distinguishes and selects its members largely by their language. What this means of course is that common discourse can both include and exclude, and in fact the Beat Generation is a very exclusive club, rather like our image of the traditional aristocracy. This sort of distinction by language has of course always existed, and it suggests that even in a classless society a hierarchy of discourse will survive. The assumption that those who are not *with it* are against it, that *them* is in no way a part of *us*, that the squares and the phoneys and the establishment—or the masses and the hoi polloi and the untutored—are by definition in another camp, means that language retains one of its essential functions. It reassures those who share our words with the warmth of phatic communion; it separates those who do not into their rightful place—beyond the pale.

In fact, of course, these two different languages represent two different functions of speech. The older language tends to be in character a language of idealism, of hortatory and ennobling concepts. It provides a range of discourse that is extensive and puts its users into touch with a history of language and thought. Its weakness is that it is apt to become detached from realities, to represent nothing but the will to speak. The second language tends, however, in the opposite direction. It is not a language of power, and is poor in abstract concepts. It tends to be anti-cultural. It is a language of uncertainty and scepticism to set off against the discourse of the confident. Its emphasis falls on realism rather than idealism, on descriptive rather than enlarging concepts. Its words for relations outside the self are often thin and indeterminate, and in some auditors it produces an impression akin to disturbed silence. Its best words are those which have to do with immediacy, spontaneity, and the presentation of disguised emotions and indignations. It stresses the value of being in touch and ready with a response. It closes off large areas of traditional thought and speech. Holden Caulfield, with all the resources of the English language behind him, can scarcely get beyond the word *phoney* to describe what he distrusts; we are invited to value him for his immediate touchstones, his vernacular of scepticism, though we tend to note too how narrow a discourse it is. It seems a thin discourse on which to pin a moral life; but the other discourse, with its heavily rhetorical note, its genial gestures toward meaning, can be a language quite as flat. The modern speaker needs to be quite as careful today as in the days when to use the word "notepaper" was enough to damn a man socially for life.

2

Felix Cohen

The Vocabulary of Prejudice

Mr. Cohen examines an obvious area of prejudice, in which most of us are generally pretty careful of the overtones of the words we use. But his point can be extended to our writing on any topic. Nowhere do we more fully expose ourselves for what we are — for what we think and feel — than in our choice of words and the way we put them together. Our prejudices, biases, and stupidities are there for all to see. Buffon's famous definition, "The style is the man," encapsules this idea.

Since you are judged by what you say and the way you say it, don't be caught with your verbal pants down. Ideally, you should be as careful in everything you write as you are in the area discussed by Mr. Cohen. This is not a recommendation for cautious or colorless writing; rather it is an exhortation to be more fully aware of the nuances of the choices open to you in your vocabulary and sentence structure. Take pains in your writing not to appear a bigger fool than you can help.

For some years I have been asking my students whether any of them had any prejudices, and I have not by this method of inquiry found anybody who had any prejudices and admitted to having them. I can think of only three possible explanations of this fact: (1) that my students have prejudices and know they have them, but are attempting to conceal this fact from me; (2) that my students are actually without prejudices; and (3) that it is normal for people not to see their own prejudices.

As my students are, generally speaking, of the highest moral character, I must reject this first alternative theory, that of conscious deception. And as my students are a fair cross-section of humanity, I must reject the second alternative possibility, that they are in fact unprejudiced. This leaves me with the third alternative, which I will accept as a working hypothesis, namely, that prejudice is something we are more apt to recognize in others than in ourselves.

In this respect prejudice is not unique. Take the relation, for instance, of fact to theory, of reverence to idolatry, of orthodoxy to heterodoxy. Generally, the theories we believe we call facts, and the facts we disbelieve we call theories; the attitude of respect for objects we respect we call reverence, and the attitude of respect for objects which we hold in contempt we call idolatry; we are all familiar, of course, with the observation that orthodoxy is my doxy and heterodoxy is the other fellow's doxy.

As the field of racial and national feeling is generally conceded to be a field in which prejudice plays a major role, it may be helpful to examine some of the semantic data in this field to see what light such data may throw upon the problem of prejudice identification.

Perhaps the simplest way to recognize racial or national prejudice (in others) is to notice the ways in which people refer to other people. A person who uses the common contemptuous or patronizing terms, *nigger, coon, darkie, redskin, paleface, Chink, Jap, Wop, Spick, Dago, Hunkie, Kraut, half-breed, Gook, Frog,* etc., may be quite unaware of the value-overtones of these terms, but the sensitive listener, especially if he has been sensitized in a particular direction by the repeated impact of these barbed words against himself, immediately spots the attitude of contempt that these terms convey.

"The Vocabulary of Prejudice" from *Fellowship*, November 1953. Reprinted with permission of Fellowship publications and Felix Cohen.

"Innocent" repeitition. Of course, the user of such terms, when challenged, may reply that these are the terms in common usage in his group, and that he means no offense by them. He "didn't know they were loaded." Almost all of us repeatedly offend others by a word, a tone, or a gesture, without being aware of the fact. It is reasonable to suppose, however, that one who takes up, however innocently, from his environment various word usages that offend others also commonly takes up, perhaps just as innocently, the implicit racial and national attitudes of separateness, distance, and direction that prevail in that environment.

Repelling associations. Why, one may ask, should the use of these terms indicate an attitude of contempt? In some cases, this question is easily answered. The name itself may indicate association with something mean or revolting or contemptible in the experience of the name-caller, perhaps with something that typifies the basic avoidance reaction which human and other animals exhibit toward various forms of filth and danger.

Such is the case, for instance, with words associating the eating habits of a racial group with some cheap or, to the word-user, bad-smelling or repelling food, as for example, *Frog, Kraut, Spick,* or *Greaser.* In other words the name itself has a downward pointing direction, e.g., *coon* (likening a person to a sub-human animal) or *half-breed* (animals breed; humans marry and bear children) or *Siwash* (corruption of *sauvage*, French for savage).

The irrelevant adjective. In still other cases, the name identifies a human being with what he justly regards as a trivial aspect of himself, such as his skin color, as in the terms *Negro, darkie, redskin,* or *paleface.* The moral tone of the designation is: the person so designated is peculiar; his outstanding characteristic is the abnormality of his skin. Such overtones may be created by repeated usage. The practice of most American newspapers of referring to arrested or suspected criminals as "Negro" or "alien," if they are either, but not as "white" or "seventh generation American" or "Protestant" or "freckled," is a technique that builds popular impressions as from the facts. What may be called "the technique of the irrelevant adjective" is a smear technique that is difficult to answer. When a New York Congressman objected to Congressman Rankin's referring to him as a "Jewish Congressman from New York," Congressman Rankin's answer was, in effect: "Well, you are Jewish, aren't you? Why be ashamed of it?"

The real issue here is not whether a racial or religious adjective is accurately descriptive of an individual, but whether the adjective is properly relevant to the context in which it is used. The adjective, Negro, may be perfectly relevant to a discussion of the medical effects of sunburn, and the adjective, Jewish, may be entirely relevant to a discussion of religious ritual. The relevance of these adjectives to a report of a crime wave, however, may depend upon the inarticulate premise that Negroes and Jews are especially disposed to criminal activity.

In some other instances, it is more difficult to understand why the racial designation should be felt as a term of disparagement. *Dago*, for instance, began apparently as a shortening of the honored Italian name, Diego, and *Wop* as an abbreviation of *guapo* (meaning handsome), yet both terms now carry definitely disparaging overtones, as do such originally harmless abbreviations as *Jap, Chink*, and *Hunkie*.

Is there something about the sound of certain words that makes them carry overtones of contempt? Is it merely a coincidence that the English language uses one-syllable words ending in *-unk* to designate so many unhonored objects, e.g., bunk, chunk, dunk, drunk, flunk, junk, punk, sunk, skunk, stunk? Does a one-syllable word that can be uttered in less time than it takes to think perhaps carry an overtone of contempt more easily than a polysyllabic word or a precise phrase, e.g., American of Chinese descent, instead of Chink?

What words reveal.   Bertrand Russell has called attention to the possibility of conjugating value-weighted adjectives in such form as: (1) I am firm; (2) You are obstinate; (3) He is a pig-headed fool. More generally, we can say that almost any human characteristic can be described either in honorific or pejorative terms. Consider, for example, how the choice between up-grading, down-grading, and neutral words may reflect a speaker's value judgment as he describes a given human trait:

Up-Grading	*Neutral*	*Down-Grading*
Loyal	Obedient	Slavish
Devoted	Self-subordinating	Fanatical
Tolerant	Non-discriminating	Nigger-lover
Courageous	Bold	Reckless, foolhardy
Humanitarian	Idealistic	Do-gooder
Realistic	Suspicious	Cynical

More subtle than the choice of adjectives is the value orientation that is involved in the choice of a noun or verb to describe a given activity, operation, or institution:

Up-Grading	*Neutral*	*Down-Grading*
Official	Office-holder	Bureaucrat
Statesman	Policy-maker	Politician
Investigator	Detective	Flatfoot
Business executive	Employer	Boss
Financial leader	Banker	Money-lender
Orator	Influential leader	Rabble-rouser

Peculiar individual tastes have relatively little permanent impact upon a social institution like language. But where many individuals in a society share a common value standard, it is natural for them to develop a common code. These codes are particularly important in a political campaign. Our candidates may *inspire;* they never *inflame,* as do the other fellow's candidates. Our candidates may *demonstrate;* only the opposing candidates allege. Our candidates may *clarify;* only the opponents will *admit error.* California's Governor Warren is reported to have made the sage observation: "When government does something for us, that's social progress; when it does something for the other fellow, that's socialism."

The language of colonial administrators offers a particularly impressive exhibition of double book-keeping in the political field, for here professional and political value standards are largely reinforced by racial or national prides and prejudices. Even in the United States today, where at least lip service must be paid to the traditional American dislike for colonialism, a highly-developed system of administrative double-talk has made it possible for our colonial officials to profess a firm resolve to liquidate their jobs and allow their so-called wards (for example, American Indians) full rights of citizenship, while in practice they press steadily for increased powers and increased appropriations.

Two vocabularies. Under this system of double-talk, colonial officials *assist, counsel, serve,* and *enlighten* natives, while other persons never assist, but only *abet,* never advise but only *incite,* never serve but only *interfere,* never enlighten but only *propagandize.* When native chiefs or councils make decisions for themselves, this is called *politics;* when decisions are made by colonial officials, this is called *policy-making.* When decisions are put into practice by the natives, this is called *manipulation;* when colonial officials handle such matters the preferred term is *administration.* When native property is handled so as to increase its productive yield, this is called *development* if colonial officials or their licensees are doing the handling, and *exploitation* if someone else is doing the handling. When natives take advice from the colonial officials, they are *cooperating;* when they take advice from others, they are *conspiring.*

By carefully keeping the two vocabularies distinct it is generally possible for a professionally trained group of administrators to persuade the public that pays its salaries that its "wards" are not yet ready to run their own businesses, manage their own lands, hold their own free elections, make their own contracts, or even decide when to go to bed and when to get up in the morning, and that increasing appropriations and powers should be granted to white officials to enable them to make such decisions for their non-white subjects. Any white man who speaks up in defense of native freedom is officially classified as either a *crank* or a *grafter* or a *paid agitator*—a *grafter* if the natives pay him for help, a *paid agitor* if white sympathizers pay him, and a *crank* if nobody pays him.

Generally speaking, eulogistic or up-grading words may be classed as "we" words. They are words which we apply customarily to our own actions and to the actions of those for whom we have a strong fellow-feeling. Dyslogistic, or down-grading words, on the other hand, are "they" words, used to describe the actions of those from whom we are inclined to separate ourselves. Just as the choice between "we have sinned" and "you have sinned" so often may mark the difference between effective shared effort at reform and the kind of preaching that moves only the preacher, so the subtler choice between "we" words and "they" words can often reveal moral premises of which the speaker himself may be quite unaware.

Are Indians people?   When, for example, a court begins an opinion in an Indian property case by referring to Indians moving from one place to another as *roaming, wandering,* or *roving,* we can be pretty sure that it will end up denying the claimed property rights of the Indians. For these words are words which are commonly applied to buffalo, wolves, and other sub-human animals. They suggest that the relation of an Indian to land is purely a physical relation and not a social one. They are plainly "out-grouping" or "they" words to describe movements which most of us, thinking of ourselves, would describe by means of such words as *traveling, vacationing, commuting,* words that we would not apply to animals, words distinctly human. These latter words connote purpose in movement. Only when we regard a person as strange or perhaps sub-human do we customarily impute aimless motion to him.

Our point of view.   Thus, if I or a friend should move from one place to another, this physical motion would ordinarily either be described in "we" terms or be assimilated into a more highly descriptive term. We may speak of ourselves as transporting merchandise, or surveying, or berry-picking, or selling life insurance, or settling the West, depending on the occasion and purpose of the physical motion. An unfriendly Indian might disregard all these nuances and describe our action in "they" terms as *trespassing* or *invading the Indian country*. And conversely, white judges or white settlers who do not consider Indians quite human will be apt to disregard the purposes and occasions of Indian motion and refer to any travelling Indian as a *nomad,* thereby implicitly justifying the taking of the Indian lands and homes by more civilized "settlers."

We may say that each of us is likely to place himself and those to whom he is especially attached closer to the top than to the bottom of our value words. This means that "we" words will generally have a higher value direction than "they" words. For example, when a white judge refers to a defendant as a Negro, Indian or savage, he is using an "out-grouping" line of demarcation that separates himself from the defendant. On the other hand, a judge who refers to the same defendant as a citizen, a taxpayer, a father, a husband, or a veteran, is using an "in-grouping" delineation that includes himself and honored friends. Perhaps the most significant effort of attorneys on opposite sides of a case is the effort to persuade the judge or the jury or both to think of the defendant in "we" or "they" terms. This, however, is not yet part of what is generally taught in the law schools of our country. Perhaps it is not yet part of what is generally understood in law schools.

Hope for the future.   The technique of semantic analysis, as I have tried to present it here, will not of itself eliminate human prejudice. But it may help us to uncover the inarticulate value premises of ourselves and others. Such understanding may itself lead to greater tolerance of cultural diversity. At the same time, it may help us to see more clearly the moral implications of our human egocentric limitations. Having achieved such understanding of our own limitations and distortions, we may be in a better position to help others to see theirs. To that extent, semantic analysis may help us, in the long run, in achieving a greater degree of tolerance and freedom for our society.

Ossie Davis

The English Language Is My Enemy

This short essay is included here to help convince you that words do count in the real world. The fact that Mr. Davis is wrong, or at least overstates his case, doesn't matter. What matters is that he thinks he's right, and so do millions of other people. "There is nothing either right or wrong, but thinking makes it so" is the most pragmatic line Hamlet ever got off.

As an exercise, you might try writing a lucid, reasoned, and dispassionate refutation of Mr. Davis' point. You could begin by checking your thesaurus for white, black, *and other colors as well. If Mars is red, does that mean that Communism controls the cosmos? Try your dictionary for the etymology of* Negro *and* black. *You might also consider primitive man, day and night, and archetypal imagery. If man had evolved with infra-red vision so that he could see only in the dark, it is probable that* whiteness *would now carry all the adverse connotations. Read* Moby Dick, *Chapter 42, "On the Whiteness of the Whale."*

Unless, of course, you're so lily-livered that you turn white with fear and show the white feather of cowardice at the thought of all that reading.

A superficial examination of Roget's Thesaurus of the English Language reveals the following facts: the word WHITENESS has 134 synonyms, 44 of which are favorable and pleasing to contemplate, i.e., purity, cleanness, immaculateness, bright, shining, ivory, fair, blonde, stainless, clean, clear, chaste, unblemished, unsullied, innocent, honorable, upright, just, straight-forward, fair, genuine, trustworthy (a white man-colloquialism). Only ten synonyms for WHITENESS appear to me to have negative implications—and these only in the mildest sense: gloss over, whitewash, gray, wan, pale, ashen, etc.

The word BLACKNESS has 120 synonyms, 60 of which are distinctly unfavorable, and none of them even mildly positive. Among the offending 60 were such words as: blot, blotch, smut, smudge, sully, begrime, soot, becloud, obscure, dingy, murky, low-toned, threatening, frowning, foreboding, forbidden, sinister, baneful, dismal, thundery, evil, wicked, malignant, deadly, unclean, dirty, unwashed, foul, etc. . . . not to mention 20 synonyms directly related to race, such as: Negro, Negress, nigger, darky, blackamoor, etc.

When you consider the fact that *thinking* itself is sub-vocal speech—in other words, one must use *words* in order to think at all—you will appreciate the enormous heritage of racial prejudgement that lies in wait for any child born into the English Language. Any teacher, good or bad, white or black, Jew or Gentile, who uses the English Language as a medium of communication is forced, willy-nilly, to teach the Negro child 60 ways to despise himself, and the white child 60 ways to aid and abet him in the crime.

Who speaks to me in my Mother Tongue damns me indeed! . . . the English Language—in which I cannot conceive myself as a black man without, at the same time, debasing myself . . . my enemy, with which to survive at all I must continually be at war.

"The English Language Is My Enemy" from the *Negro History Bulletin*, April 1967. Copyright © by the Association for the Study of Negro Life and History. Reprinted with permission of the publisher.

4

Arthur M. Schlesinger, Jr.

A Note on Language

President Kennedy was a man with a care for the written word and with considerable grace and style of his own. Mr. Schlesinger, historian and adviser to President Kennedy, shared that concern.

In this essay he speaks with resignation of the losing battle against gobbledygook. Note in his first sentence, and throughout the essay, his implicit recognition of the reciprocal relationship between thought and word. Note also the list of standard symptoms: cliché, repetition, the passive voice, bad spelling, and grammar.

The intellectual exhaustion of the Foreign Service expressed itself in the poverty of the official rhetoric. In meetings the men from State would talk in a bureaucratic patois borrowed in large part from the Department of Defense. We would be exhorted to "zero in" on "the purpose of the drill" (or of the "exercise" or "operation"), to "crank in" this and "phase out" that and "gin up" something else, to "pinpoint" a "viable" policy and, behind it, a "fall-back position," to ignore the "flak" from competing government bureaus or from the communists, to refrain from "nit-picking" and never to be "counterproductive." Once we were "seized of the problem," preferably in as "hard-nosed" a manner as possible, we would review "options," discuss "over-all" objectives, seek "breakthroughs," consider "crash programs," "staff out" policies—doing all these things preferably "meaningfully" and "in depth" until we were ready to "finalize" our deliberations, "sign on to" or "sign off on" a conclusion (I never could discover the distinction, if any, between these two locutions) and "implement" a decision. This was not just shorthand; part of the conference-table vocabulary involved a studied multiplication of words. Thus one never talked about a "paper" but always a "piece of paper," never said "at this point" but always "at this point in time."

Graceless as this patois was, it did have a certain, if sometimes spurious, air of briskness and efficiency. The result was far worse when the Department stopped talking and started writing. Whether drafting memoranda, cables or even letters or statements for the President, the Department fell into full, ripe, dreariness of utterance with hideous ease. The recipe was evidently to take a handful of clichés (saying something in a fresh way might create unforeseen troubles), repeat at five-minute intervals (lest the argument become clear or interesting), stir in the dough of the passive voice (the active voice assigns responsibility and was therefore hazardous) and garnish with self-serving rhetoric (Congress would be unhappy unless we constantly proclaimed the rectitude of American motives).

After the Bay of Pigs, the State Department sent over a document entitled "The Communist Totalitarian Government of Cuba as a Source of International Tension in the Americas," which it had approved for distribution to NATO, CENTO, SEATO, the OAS and the free governments of Latin America and eventually for public release. In addition to the usual defects of Foggy Bottom prose, the paper was filled with bad spelling and grammar. Moreover, the narrative, which mysteriously stopped at the beginning of April 1961, contained a self-righteous condemnation of Castro's interventionist activities in the Caribbean that an unfriendly critic, alas! could have applied, without changing a word, to more recent actions by the United States. I responded on behalf of the White House:

> *It is our feeling here that the paper should not be disseminated in its present form....*
>
> *Presumably the document is designed to impress, not an audience which is already passionately anti-Castro, but an audience which has not yet finally made up its mind on the gravity of the problem. Such an audience is going to be persuaded, not by rhetoric, but by evidence. Every effort to heighten the evidence by rhetoric only impairs the persuasive power of the document. Observe the title: "The Communist Totalitarian Government of Cuba..." This title presupposes the conclusion which the paper seeks to establish. Why not call it "The Castro Regime in Cuba" and let the reader draw his own conclusions from the evidence? And why call it both "Communist" and "totalitarian"? All Communist governments are totalitarian. The paper, in our view, should be understated rather than overstated; it should eschew cold war jargon; the argument should be carried by facts, not exhortations. The writing is below the level we would hope for in papers for dissemination to other countries. The writing of lucid and forceful English is not too arcane an art.*

The President himself, with his sensitive ear for style, led the fight for literacy in the Department; and he had the vigorous support of some State Department officials, notably George Ball, Harriman and William R. Tyler. But the effort to liberate the State Department from automatic writing had little success. As late as 1963, the Department could submit as a draft of a presidential message on the National Academy of Foreign Affairs a text which provoked this resigned White House comment:

> *This is only the latest and worst of a long number of drafts sent here for Presidential signature. Most of the time it does not matter, I suppose, if the prose is tired, the thought banal and the syntax bureaucratic; and, occasionally when it does matter, State's drafts are very good. But sometimes, as in this case, they are not.*
>
> *A message to Congress is a fairly important form of Presidential communication. The President does not send so many—nor of those*

he does send, does State draft so many—that each one cannot re-
ceive due care and attention. My own old-fashioned belief is that
every Presidential message should be a model of grace, lucidity and
taste in expression. At the very least, each message should be (a) in
English, (b) clear and trenchant in its style, (c) logical in its structure
and (d) devoid of gobbledygook. The State Department draft on the
Academy failed each one of these tests (including, in my view, the
first).

Would it not be possible for someone in the Department with at
least minimal sensibility to take a look at pieces of paper designed for
Presidential signature before they are sent to the White House?

It was a vain fight; the plague of gobbledygook was hard to shake off.
I note words like "minimal" (at least not "optimal") and "pieces of paper"
in my own lament. I can only testify with what interest and relief the President and the White House read cables from ambassadors who could write
—Galbraith from New Delhi with his suave irony, David Bruce from London
with his sharp wit, Kennan from Belgrade with his historical perspective
and somber eloquence, John Bartlow Martin from Santo Domingo and
William Attwood from Guinea with their vivid journalistic touch.

Theodore H. White summed it all up in a letter he sent me from the
Far East in the summer of 1961—a dispatch the President read with great
interest. "The State Department and its competitive instruments," White
wrote, "have in the years since I worked with them become so tangled as
to be almost unfit for any policy-making purpose or decision. . . . Somewhere there exists in the State Department a zone, or a climate, or inertia,
which prevents it from thinking in terms of a new kind of politics, new de-
partures in technique, an inertia which binds it rigidly to the fossil routine of
conferences, negotiations, frozen positions. What must be changed must be
changed first in Washington, at the center."

5

Alexis de Tocqueville

How American Democracy Has Modified the English Language

In the early nineteenth century, de Tocqueville toured America and wrote an extensive report on his observations. Democracy in America is a fascinating book, filled with the most level-headed observations and uncannily accurate in some of its predictions.

De Tocqueville was not a socio-linguist, but his speculations on the relation of political systems to language have been confirmed by research. The predilection of democratic societies for abstract words is an interesting phenomenon. In a later essay, George Orwell will deal with some of its implications.

J f the reader has rightly under-stood what I have already said on the subject of literature in general, he will have no difficulty in understanding that species of influence which a democratic social condition and democratic institutions may exercise over language itself, which is the chief instrument of thought.

Englishmen of education, and more competent judges than I can be of the nicer shades of expression, have frequently assured me that the lan-guage of the educated classes in the United States is notably different from that of the educated classes in Great Britain. They complain, not only that the Americans have brought into use a number of new words (the differ-ence and the distance between the two countries might suffice to explain that much), but that these new words are more especially taken from the jargon of parties, the mechanical arts, or the language of trade. In addition to this, they assert that old English words are often used by the Americans in new acceptations; and lastly, that the inhabitants of the United States frequently intermingle phraseology in the strangest manner, and sometimes place words together which are always kept apart in the language of the mother country. These remarks, which were made to me at various times by persons who appeared to be worthy of credit, led me to reflect upon the subject; and my reflections brought me, by theoretical reasoning, to the same point at which my informants had arrived by practical observation.

In aristocracies language must naturally partake of that state of repose in which everything remains. Few new words are coined because few new things are made; and even if new things were made, they would be desig-nated by known words, whose meaning had been determined by tradition. If it happens that the human mind bestirs itself at length or is roused by light breaking in from without, the novel expressions that are introduced have a learned, intellectual, and philosophical character, showing that they do not originate in a democracy. After the fall of Constantinople had turned the tide of science and letters towards the west, the French language was almost immediately invaded by a multitude of new words, which all had Greek and Latin roots. An erudite neologism then sprang up in France, which was confined to the educated classes, and which produced no sensi-ble effect, or at least a very gradual one, upon the people.

All the nations of Europe successively exhibited the same change. Milton alone introduced more than six hundred words into the English lan-

"How American Democracy Has Modified the English Language" from *Democracy in Amer-ica*, Vol. II, by Alexis de Tocqueville, John Allyn, Publisher, 1882, Boston.

guage, almost all derived from the Latin, the Greek, or the Hebrew. The constant agitation that prevails in a democratic community tends unceasingly, on the contrary, to change the character of the language, as it does the aspect of affairs. In the midst of this general stir and competition of minds, many new ideas are formed, old ideas are lost, or reappear, or are subdivided into an infinite variety of minor shades. The consequence is that many words must fall into desuetude, and others must be brought into use.

Besides, democratic nations love change for its own sake, and this is seen in their language as much as in their politics. Even when they have no need to change words, they sometimes have the desire.

The genius of a democratic people is not only shown by the great number of words they bring into use, but also by the nature of the ideas these new words represent. Among such a people the majority lays down the law in language as well as in everything else; its prevailing spirit is as manifest in this as in other respects. But the majority is more engaged in business than in study, in political and commercial interests than in philosophical speculation or literary pursuits. Most of the words coined or adopted for its use will bear the mark of these habits; they will mainly serve to express the wants of business, the passions of party, or the details of the public administration. In these departments the language will constantly grow, while it will gradually lose ground in metaphysics and theology.

As to the source from which democratic nations are accustomed to derive their new expressions and the manner in which they coin them, both may easily be described. Men living in democratic countries know but little of the language that was spoken at Athens or at Rome, and they do not care to dive into the lore of antiquity to find the expression that they want. If they sometimes have recourse to learned etymologies, vanity will induce them to search for roots from the dead languages; but erudition does not naturally furnish them its resources. The most ignorant, it sometimes happens, will use them most. The eminently democratic desire to get above their own sphere will often lead them to seek to dignify a vulgar profession by a Greek or Latin name. The lower the calling is and the more remote from learning, the more pompous and erudite is its appellation. Thus the French rope-dancers have transformed themselves into *acrobates* and *funambules*.

Having little knowledge of the dead languages, democratic nations are apt to borrow words from living tongues, for they have constant mutual intercourse, and the inhabitants of different countries imitate each other the more readily as they grow more like each other every day.

110

But it is principally upon their own languages that democratic nations attempt to make innovations. From time to time they resume and restore to use forgotten expressions in their vocabulary, or they borrow from some particular class of the community a term peculiar to it, which they introduce with a figurative meaning into the language of daily life. Many expressions which originally belonged to the technical language of a profession or a party are thus drawn into general circulation.

The most common expedient employed by democratic nations to make an innovation in language consists in giving an unwonted meaning to an expression already in use. This method is very simple, prompt, and convenient; no learning is required to use it correctly and ignorance itself rather facilitates the practice; but that practice is most dangerous to the language. When a democratic people double the meaning of a word in this way, they sometimes render the meaning which it retains as ambiguous as that which it acquires. An author begins by a slight deflection of a known expression from its primitive meaning, and he adapts it, thus modified, as well as he can to his subject. A second writer twists the sense of the expression in another way; a third takes possession of it for another purpose; and as there is no common appeal to the sentence of a permanent tribunal that may definitively settle the meaning of the word, it remains in an unsettled condition. The consequence is that writers hardly ever appear to dwell upon a single thought, but they always seem to aim at a group of ideas, leaving the reader to judge which of them has been hit.

This is a deplorable consequence of democracy. I had rather that the language should be made hideous with words imported from the Chinese, the Tatars, or the Hurons than that the meaning of a word in our own language should become indeterminate. Harmony and uniformity are only secondary beauties in composition: many of these things are conventional, and, strictly speaking, it is possible to do without them; but without clear phraseology there is no good language.

The principle of equality necessarily introduces several other changes into language.

In aristocratic ages, when each nation tends to stand aloof from all others and likes to have a physiognomy of its own, it often happens that several communities which have a common origin become nevertheless strangers to each other; so that, without ceasing to understand the same language, they no longer all speak it in the same manner. In these ages each nation is divided into a certain number of classes, which see but little of each other and do not intermingle. Each of these classes contracts and invariably retains habits of mind peculiar to itself and adopts by choice certain terms which afterwards pass from generation to generation, like their estates. The same idiom then comprises a language of the poor and a language of the rich, a language of the commoner and a language of the nobility, a learned language and a colloquial one. The deeper the divisions and the more impassable the barriers of society become, the more must this be the case. I would lay a wager that among the castes of India there are amazing variations of language, and that there is almost as much difference between the language of a pariah and that of a Brahmin as there is in their dress.

When, on the contrary, men, being no longer restrained by ranks, meet on terms of constant intercourse, when castes are destroyed and the classes of society are recruited from and intermixed with each other, all the words of a language are mingled. Those which are unsuitable to the greater number perish; the remainder form a common store, whence everyone chooses pretty nearly at random. Almost all the different dialects that divided the idioms of European nations are manifestly declining; there is no patois in the New World, and it is disappearing every day from the old countries.

The influence of this revolution in social condition is as much felt in style as it is in language. Not only does everyone use the same words, but a habit springs up of using them without discrimination. The rules which style had set up are almost abolished: the line ceases to be drawn between expressions which seem by their very nature vulgar and others which appear to be refined. Persons springing from different ranks of society carry with them the terms and expressions they are accustomed to use into whatever circumstances they may enter; thus the origin of words is lost like the origin of individuals, and there is as much confusion in language as there is in society.

I am aware that in the classification of words there are rules which do not belong to one form of society any more than to another, but which are derived from the nature of things. Some expressions and phrases are vulgar because the ideas they are meant to express are low in themselves; others are of a higher character because the objects they are intended to designate are naturally lofty. No intermixture of ranks will ever efface these differences. But the principle of equality cannot fail to root out whatever is merely conventional and arbitrary in the forms of thought. Perhaps the necessary classification that I have just pointed out will always be less respected by a democratic people than by any other, because among such a people there are no men who are permanently disposed, by education, culture, and leisure, to study the natural laws of language and who cause those laws to be respected by their own observance of them.

I shall not leave this topic without touching on a feature of democratic languages that is, perhaps, more characteristic of them than any other. It has already been shown that democratic nations have a taste and sometimes a passion for general ideas, and that this arises from their peculiar merits and defects. This liking for general ideas is displayed in democratic languages by the continual use of generic terms or abstract expressions and by the manner in which they are employed. This is the great merit and the great imperfection of these languages.

Democratic nations are passionately addicted to generic terms and abstract expressions because these modes of speech enlarge thought and assist the operations of the mind by enabling it to include many objects in a small compass. A democratic writer will be apt to speak of *capacities* in the abstract for men of capacity and without specifying the objects to which their capacity is applied; he will talk about *actualities* to designate in one word the things passing before his eyes at the moment; and, in French, he will comprehend under the term *éventualités* whatever may happen in the universe, dating from the moment at which he speaks. Democratic writers are perpetually coining abstract words of this kind, in which they sublimate into further abstraction the abstract terms of the language. Moreover, to render their mode of speech more succinct, they personify the object of these abstract terms and make it act like a real person. Thus they would say in French: *La force des choses veut que les capacités gouvernent.*

I cannot better illustrate what I mean than by my own example. I have frequently used the word *equality* in an absolute sense; nay, I have personified equality in several places; thus I have said that equality does such and such things or refrains from doing others. It may be affirmed that the writers of the age of Louis XIV would not have spoken in this manner; they would never have thought of using the word *equality* without applying it to some particular thing; and they would rather have renounced the term altogether than have consented to make it a living personage.

These abstract terms which abound in democratic languages, and which are used on every occasion without attaching them to any particular fact, enlarge and obscure the thoughts they are intended to convey; they render the mode of speech more succinct and the idea contained in it less clear. But with regard to language, democratic nations prefer obscurity to labor.

I do not know, indeed, whether this loose style has not some secret charm for those who speak and write among these nations. As the men who live there are frequently left to the efforts of their individual powers of mind, they are almost always a prey to doubt; and as their situation in life is forever changing, they are never held fast to any of their opinions by the immobility of their fortunes. Men living in democratic countries, then, are apt to entertain unsettled ideas, and they require loose expressions to convey them. As they never know whether the idea they express today will be appropriate to the new position they may occupy tomorrow, they naturally acquire a liking for abstract terms. An abstract term is like a box with a false bottom; you may put in it what ideas you please, and take them out again without being observed.

Among all nations generic and abstract terms form the basis of language. I do not, therefore, pretend that these terms are found only in democratic languages; I say only that men have a special tendency in the ages of democracy to multiply words of this kind, to take them always by themselves in their most abstract acceptation, and to use them on all occasions, even when the nature of the discourse does not require them.

6

John Kenneth Galbraith

The Age of the Wordfact

We have said that words count in the real world. In this essay, Galbraith shows how words can be used to distort the real world, and how dangerous that ability can be.

You may recall Milton's Belial: "But all was false and hollow, though his tongue dropped manna, and could make the worse appear the better reason."

After the loss of New York and Long Island to Howe in 1776, General Washington made no effort to picture this misfortune as an important gain for the Continental army. Lincoln was similarly remiss after the debacle at First Manassas. In 1919 Wilson succeeded in persuading a clear majority of the Senate to vote in favor of the Covenant of the League of Nations, although not the necessary two-thirds majority. Nothing whatever was made of this moral victory.

Things are different today. In June of 1960 President Eisenhower returned from a trip to the Pacific which would seem, superficially, to have been an unparalleled disaster of its kind. Japan, which was the principal object of his tour, had been beset by violent riots over the visit, and in the end it had been forced to urge him not to come. With the aid of his press secretary, however, the President was able to report on his return that the trip had been a success. A small number of Communists, acting under outside orders, had made things a trifle sour in Japan. But that was because they knew how powerful was the impression Mr. Eisenhower made on his trips to other lands, and they determined, as a result, that no such impression would be made on Japan. This was not the first time this kind of thing had happened. Two years earlier, Communists in South American had been forced to take similar preventive action because of the overwhelming appeal of Mr. Nixon to the Latin populace.

Some will perhaps conclude from this comparison that Mr. Eisenhower (and also Mr. Nixon and Mr. Hagerty) has a deeper and more perceptive insight into the ultimate meaning of events than did Washington, Lincoln, or Wilson. After all, the battles of Long Island, of Bull Run, and over the League all occurred in wars that were eventually won. Such a conclusion would be wrong. The earlier Presidents operated, in fact, without the help and support of one of the most important modern instruments of public administration. Just possibly they would not have used it, but the issue is academic, for it had not been invented. I refer to the institution of the "wordfact."

The wordfact makes words a precise substitute for reality. This is an enormous convenience. It means that to say that something exists is a substitute for its existence. And to say that something will happen is as good as having it happen. The saving in energy is nearly total.

There is a distinct possibility that the inventor of the wordfact was an editor or a newspaperman. But whatever its origins, it has come to have present-day importance less in journalism than in government. A press that fully accepts the institution is essential to its employment, but one of the principal functions of the modern public leader is to find the language which adequately improves the reality. Where once it was said of a statesman that he suited action to the words, now he suits the words to the action. If past action (or inaction) has failed to produce the desired result, then, by resort to wordfact, he quickly establishes that the undesired result was more desirable than the desired result.

Lest any of this seem farfetched or complicated, let us remind ourselves of some of the achievements of wordfact in these last years. We agree, of course, that any manifestation of anti-American sentiment abroad is the work of a misguided minority. And until last summer there was no misunderstanding that could not be cured, no resentment that could not be alleviated, no fear that could not be dissipated by a smiling visit of two days to the capital of the country. It would then be stated with appropriate solemnity that the visit was a success; the papers would report that it was a great success; the problems then were presumably gone. Perhaps never before in history had diplomacy become so simple.

But not even traveling has always been necessary. By a bold use of wordfact, we were long able to convert South American dictators into bulwarks of the free world, although on occasion it was thought necessary to drive home the point by decorating them. The recent rise of military regimes in Asia is not a setback for democracy. Rather, it reflects the natural and inevitable difficulty in these countries of basing government on the consent of the governed.

Here at home it is no longer easy to think of unemployment as a misfortune. It reflects the introduction of needed and desirable slack in the system. No properly run economy can be without it. The drastic decline in farm income in recent years has become a manifestation of the vitality of the market system. Though farmers have been leaving their farms at an unprecedented rate, the forces making for this migration have been favorably described by the Secretary of Agriculture in a book with the agreeable title *Freedom to Farm*. Bad television programs were strongly defended early this year by the Federal Communications Commission as a precious manifestation of the freedom of speech. The networks found this a more than satisfactory substitute for any improvement in their programs. They are said, as a result, to be coming up with autumn offerings of unparalleled banality and horror. One hopes that some Sunday afternoon they will have a statesmanlike salute to the principal modern architects of the wordfact.

However, as an indication of what can be done by skillful deployment of the wordfact, with the air of an acquiescent press, it is unlikely that any recent event matches that of the ill-fated U-2. Until Francis Powers made his unpremeditated landing, the sending of military or paramilitary aircraft by one country over another without the permission of the latter would have been considered a somewhat provocative act. (Even now the appearance of such planes over the United States would not be regarded with any real warmth and enthusiasm.) To have an aircraft shot down in the course of such an excursion into another country would have been regarded as a serious misfortune from which little comfort or reward of any kind could possibly be gleaned.

Yet in the days immediately following the last flight of the U-2, by the massive use of wordfact all of the relevant circumstances were changed. Flying planes over other countries became a kind of fifth freedom, to be justified, not without sanctimony, by the secrecy of the other country. The information gained justified the danger incurred and the mistrust aroused among our friends. Indeed, the flights would have to continue. The loss of the plane had proved, as nothing else, the weakness of the opposing defenses. The flights were then suspended, and this became an act of wise restraint. At this stage, the information being gathered ceased to be important as compared with the danger involved and the discomfort and mistrust created among our allies.

Such is the service of wordfact in transforming misfortune into fortune. But it has at least an equal value in transforming inaction into action. Thus, for a year and half now, a cabinet committee headed by Vice President Nixon has been dealing with the problem of inflation. This it has done all but exclusively by denouncing it, and so great has been the fury of its denunciation that it has not deemed it necessary to propose any concrete remedies of importance. In recent years, medical care for the aged has become a major political issue. As this is written, both parties in Congress are endeavoring to make a record on the issue. Records are made not by enacting legislation but by indicating an all but uncontrollable desire to enact legislation. Yet there is a difference, which is recognizable to those who are old and ill and faced with a terrible medical bill. Strong statements in favor of school integration and voting rights for Negroes are a widely accepted substitute for progress, and much less complicated in practice. To most congressional and campaign strategists, it would be considered little short of eccentric to inquire what might be accomplished. The important thing is to find the form of words that will satisfy, and if possible inspire, the Negro voters. One imagines, incidentally, that the invasion of the lunch counters by Negro students is related to the discovery that much of the civil rights discussion is purely inspirational.

On occasion, as when Republicans opposed slavery and Democrats favored alcohol, political platforms in the past have been a guide to ensuing action. But these, too, have been taken over by wordfact. In those hammered out this summer at Los Angeles and Chicago, little thought was given to whether the good things mentioned in them could or would be done. It would have been a jarring note had anyone on either platform committee asked: "Are we sure we can keep this promise?" (It *was* a jarring note at Los Angeles when Paul Ziffren, the California Democratic national committeeman, said that it was less important to write platforms than to get them enacted.) In the case of the platforms, the people appear to be fully aware of the use of wordfact. As a result, they pay them only the most perfunctory attention. It is unfortunate, but words have value only if they have some nexus, however tenuous, with action.

This truth is well illustrated on a global and tragic basis by the discussion of disarmament. Here it is all but taken for granted that no one means what he says, that proposals are made for their effect on public opinion and not on the arms race. And, as a result, people have ceased to pay any attention to the proposals. Civilized survival may in this instance depend on our ability to redeem this problem from the practitioners of wordfact.

But the redemption had better be general. To some extent, of course, it is automatic. It cannot be supposed that the vast verbal fallout of recent years is intrinsically attractive. It is certain to breed a reaction. Convention viewers doubtless saw the beginning of such a reaction this year in the massive inattention that was accorded these wordy proceedings. One sees it also in the tendency to assume, when the government explains that all is well, that something must be wrong.

In part, the control of wordfact requires only that our leaders be slightly more sensible in their approach to the American people. It would be to their own interest. When President Eisenhower described his trip to the vicinity of Japan as a success, he was fooling no one capable of consecutive thought. He did risk giving the impression that he was susceptible to such nonsensical conclusions. And certainly he revealed an unflattering attitude toward the gullibility of the American people.

This, to some extent, was their—or our—fault. We have come to suffer nonsense gladly, and pompous nonsense far too gladly. Elaborate rationalizations of failure should not be met by bored silence or even by a fishy stare. They should be greeted by loud and vulgar laughter, followed immediately by equally uncouth speeches and letters and, if nothing else is possible, by scribbling on walls. All who proclaim good intentions should be immediately asked for their program as to performance. Speeches of candidates for public office this autumn should be scrupulously clipped and saved—and sent to them at intervals over the next couple of years with a request for a progress report. Four years from now, when the parties meet to write their programs, a large number of articulate citizens must be on hand to inquire what in hell happened to the pious promises of 1960. They should have this year's copies in hand.

Perhaps, having organizations for almost everything else, we should have an organization for enforcing election promises and for fingering the man who imagines that he can make his record with words. At a minimum, however, we must reconstruct our hierarchy of political delinquency. The most serious delinquent, the man now to be marked for extinction even before the Florida free-loader, is the man of any political faith or persuasion whose talk shows any sign of being unmatched by intention. The windy liberal should go, along with the windy conservative, and, as a liberal, I devoutly hope that he will go first. And while dealing kindly with all who confess honest error, we should make a special bipartisan onslaught on any man who defends his mistakes by saying that the unintended was better than the intended and that it was really planned all along.

7

George Orwell

Politics and the English Language

If Professor Thorp's essay was a convenient opening survey, this famous essay by George Orwell is a magnfiicent summary of everything we have been talking about in the last two sections. And the six rules for writing that he gives at the end of his essay serve as an introduction to the following section of prescriptions for good style.

Notice that Orwell also relates ideas and style, and subscribes to the main idea of this book that if you write better it will be reflected in your ideas. If one gets rid of bad habits in writing, he says, "one can think better." If this essay doesn't convince you that style is important, nothing will.

In 1984, his famous political novel, Orwell develops the relationship of thought and language. You might want to read it, if you haven't already, especially the appendix in which the purpose of the deliberate debasement of language is most fully developed.

Most people who bother with the matter at all would admit that the English language is in a bad way, but it is generally assumed that we cannot by conscious action do anything about it. Our civilization is decadent and our language—so the argument runs— must inevitably share in the general collapse. It follows that any struggle against the abuse of language is a sentimental archaism, like preferring candles to electric light or hansom cabs to aeroplanes. Underneath this lies the half-conscious belief that language is a natural growth and not an instrument which we shape for our own purposes.

Now, it is clear that the decline of a language must ultimately have political and economic causes: it is not due simply to the bad influence of this or that individual writer. But an effect can become a cause, reinforcing the original cause and producing the same effect in an intensified form, and so on indefinitely. A man may take to drink because he feels himself to be a failure, and then fail all the more completely because he drinks. It is rather the same thing that is happening to the English language. It becomes ugly and inaccurate because our thoughts are foolish, but the slovenliness of our language makes it easier for us to have foolish thoughts. The point is that the process is reversible. Modern English, especially written English, is full of bad habits which spread by imitation and which can be avoided if one is willing to take the necessary trouble. If one gets rid of these habits one can think more clearly, and to think clearly is a necessary first step towards political regeneration: so that the fight against bad English is not frivolous and is not the exclusive concern of professional writers. I will come back to this presently, and I hope that by that time the meaning of what I have said here will have become clearer. Meanwhile, here are five specimens of the English language as it is now habitually written.

These five passages have not been picked out because they are especially bad—I could have quoted far worse if I had chosen—but because they illustrate various of the mental vices from which we now suffer. They are a little below the average, but are fairly representative samples. I number them so that I can refer back to them when necessary:

> *(1) I am not, indeed, sure whether it is not true to say that the Milton who once seemed not unlike a seventeenth-century Shelley*

had not become, out of an experience ever more bitter in each year, more alien [sic] *to the founder of that Jesuit sect which nothing could induce him to tolerate. Professor Harold Laski (Essay in* Freedom of Expression*)*

(2) Above all, we cannot play ducks and drakes with a native battery of idioms which prescribes such egregious collocations of vocables as the Basic put up with *for* tolerate *or* put at a loss *for* bewilder. *Professor Lancelot Hogben (*Interglossa*)*

(3) On the one side we have the free personality: by definition it is not neurotic, for it has neither conflict nor dream. Its desires, such as they are, are transparent, for they are just what institutional approval keeps in the forefront of consciousness; another institutional pattern would alter their number and intensity; there is little in them that is natural, irreducible, or culturally dangerous. But on the other side, the social bond itself is nothing but the mutual reflection of these self-secure integrities. Recall the definition of love. Is not this the very picture of a small academic? Where is there a place in this hall of mirrors for either personality or fraternity? Essay on psychology in Politics *(New York)*

(4). All the "best people" from the gentlemen's clubs, and all the frantic fascist captains, united in common hatred of Socialism and bestial horror of the rising tide of the mass revolutionary movement, have turned to acts of provocation, to foul incendiarism, to medieval legends of poisoned wells, to legalize their own destruction of proletarian organizations, and rouse the agitated petty-bourgeoisie to chauvinistic fervor on behalf of the fight against the revolutionary way out of the crisis. Communist pamphlet

(5) If a new spirit is to be infused into this old country, there is one thorny and contentious reform which must be tackled, and that is the humanization and galvanization of the B.B.C. Timidity here will bespeak canker and atrophy of the soul. The heart of Britain may be sound and of strong beat, for instance, but the British lion's roar at present is like that of Bottom in Shakespeare's Midsummer Night's Dream—*as gentle as any sucking dove. A virile new Britain cannot continue indefinitely to be traduced in the eyes or rather ears of the world by the effete languors of Langham Place, brazenly masquerading as "standard English." When the Voice of Britain is heard at nine*

o'clock, better far and infinitely less ludicrous to hear aitches honestly dropped than the present priggish, inflated, inhibited, school-ma'amish arch braying of blameless bashful mewing maidens!
Letter in Tribune

Each of these passages has faults of its own, but, quite apart from avoidable ugliness, two qualities are common to all of them. The first is staleness of imagery; the other is lack of precision. The writer either has a meaning and cannot express it, or he inadvertently says something else, or he is almost indifferent as to whether his words mean anything or not. This mixture of vagueness and sheer incompetence is the most marked characteristic of modern English prose, and especially of any kind of political writing. As soon as certain topics are raised, the concrete melts into the abstract and no one seems able to think of turns of speech that are not hackneyed: prose consists less and less of *words* chosen for the sake of their meaning, and more and more of *phrases* tacked together like the sections of a prefabricated hen-house. I list below, with notes and examples, various of the tricks by means of which the work of prose-construction is habitually dodged:

Dying metaphors. A newly invented metaphor assists thought by evoking a visual image, while on the other hand a metaphor which is technically "dead" (e.g., *iron resolution*) has in effect reverted to being an ordinary word and can generally be used without loss of vividness. But in between these two classes there is a huge dump of worn-out metaphors which have lost all evocative power and are merely used because they save people the trouble of inventing phrases for themselves. Examples are: *ring the changes on, take up the cudgels for, toe the line, ride roughshod over, stand shoulder to shoulder with, play into the hands of, no axe to grind, grist to the mill, fishing in troubled waters, on the order of the day, Achilles' heel, swan song, hotbed.* Many of these are used without knowledge of their meaning (what is a "rift," for instance?), and incompatible metaphors are frequently mixed, a sure sign that the writer is not interested in what he is saying. Some metaphors now current have been twisted out of their original meaning without those who use them even being aware of the fact. For example, *toe the line* is sometimes written *tow the line.* Another example is *the hammer and the anvil,* now always used with the implication that the anvil gets the worst of it. In real life it is always the anvil that breaks the hammer, never the other way about: a writer who stopped to think what he was saying would be aware of this, and would avoid perverting the original phrase.

Operators or *verbal false limbs.* These save the trouble of picking out appropriate verbs and nouns, and at the same time pad each sentence with extra syllables which give it an appearance of symmetry. Characteristic phrases are *render inoperative, militate against, make contact with, be subjected to, give rise to, give grounds for, have the effect of, play a leading part (role) in, make itself felt, take effect, exhibit a tendency to, serve the purpose of, etc., etc.* The keynote is the elimination of simple verbs. Instead of being a single word, such as *break, stop, spoil, mend, kill,* a verb becomes a *phrase,* made up of a noun or adjective tacked on to some general purposes verb such as *prove, serve, form, play, render.* In addition, the passive voice is wherever possible used in preference to the active, and noun constructions are used instead of gerunds (*by examination of* instead of *by examining*). The range of verbs is further cut down by means of the *-ize* and *de-* formations, and the banal statements are given an appearance of profundity by means of the *not un-* formation. Simple conjunctions and prepositions are replaced by such phrases as *with respect to, having regard to, the fact that, by dint of, in view of, in the interests of, on the hypothesis that;* and the ends of sentences are saved by anticlimax by such resounding common-places as *greatly to be desired, cannot be left out of account, a development to be expected in the near future, deserving of serious consideration, brought to a satisfactory conclusion,* and so on and so forth.

Pretentious diction. Words like *phenomenon, element, individual* (as noun), *objective, categorical, effective, virtual, basic, primary, promote, constitute, exhibit, exploit, utilize, eliminate, liquidate,* are used to dress up simple statement and give an air of scientific impartiality to biased judgments. Adjectives like *epoch-making, epic, historic, unforgettable, triumphant, age-old, inevitable, inexorable, veritable,* are used to dignify the sordid processes of international politics, while writing that aims at glorifying war usually takes on an archaic color, its characteristic words being: *realm, throne, chariot, mailed fist, trident, sword, shield, buckler, banner, jackboot, clarion.* Foreign words and expressions such as *cul de sac, ancien régime, deus ex machina, mutatis mutandis, status quo, gleichschaltqng, weltanschauung,* are used to give an air of culture and elegance. Except for the useful abbreviations *i.e., e.g.,* and *etc.,* there is no real need for any of the hundreds of foreign phrases now current in English. Bad writers, and especially scientific, political and sociological writers, are nearly always haunted by the notion that Latin or Greek words are grander than Saxon ones, and unnecessary words like *expedite, ameliorate, predict, extraneous, deracinated, clandestine, subaqueous* and hundreds of others constantly gain ground from their Anglo-Saxon opposite numbers.[1] The jargon peculiar to Marxist writing (*hyena, hangman, cannibal, petty bourgeois, these gentry, lacquey, flunkey, mad dog, White Guard,* etc.) consists largely of words and phrases translated from Russian, German or French; but the normal way of coining a new word is to use a Latin or Greek root with the appropriate affix and, where necessary, the size formation. It is often easier to make up words of this kind (*deregionalize, impermissible, extramarital, non-fragmentary* and so forth) than to think up the English words that will cover one's meaning. The result, in general, is an increase in slovenliness and vagueness.

Meaningless words. In certain kinds of writing, particularly in art criticism and literary criticism, it is normal to come across long passages which are almost completely lacking in meaning.[2] Words like *romantic, plastic, values, human, dead, sentimental, natural, vitality,* as used in art criticism, are strictly meaningless, in the sense that they not only do not point to any discoverable object, but are hardly ever expected to do so by the reader. When one critic writes, "The outstanding feature of Mr. X's work is its living quality," while another writes, "The immediately striking thing about Mr. X's work is its peculiar deadness," the reader accepts this as a simple difference of opinion. If words like *black* and *white* were involved, instead of the jargon words *dead* and *living,* he would see at once that language was being used in an improper way. Many political words are similarly abused. The word *Fascism* has now no meaning except in so far as it signifies "something not desirable." The words *democracy, socialism, freedom, patriotic, realistic, justice,* have each of them several different meanings which cannot be reconciled with one another. In the case of a word like *democracy,* not only is there no agreed definition, but the attempt to make one is resisted from all sides. It is almost universally felt that when we call a country democratic we are praising it: consequently the defenders of every kind of régime claim that it is a democracy, and fear that they might have to stop using the word if it were tied down to any one meaning. Words of this kind are often used in a consciously dishonest way. That

---

[1] An interesting illustration of this is the way in which the English flower names which were in use till very recently are being ousted by Greek ones, *snapdragon* becoming *antirrhinum,* *forget-me-not* becoming *myosotis,* etc. It is hard to see any practical reason for this change of fashion: it is probably due to an instinctive turning-away from the more homely word and a vague feeling that the Greek word is scientific.

[2] Example: "Comfort's catholicity of perception and image, strangely Whitmanesque in range, almost the exact opposite in aesthetic compulsion, continues to evoke that trembling atmospheric accumulative hinting at a cruel, an inexorably serene timelessness. . . . Wrey Gardiner scores by aiming at simple bull's-eyes with precision. Only they are not so simple, and through this contented sadness runs more than the surface bitter-sweet of resignation." *(Poetry Quarterly)*

is, the person who uses them has his own private definition, but allows his hearer to think he means something quite different. Statements like *Marshal Pétain was a true patriot, The Soviet Press is the freest in the world, The Catholic Church is opposed to persecution,* are almost always made with intent to deceive. Other words used in variable meanings, in most cases more or less dishonestly, are: *class, totalitarian, science, progressive, reactionary, bourgeois, equality.*

Now that I have made this catalogue of swindles and perversions, let me give another example of the kind of writing that they lead to. This time it must of its nature be an imaginary one. I am going to translate a passage of good English into modern English of the worst sort. Here is a well-known verse from *Ecclesiastes:*

> *I returned and saw under the sun, that the race is not to the swift, nor the battle to the strong, neither yet bread to the wise, nor yet riches to men of understanding, nor yet favour to men of skill; but time and chance happeneth to them all.*

Here it is in modern English:

> *Objective considerations of contemporary phenomena compels the conclusion that success or failure in competitive activities exhibits no tendency to be commensurate with innate capacity, but that a considerable element of the unpredictable must invariably be taken into account.*

This is a parody, but not a very gross one. Exhibit (3), above, for instance, contains several patches of the same kind of English. It will be seen that I have not made a full translation. The beginning and ending of the sentence follow the original meaning fairly closely, but in the middle the concrete illustrations—race, battle, bread—dissolve into the vague phrase "success or failure in competitive activities." This had to be so, because no modern writer of the kind I am discussing—no one capable of using phrases like "objective consideration of contemporary phenomena"—would ever tabulate his thoughts in that precise and detailed way. The whole tendency of modern prose is away from concreteness. Now analyse these two sentences a little more closely. The first contains forty-nine words but only sixty syllables, and all its words are those of everyday life. The second contains thirty-eight words of ninety syllables: eighteen of its words are from Latin roots, and one from Greek. The first sentence contains six vivid images, and only one phrase ("time and chance") that could be called vague. The second contains not a single fresh, arresting phrase, and in spite of its ninety syllables it gives only a shortened version of the meaning contained in the first. Yet without a doubt it is the second kind of sentence that is gaining ground in modern English. I do not want to exaggerate. This kind of writing is not yet universal, and outcrops of simplicity will occur here and there in the worst-written page. Still, if you or I were told to write a few lines on the uncertainty of human fortunes, we should probably come much nearer to my imaginary sentence than to the one from *Ecclesiastes*.

As I have tried to show, modern writing at its worst does not consist in picking out words for the sake of their meaning and inventing images in order to make the meaning clearer. It consists in gumming together long strips of words which have already been set in order by someone else, and making the results presentable by sheer humbug. The attraction of this way of writing is that it is easy. It is easier—even quicker, once you have the habit—to say *In my opinion it is not an unjustifiable assumption that* than to say *I think*. If you use ready-made phrases, you not only don't have to hunt about for words; you also don't have to bother with the rhythms of your sentences, since these phrases are generally so arranged as to be more or less euphonious. When you are composing in a hurry—when you are dictating to a stenographer, for instance, or making a public speech—it is natural to fall into a pretentious, Latinized style. Tags like *a consideration which we should do well to bear in mind* or *a conclusion to which all of us would readily assent* will save many a sentence from coming down with a bump. By using stale metaphors, similes and idioms, you save much mental effort, at the cost of leaving your meaning vague, not only for your reader but for yourself. This is the significance of mixed metaphors. The sole aim of a metaphor is to call up a visual image. When these images clash—as in *The Fascist octopus has sung its swan song, the jackboot is thrown into the melting pot*—it can be taken as certain that the writer is not seeing a mental image of the objects he is naming; in other words he is not really thinking. Look again at the examples I gave at the beginning of this essay. Professor Laski (1) uses five negatives in fifty-three words. One of these is superfluous, making nonsense of the whole passage, and in addition there is the slip *alien* for akin, making further nonsense, and several avoidable pieces of clumsiness which increase the general vagueness. Professor Hogben (2) plays ducks and drakes with a battery which is able to write prescriptions, and, while disapproving of the everyday phrase *put up with*, is unwilling to look *egregious* up in the dictionary and see what it means; (3), if one takes an uncharitable attitude towards it, is simply meaningless: probably one could work out its intended meaning by reading the whole of the article in which it occurs. In (4), the writer knows more or less what he wants to say, but an accumulation of stale phrases chokes him like tea leaves blocking a sink. In (5), words and meaning have almost parted company. People who write in this manner usually have a general emotional meaning—they dislike one thing and want to express solidarity with another—but they are not interested in the detail of what they are saying. A scrupulous writer, in every sentence that he writes, will ask himself at least four questions, thus: What am I trying to say? What words will express it? What image or idiom will make it clearer? Is this image fresh enough to have an effect? And he will probably ask himself two more: Could I put it more shortly? Have I said anything that is avoidably ugly? But you are not obliged to go to all this trouble. You can shirk it by simply throwing your mind open and letting the ready-made phrases come crowding in. They will construct your sentences for you—even think your thoughts for you, to a certain extent—and at need they will perform the important service of partially concealing your meaning even from yourself. It is at this point that the special connection between politics and the debasement of language becomes clear.

In our time it is broadly true that political writing is bad writing. Where it is not true, it will generally be found that the writer is some kind of rebel, expressing his private opinions and not a "party line." Orthodoxy, of whatever color, seems to demand a lifeless, imitative style. The political dialects to be found in pamphlets, leading articles, manifestos, White Papers and the speeches of under-secretaries do, of course, vary from party to party, but they are all alike in that one almost never finds in them a fresh, vivid, home-made turn of speech. When one watches some tired hack on the platform mechanically repeating the familiar phrases—*bestial atrocities, iron heel, bloodstained tyranny, free peoples of the world, stand shoulder to shoulder*—one often has a curious feeling that one is not watching a live human being but some kind of dummy: a feeling which suddenly becomes stronger at moments when the light catches the speaker's spectacles and turns them into blank discs which seem to have no eyes behind them. And this is not altogether fanciful. A speaker who uses that kind of phraseology has gone some distance towards turning himself into a machine. The appropriate noises are coming out of his larynx, but his brain is not involved as it would be if he were choosing his words for himself. If the speech he is making is one that he is accustomed to make over and over again, he may be almost unconscious of what he is saying, as one is when one utters the responses in church. And this reduced state of consciousness, if not indispensable, is at any rate favorable to political conformity.

130

In our time, political speech and writing are largely the defence of the indefensible. Things like the continuance of British rule in India, the Russian purges and deportations, the dropping of the atom bombs on Japan, can indeed be defended, but only by arguments which are too brutal for most people to face, and which do not square with the professed aims of political parties. Thus political language has to consist largely of euphemism, question-begging and sheer cloudy vagueness. Defenceless villages are bombarded from the air, the inhabitants driven out into the countryside, the cattle machine-gunned, the huts set on fire with incendiary bullets: this is called *pacification*. Millions of peasants are robbed of their farms and sent trudging along the roads with no more than they can carry: this is called *transfer of population* or *rectification of frontiers*. People are imprisoned for years without trial, or shot in the back of the neck or sent to die of scurvy in Arctic lumber camps: this is called *elimination of unreliable elements*. Such phraseology is needed if one wants to name things without calling up mental pictures of them. Consider for instance some comfortable English professor defending Russian totalitarianism. He cannot say outright, "I believe in killing off your opponents when you can get good results by doing so." Probably, therefore, he will say something like this:

> While freely conceding that the Soviet régime exhibits certain features which the humanitarian may be inclined to deplore, we must, I think, agree that a certain curtailment of the right to political opposition is an unavoidable concomitant of transitional periods, and that the rigors which the Russian people have been called upon to undergo have been amply justified in the sphere of concrete achievement.

The inflated style is itself a kind of euphemism. A mass of Latin words falls upon the facts like soft snow, blurring the outlines and covering up all the details. The great enemy of clear language is insincerity. When there is a gap between one's real and one's declared aims, one turns as it were instinctively to long words and exhausted idioms, like a cuttlefish squirting out ink. In our age there is no such thing as "keeping out of politics." All issues are political issues, and politics itself is a mass of lies, evasions, folly, hatred and schizophrenia. When the general atmosphere is bad, language must suffer. I should expect to find—this is a guess which I have not sufficient knowledge to verify—that the German, Russian and Italian languages have all deteriorated in the last ten or fifteen years, as a result of dictatorship.

But if thought corrupts language, language can also corrupt thought. A bad usage can spread by tradition and imitation, even among people who

should and do know better. The debased language that I have been discussing is in some ways very convenient. Phrases like *a not unjustifiable
assumption, leaves much to be desired, would serve no good purpose, a
consideration which we should do well to bear in mind,* are a continuous
temptation, a packet of aspirins always at one's elbow. Look back through
this essay, and for certain you will find that I have again and again committed the very faults I am protesting against. By this morning's post I have
received a pamphlet dealing with conditions in Germany. The author tells
me that he "felt impelled" to write it. I open it at random, and here is almost the first sentence that I see: "[The Allies] have an opportunity not
only of achieving a radical transformation of Germany's social and political
structure in such a way as to avoid a nationalistic reaction in Germany itself, but at the same time of laying the foundations of a co-operative and
unified Europe." You see, he "feels impelled" to write—feels, presumably,
that he has something new to say—and yet his words, like cavalry horses
answering the bugle, group themselves automatically into the familiar
dreary pattern. This invasion of one's mind by ready-made phrases (*lay the
foundations, achieve a radical transformation*) can only be prevented if one
is constantly on guard against them, and every such phrase anaesthetizes a
portion of one's brain.

I said earlier that the decadence of our language is probably curable.
Those who deny this would argue, if they produced an argument at all, that
language merely reflects existing social conditions, and that we cannot influence its development by any direct tinkering with words and constructions. So far as the general tone or spirit of a language goes, this may be
true, but it is not true in detail. Silly words and expressions have often disappeared, not through any evolutionary process but owing to the conscious
action of a minority. Two recent examples were *explore every avenue* and
leave no stone unturned, which were killed by the jeers of a few journalista.
There is a long list of flyblown metaphors which could similarly be got rid
of if enough people would interest themselves in the job and it should also
be possible to laugh the *not un-* formation out of existence,[3] to reduce the
amount of Latin and Greek in the average sentence, to drive out foreign
phrases and strayed scientific words, and, in general, to make pretentiousness unfashionable. But all these are minor points. The defence of the English language implies more than this, and perhaps it is best to start by saying what it does *not* imply.

---

[3] One can cure oneself of the *not un-* formation by memorizing this sentence: *A not
unblack dog was chasing a not unsmall rabbit across a not ungreen field.*

To begin with it has nothing to do with archaism, with the salvaging of obsolete words and turns of speech, or with the setting up of a "standard English" which must never be departed from. On the contrary, it is especially concerned with the scrapping of every word or idiom which has outworn its usefulness. It has nothing to do with correct grammar and syntax, which are of no importance so long as one makes one's meaning clear, or with the avoidance of Americanisms, or with having what is called a "good prose style." On the other hand it is not concerned with fake simplicity and the attempt to make written English colloquial. Nor does it even imply in every case preferring the Saxon word to the Latin one, though it does imply using the fewest and shortest words that will cover one's meaning. What is above all needed is to let the meaning choose the word, and not the other way about. In prose, the worst thing one can do with words is to surrender to them. When you think of a concrete object, you think wordlessly, and then, if you want to describe the thing you have been visualizing you probably hunt about till you find the exact words that seem to fit it. When you think of something abstract you are more inclined to use words from the start, and unless you make a conscious effort to prevent it, the existing dialect will come rushing in and do the job for you, at the expense of blurring or even changing your meaning. Probably it is better to put off using words as long as possible and get one's meaning as clear as one can through pictures or sensations. Afterwards one can choose—not simply *accept*—the phrases that will best cover the meaning, and then switch round and decide what impression one's words are likely to make on another person. This last effort of the mind cuts out all stale or mixed images, all prefabricated phrases, needless repetitions, and humbug and vagueness generally. But one can often be in doubt about the effect of a word or a phrase, and one needs rules that one can rely on when instinct fails. I think the following rules will cover most cases:

(i) Never use a metaphor, simile or other figure of speech which you are used to seeing in print.

(ii) Never use a long word where a short one will do.

(iii) If it is possible to cut a word out, always cut it out.

(iv) Never use the passive where you can use the active.

(v) Never use a foreign phrase, a scientific word or a jargon word if you can think of an everyday English equivalent.

(vi) Break any of these rules sooner than say anything outright barbarous.

These rules sound elementary, and so they are, but they demand a deep change of attitude in anyone who has grown used to writing in the style now fashionable. One could keep all of them and still write bad English, but one could not write the kind of stuff that I quoted in those five specimens at the beginning of this article.

I have not here been considering the literary use of language, but merely language as an instrument for expressing and not for concealing or preventing thought. Stuart Chase and others have come near to claiming that all abstract words are meaningless, and have used this as a pretext for advocating a kind of political quietism. Since you don't know what Fascism is, how can you struggle against Fascism? One need not swallow such absurdities as this, but one ought to recognize that the present political chaos is connected with the decay of language, and that one can probably bring about some improvement by starting at the verbal end. If you simplify your English, you are freed from the worst follies of orthodoxy. You cannot speak any of the necessary dialects, and when you make a stupid remark its stupidity will be obvious, even to yourself. Political language—and with variations this is true of all political parties, from Conservatives to Anarchists—is designed to make lies sound truthful and murder respectable, and to give an appearance of solidity to pure wind. One cannot change this all in a moment, but one can at least change one's own habits, and from time to time one can even, if one jeers loudly enough, send some worn-out and useless phrase—some *jackboot, Achilles' heel, hotbed, melting pot, acid test, veritable inferno* or other lump of verbal refuse—into the dustbin where it belongs.

Three

SOME REMEDIES
AND PRESCRIPTIONS

> . . . where every word is at home,
> Taking its place to support the others,
> The word neither diffident
>   nor ostentatious,
> And easy commerce of the old
>   and the new,
> The common word exact without vulgarity,
> The formal word precise but not pedantic,
> The complete consort dancing together . . .
>
> —T. S. Eliot, *Four Quartets*

> True ease in writing comes from art,
>   not chance,
> As those move easiest who have
>   learned to dance.
>
> — Alexander Pope, *Essay on Criticism*

No one likes to be told exactly what to do. And especially in writing, where so much of style is personal choice, too much direction can be crippling. So none of the following essays is dictatorial. Only in the final selection are any specific directions offered, and even there they are in the form of questions for the writer to ask himself. However, since all but one of the authors below can be considered a professional—and that one is a professional student of writing—it might be of benefit to you to listen to some of their ideas.

If you do, you will notice several things. First, they seem to agree on the interrelationship of thought and style with which this book has been primarily concerned. Apparently they all think that fine thoughts are not enough. Second, you will notice that most of them emphasize many of the same points—points you have heard mentioned before—clarity, conciseness, simplicity, concern for the reader. Finally, notice that they agree with Pope: good writing is not due to chance. It depends on practice, re-writing, and care.

As they themselves point out, there is more than one way to write well. Neither they nor anyone else claim to have a corner on the market. But their suggestions are uncomplicated and reasonable, and have worked for them. It's as good a place as any to start thinking about the matter.

Harold Whitehall

Writing and Speech

Mr. Whitehall makes some interesting observations on the advantages and disadvantages of the relative homogeneity of American speech. Compared to the speech of England, for instance, this homogeneity makes people more unwilling to accept the need for standard written English.

Notice that he makes no bones about standard written English being a specialized variety of the language, but pay attention to his claims for its importance. He posits a real difference between speech and writing, a claim denied by Mencken in a later essay.

All of us have a grammar. The fact that we use and understand English in daily affairs means that we use and understand, for the most part unconsciously, the major grammatical patterns of our language. Yet because of the effects of education, many of us have come to think of a relatively formal written English and its reflection among those who "speak by the book" as the only genuine English, and to consider its grammar as the only acceptable English grammar. That is by no means true. The basic form of present-day American English is the patterned, rhythmed, and segmented code of voice signals called *speech*—speech as used in everyday conversation by highly educated people (*cultivated speech*), by the general run of our population (*common speech*), or by some rural persons in such geographically isolated areas as the Ozark Plateau, the Appalachian Mountains, or the woodland areas of northern New England (*folk speech*). From the code of speech, the language of formal writing is something of an abstraction, differing in details of grammar and vocabulary and lacking clear indication of the bodily gestures and meaningful qualities of the voice which accompany ordinary conversation. Thus, serious written English may be regarded as a rather artificial dialect of our language. To acquire that dialect, the would-be writer needs to know a good deal about its structural details, and particularly about those in which it differs from the less formal varieties of speech.

Even a moment's reflection will show that the spoken American language is backed by expressive features lacking in the written language: the rise or fall of the voice at the ends of phrases and sentences; the application of vocal loudness to this or that word or part of a word; the use of gesture; the meaningful rasp or liquidity, shouting or muting, drawing or clipping, whining or breaking, melody or whispering imparted to the quality of the voice. Written English, lacking clear indication of such features, must be so managed that it compensates for what it lacks. It must be more carefully organized than speech in order to overcome its communicative deficiencies as compared with speech. In speech, we safeguard meaning by the use of intonation, stress, gesture, and voice qualities. In writing, we must deal with our medium in such a way that the meaning cannot possibly be misunderstood. In the absence of an actual hearer capable of interrupting and demanding further explanation, a clear writer is always conscious of "a reader over his shoulder." All this despite the fact that writing, being permanent, as compared with speech, which is evanescent, allows not only reading but also rereading.

Nor is this all. If written English is somewhat abstract, somewhat artificial, it is also generalized—national, not geographically or socially limited in scope. We must realize that comparatively few of us make use in our day-to-day affairs of a generalized spoken American English that is at all comparable with it. Such a language—a Received Standard Spoken English—exists, but not for the most part in this country where the practical need for it is slight. It exists in England, where the practical need for it is great. In England, many people still start their linguistic careers speaking one or another of the regional dialects, dialects so different from each other in vocabulary and grammar, so quilt-crazy in their distribution, that they form real barriers to generalized, national communication. Yet, in a modern, democratic country, general communication is a necessity. For that reason, Englishmen are willing to accept the notion both of a generalized spoken and a generalized written form of expression on a level above the dialects, and are willing to make the effort of learning them in school and elsewhere. We would be equally willing if our everyday speech happened to resemble this specimen from the English county of Lancaster:

> *Nay! my heart misgi'es me! There's summat abeawt this neet's wark as is noan jannock. Look thee here! Yon chap's noan t' first sheep theaw's lifted tax-free fro't' mooar, an' aw've niver been one to worrit abeawt it, that aw hav'nt. But toneet, someheaw, it's noan t' same. There's summat beawn't 'appen—aw con feel it i' my booans. This een, an unconny wind wor burrin' i' t'ling, an' not a cleawd i' t' sky; an' whin aw went deawn to' t' well for watter, t'bats wor flyin' reawn it in a widdershins ring. Mark my words, there's mooar to coom.*

In the United States, our language situation is quite different. Ours is probably the only country on earth in which three thousand miles of travel will bring no difficulty of spoken communication. We do have, of course, regional and social differences of language. The speech of Maine does not coincide in all points with that of Texas, nor the speech of Georgia with that of Minnesota. The speech of cultivated people in urban centers is not precisely that of the general mass of our citizens, nor that of rural residents of limited education in geographically secluded areas. Yet, unless we deliberately choose to emphasize disparities for social or other reasons, our regional and social speech differences create no great barriers to the free exchange of opinions and ideas. They consist of flavoring rather than substance.

Precisely for that reason, pressures for the adoption of a generalized national spoken American English comparable in acceptance and prestige with Received Standard Spoken British have proved largely unavailing. In American life, one may use cultivated or common speech Southern, cultivated or common speech Northeastern, or cultivated or common speech North Middle Western without encountering any great practical disadvantage. Our standards of speech are mainly regional standards, and most of us, in actual fact, speak some kind of a patois in which one or another of the cultivated or common speech regional varieties of American English blends quite happily with elements absorbed from reading and the educational process. We are very fortunate in this—fortunate that American historical and sociological conditions have removed difficulties of spoken communication found in most other parts of the world.

In a lesser sense, however, our good fortune is something of a misfortune. Because an American can understand other Americans no matter what regional or social class they come from, he is apt to underestimate the necessity for a generalized and abstract written American English. Because he finds no pressing reason for standardizing his speech, he is likely to misunderstand the necessity for standardizing his writing. He would like to write as he speaks. Moreover, the differences between the various regional and social varieties of American speech, being slight, are often of so subtle a nature that he tends to find difficulty in discriminating them. Slight as they are, when transferred to writing they are sufficient to make a reader pause, to induce a momentary feeling of unfamiliarity, to interrupt his consideration of the *matter* of expression by unwittingly calling attention to the *manner* of expression. Outside frankly literary writing (particularly the writing of poetry), such pauses, such unfamiliarities, such interruptions will hinder rather than help the writer's communicative purpose. If writing must be generalized, it must be generalized with a good reason: to speak with a local accent is not disadvantageous; to write serious prose with a local accent definitely is.

The moral of all this is clear. To gain command of serious written English is to acquire, quite deliberately, an abstract and generalized variety of the language differing by nature and purpose from any social or regional variety whatsoever. It is to sacrifice the local for the general, the spontaneous for the permanent. It is to bring to the study of written American English something of the perspective we normally reserve for the study of foreign languages. It is to master a set of grammatical and vocabulary patterns not because they are "correct" but because experience has proved them efficient in the communicative activity of writing.

The word "correct" is deliberately introduced here. The clear distinctions between spoken and written language mentioned in the paragraphs above have been all too often masked by the pernicious doctrine of "correctness." Perhaps that is to be expected. Without the flexible medium of language, a human society in human terms would be impossible. Without language, there could be no continuous record of experience, no diversification of labor, no great social institutions—the humanity of man could never have been achieved. But social activities breed social rituals and social judgments. Because language is *the* basic social instrument, it has inevitably acquired social attitudes so complex and variegated that they have often been allowed to obscure its primary communicative function. For far too many of us, knowledge of language is confused with knowledge of judgments on language that are socially acceptable. Education in the English language has become, for the most part, education in linguistic niceties —a poor substitute for that real linguistic education which ought to show us the major and minor patterns of our language, the way in which they interlock in function, the ways in which they can be manipulated for effective expression. As a result, the instrument of communication which should be every man's servant has become most men's master. This need not be so. Our self-confidence is immediately bolstered, our attitudes towards the study of writing techniques tremendously improved, once we realize that the difficulties of writing English do not spring from faulty nurture, restricted intelligence, or beyond-the-tracks environment but from the necessary change-over from one kind of English to another—that they are neither unpardonable nor irremediable.

No matter what irrationalities surround the details and the perspectives by which English is normally viewed, the fact that it has so admirably served and is still serving the needs of many fine writers guarantees that it is neither an impossible nor an unworthy instrument of human expression. Let us admit that all languages, spoken or written, are man-made things, that their weaknesses as well as their strengths are implicit in their human origin. Let us admit that the world has never known either a faultless language nor one constructed on what to us seems a strictly logical system. The proper approach to written English is first to understand what the medium is; then to concede its limitations and to use its strengths to the best possible effect. Every communicative medium has a set of resistances that the communicator must overcome. Marble is hard; paint relatively unmanageable; music barely descriptive. No small part of any kind of composition is contributed directly by tensions set up between the craftsman's demands on his medium on the one hand and its inherent resistances on the other. To this, the science, craft, and art of expression in written American English is no exception.

2

Francis Bacon

Of Studies

This is a classic essay, and it is included here out of deference to tradition as much as for any other reason. Every schoolchild in the country used to have to read this, and every one of them loathed it. He makes at least one pertinent point, however. "Writing maketh an exact man."

Notice also that he advocates exercise. Back to the sound body idea. The more you write, the better you get at it, and occasionally it even gets easier. In general he favors the exercise of style and claims you can improve.

$\mathcal{S}$tudies serve for delight, for ornament, and for ability. Their chief use for delight, is in privateness and retiring; for ornament, is in discourse; and for ability, is in the judgment and disposition of business. For expert men can execute, and perhaps judge of particulars, one by one; but the general counsels, and the plots and marshalling of affairs, come best from those that are learned. To spend too much time in studies is sloth; to use them too much for ornament, is affectation; to make judgment wholly by their rules, is the humour of a scholar. They perfect nature, and are perfected by experience: for natural abilities are like natural plants, that need proyning by study; and studies themselves do give forth directions too much at large, except they be bounded in by experience. Crafty men contemn studies, simple men admire them, and wise men use them; for they teach not their own use; but that is a wisdom without them, and above them, won by observation. Read not to contradict and confute; nor to believe and take for granted; nor to find talk and discourse; but to weigh and consider.

Some books are to be tasted, others to be swallowed, and some few to be chewed and digested; that is, some books are to be read only in parts; others to be read, but not curiously; and some few to be read wholly, and with diligence and attention. Some books also may be read by deputy, and extracts made of them by others; but that would be only in the less important arguments, and the meaner sort of books; else distilled books are like common distilled waters, flashy things. Reading maketh a full man; conference a ready man; and writing an exact man. And therefore, if a man write little, he had need have a great memory; if he confer little, he had need have a present wit: and if he read little, he had need have much cunning, to seem to know that he doth not. Histories make men wise; poets witty; the mathematics subtile; natural philosophy deep; moral grave; logic and rhetoric able to contend. *Abeunt studia in mores.* Nay there is no stond or impediment in the wit, but may be wrought out by fit studies: like as diseases of the body may have appropriate exercises.

Bowling is good for the stone and reins; shooting for the lungs and breast; gentle walking for the stomach; riding for the head; and the like. So if a man's wit be wandering, let him study the mathematics; for in demonstrations, if his wit be called away never so little, he must begin again. If his wit be not apt to distinguish or find differences, let him study the schoolmen; for they are *cymini sectores*. If he be not apt to beat over matters, and to call up one thing to prove and illustrate another, let him study the lawyers' cases. So every defect of the mind may have a special receipt.

"Of Studies" from The Essays; Colours of Good and Evil; and, Advancement of Learning of Francis Bacon, Macmillan & Co., Ltd., 1900, London.

H. L. Mencken

Literature and the Schoolmam

There are two sides to every question, and we must be fair. If Bacon thinks that practice makes perfect, Mencken doesn't. You may dislike or dispute his grounds for claiming that you will never write well, but there is only one way you can disprove them. Try it.

With precious few exceptions, all the books on style in English are by writers quite unable to write. The subject, indeed, seems to exercise a special and dreadful fascination over schoolma'ms, bucolic college professors, and other such pseudo-literates. One never hears of treatises on it by George Moore or James Branch Cabell, but the pedagogues, male and female, are at it all the time. In a thousand texts they set forth their depressing ideas about it, and millions of suffering high-school pupils have to study what they say. Their central aim, of course, is to reduce the whole thing to a series of simple rules—the overmastering passion of their melancholy order, at all times and everywhere. They aspire to teach it as bridge whist, the American Legion flag-drill and double-entry bookkeeping are taught. They fail as ignominiously as that Athenian of legend who essayed to train a regiment of grasshoppers in the goose-step.

For the essence of a sound style is that it cannot be reduced to rules—that it is a living and breathing thing, with something of the devilish in it—that it fits its proprietor tightly and yet ever so loosely, as his skin fits him. It is, in fact, quite as securely an integral part of him as that skin is. It hardens as his arteries harden. It has *Katzenjammer* on the days succeeding his indiscretions. It is gaudy when he is young and gathers decorum when he grows old. On the day after he makes a mash on a new girl it glows and glitters. If he has fed well, it is mellow. If he has gastritis it is bitter. In brief, a style is always the outward and visible symbol of a man, and it cannot be anything else. To attempt to teach it is as silly as to set up courses in making love. The man who makes love out of a book is not making love at all; he is simply imitating someone else making love. God help him if, in love or literary composition, his preceptor be a pedagogue!

The schoolma'm theory that the writing of English may be taught is based upon a faulty inference from a sound observation. The sound observation is that the great majority of American high-school pupils, when they attempt to put their thoughts upon paper, produce only a mass of confused and puerile nonsense—that they express themselves so clumsily that it is often quite impossible to understand them at all. The faulty inference is to the effect that what ails them is a defective technical equipment—that they can be trained to write clearly as a dog may be trained to walk on its hind legs. This is all wrong. What ails them is not a defective technical equipment but a defective natural equipment. They write badly simply because they cannot think clearly. They cannot think clearly because they lack the brains. Trying to teach them is as hopeless as trying to teach a dog with only one hind leg. Any human being who can speak English understandably has all the materials necessary to write English clearly, and even beautifully. There is nothing mysterious about the written language; it is precisely the same, in essence, as the spoken language. If a man can think in English at all, he can find words enough to express his ideas. The fact is proved abundantly by the excellent writing that often comes from so-called ignorant men. It is proved anew by the even better writing that is done on higher levels by persons of great simplicity, for example, Abraham Lincoln. Such writing commonly arouses little enthusiasm among pedagogues. Its transparency excites their professional disdain, and they are offended by its use of homely words and phrases. They prefer something more ornate and complex—something, as they would probably put it, demanding more thought. But the thought they yearn for is the kind, alas, that they secrete themselves—the muddled, highfalutin, vapid thought that one finds in their own text-books.

I do not denounce them because they write so badly; I merely record the fact in a sad, scientific spirit. Even in such twilight regions of the intellect the style remains the man. What is in the head infallibly oozes out of the nub of the pen. If it is sparkling Burgundy the writing is full of life and charm. If it is mush the writing is mush too. The late Dr. Harding, twenty-ninth President of the Federal Union, was a highly self-conscious stylist. He practiced prose composition assiduously, and was regarded by the pedagogues of Marion, Ohio, and vicinity as a very talented fellow. But when he sent a message to Congress it was so muddled in style that even the late Henry Cabot Lodge, a professional literary man, could not understand it. Why? Simply because Dr. Harding's thoughts, on the high and grave subjects he discussed, were so muddled that he couln't understand them himself. But on matters within his range of customary meditation he was clear and even charming, as all of us are. I once heard him deliver a brief address upon the ideals of the Elks. It was a topic close to his heart, and he had thought about it at length and *con amore*. The result was an excellent speech—clear, logical, forceful, and with a touch of wild, romantic beauty. His sentences hung together. He employed simple words, and put them together with skill. But when, at a public meeting in Washington, he essayed to deliver an oration on the subject of the late Dante Alighieri, he quickly became so obscure and absurd that even the Diplomatic Corps began to snicker. The cause was plain: he knew no more about Dante than a Tennessee county judge knows about the Institutes of Justinian. Trying to formulate ideas upon the topic, he could get together only a few disjected fragments and ghosts of ideas—here an ear, there a section of tibia, be-yond a puff of soul substance or other gas. The resultant speech was thus enigmatical, cacophonous and awful stuff. It sounded precisely like a lec-ture by a college professor on style.

A pedagogue, confronted by Dr. Harding in class, would have set him to the business of what is called improving his vocabulary—that is, to the business of making his writing even worse than it was. Dr. Harding, in point of fact, had all the vocabulary that he needed, and a great deal more. Any idea that he could formulate clearly he could convey clearly. Any idea that genuinely moved him he could invest with charm—which is to say, with what the pedagogues call style. I believe that this capacity is pos-sessed by all literate persons above the age of fourteen. It is not acquired by studying text-books; it is acquired by learning how to think. Children even younger often show it. I have a niece, now eleven years old, who al-ready has an excellent style. When she writes to me about things that in-terest her—in other words, about the things she is capable of thinking about—she puts her thoughts into clear, dignified and admirable English. Her vocabulary, so far, is unspoiled by schoolma'ms. She doesn't try to knock me out by bombarding me with hard words, and phrases filched from Addison. She is unaffected, and hence her writing is charming. But if she essayed to send me a communication on the subject, say, of Balkan politics or government ownership, her style would descend instantly to the level of that of Dr. Harding's state papers.

To sum up, style cannot go beyond the ideas which lie at the heart of it. If they are clear, it too will be clear. If they are held passionately, it will be eloquent. Trying to teach it to persons who cannot think, especially when the business is attempted by persons who also cannot think, is a great waste of time, and an immoral imposition upon the taxpayers of the nation. It would be far more logical to devote all the energy to teaching, not writing, but logic—and probably just as useless. For I doubt that the art of thinking can be taught at all—at any rate, by school-teachers. It is not acquired, but congenital. Some persons are born with it. Their ideas flow in straight channels; they are capable of lucid reasoning; when they say any-thing it is instantly understandable; when they write anything it is clear and persuasive. They constitute, I should say, about one-eighth of one per cent. of the human race. The rest of God's children are just as incapable of logi-cal thought as they are incapable of jumping over the moon. Trying to teach them to think is as vain an enterprise as trying to teach a streptococ-cus the principles of Americanism. The only thing to do with them is to make Ph.D.'s of them, and set them to writing handbooks on style.

4

Ben Jonson

On Style

Jonson has a lot to say to the beginning writer, so plow through the archaic style and diction. Notice that he urges precision and practice. He also prescribes cool revision after the heat of composition. In speaking of the harmony of all the parts, he anticipates the quotation from Eliot at the beginning of this section.

His final paragraph should sound familiar by now. Be yourself, consider your audience, and suit your tone to your subject matter.

150

For a man to write well, there are required three necessaries—to read the best authors, observe the best speakers, and much exercise of his own style. In style, to consider what ought to be written, and after what manner, he must first think and excogitate his matter, then choose his words, and examine the weight of either. Then take care, in placing and ranking both matter and words, that the composition be comely; and to do this with diligence and often. No matter how slow the style be at first, so it be labored and accurate; seek the best, and be not glad of the forward conceits, or first words, that offer themselves to us; but judge of what we invent, and order what we approve. Repeat often what we have formerly written; which beside that it helps the consequence, and makes the juncture better, it quickens the heat of imagination, that often cools in the time of setting down, and gives it new strength, as if it grew lustier by the going back. As we see in the contention of leaping, they jump farthest that fetch their race largest; or, as in throwing a dart or javelin, we force back our arms to make our loose the stronger. Yet, if we have a fair gale of wind, I forbid not the steering out of our sail, so the favor of the gale deceive us not. For all that we invent doth please us in the conception of birth, else we would never set it down. But the safest is to return to our judgment, and handle over again those things the easiness of which might make them justly suspected. So did the best writers in their beginnings; they imposed upon themselves care and industry; they did nothing rashly: they obtained first to write well, and then custom made it easy and a habit. By little and little their matter showed itself to them more plentifully; their words answered, their composition followed; and all, as in a well-ordered family, presented itself in the place. So that the sum of all is, ready writing makes not good writing, but good writing brings on ready writing. Yet, when we think we have got the faculty, it is even then good to resist it, as to give a horse a check sometimes with a bit, which doth not so much stop his course as stir his mettle. Again, whither a man's genius is best able to reach, thither it should more and more contend, lift and dilate itself; as men of low stature raise themselves on their toes, and so ofttimes get even, if not eminent. Besides, as it is fit for grown and able writers to stand of themselves, and work with their own strength, to trust and endeavor by their own faculties, so it is fit for the beginner and learner to study others and the best. For the mind and memory are more sharply exercised in comprehending another man's things than our own;

"On Style" from *Timber: or, Discoveries Made Upon Men and Matter* by Ben Jonson, edited by Felix E. Schelling, Ginn & Co., 1892, Boston.

and such as accustom themselves and are familiar with the best authors shall ever and anon find somewhat of them in themselves, and in the expression of their minds, even when they feel it not, be able to utter something like theirs, which hath an authority above their own. Nay, sometimes it is the reward of a man's study, the praise of quoting another man fitly; and though a man be more prone and able for one kind of writing than another, yet he must exercise all. For as in an instrument, so in style, there must be a harmony and consent of parts. . . .

The brief style is that which expresseth much in little; the concise style, which expresseth not enough but leaves somewhat to be understood; the abrupt style, which hath many breaches, and doth not seem to end but fall. The congruent and harmonious fitting of parts in a sentence hath almost the fastening and force of knitting and connection; as in stones well squared, which will rise strong a great way without mortar. . . .

The next property of style is perspicuity, and is oftentimes lost by affectation of some wit ill angled for, or ostentation of some hidden terms of art. Few words they darken speech, and so do too many; as well too much light hurteth the eyes, as too little; and a long bill of chancery confounds the understanding as much as the shortest note. Therefore, let not your letters be penned like English statutes, and this is obtained. These vices are eschewed by pondering your business well and distinctly concerning yourself, which is much furthered by uttering your thoughts, and letting them as well come forth to the light and judgment of your own outward senses as to the censure of other men's ears; for that is the reason why many good scholars speak but fumblingly; like a rich man, that for want of particular note and difference can bring you no certain ware readily out of his shop. Hence it is that talkative, shallow men do often content the hearers more than the wise. But this may find a speedier redress in writing, where all comes under the last examination of the eyes. First, mind it well, then pen it, then examine it, then amend it, and you may be in the better hope of doing reasonably well. Under this virtue may come plainness, which is not to be curious in the order as to answer a letter, as if you were to answer to interrogatories. As to the first, first; and to the second, secondly, etc.; but both in method to use (as ladies do in their attire) a diligent kind of negligence, and their sportive freedom; though with some men you are not to jest, or practise tricks; yet the delivery of the most important things may be carried with such a grace, as that it may yield a pleasure to the conceit of the reader. There must be store, though no excess of terms; as if you are to name store, sometimes you may call it choice, sometimes plenty, sometimes copiousness, or variety; but ever so, that the word which comes in lieu have not such difference of meaning as that it may put the sense of the first in hazard to be mistaken. . . .

The last is, respect to discern what fits yourself, him to whom you write, and that which you handle, which is a quality fit to conclude the rest, because it doth include all. And that must proceed from ripeness of judgment, which, as one truly saith, is gotten by four means, God, nature, diligence, and conversation. Serve the first well, and the rest will serve you.

5

W. Somerset Maugham

Reflections on Writing

Of the authors in this section, only Maugham made his living by writing fiction almost exclusively, and hence can claim to be a "creative writer." But apparently it matters little, for you will find in Maugham praise of the same qualities mentioned before. His opening sentence should have a familiar ring.

As you might expect from a writer of "artistic" works, he stresses euphony more than have our other authors; although you will recall that Jonson praised "harmony," and in the next essay you will note that Lucas inveighs against "jingles."

J have have never had much patience with the writers who claim from the reader an effort to understand their meaning. You have only to go to the great philosophers to see that it is possible to express with lucidity the most subtle reflections. You may find it difficult to understand the thought of Hume, and if you have no philosophical training its implications will doubtless escape you; but no one with any education at all can fail to understand exactly what the meaning of each sentence is. Few people have written English with more grace than Berkeley. There are two sorts of obscurity that you find in writers. One is due to negligence and the other to wilfulness. People often write obscurely because they have never taken the trouble to learn to write clearly. This sort of obscurity you find too often in modern philosophers, in men of science, and even in literary critics. Here it is indeed strange. You would have thought that men who passed their lives in the study of the great masters of literature would be sufficiently sensitive to the beauty of language to write if not beautifully at least with perspicuity. Yet you will find in their works sentence after sentence that you must read twice to discover the sense. Often you can only guess at it, for the writers have evidently not said what they intended.

Another cause of obscurity is that the writer is himself not quite sure of his meaning. He has a vague impression of what he wants to say, but has not, either from lack of mental power or from laziness, exactly formulated it in his mind and it is natural enough that he should not find a precise expression for a confused idea. This is due largely to the fact that many writers think, not before, but as they write. The pen originates the thought. The disadvantage of this, and indeed it is a danger against which the author must be always on his guard, is that there is a sort of magic in the written word. The idea acquires substance by taking on a visible nature, and then stands in the way of its own clarification. But this sort of obscurity merges very easily into the wilful. Some writers who do not think clearly are inclined to suppose that their thoughts have a significance greater than at first sight appears. It is flattering to believe that they are too profound to be expressed so clearly that all who run may read, and very naturally it does not occur to such writers that the fault is with their own minds which have not the faculty of precise reflection. Here again the magic of the written word obtains. It is very easy to persuade oneself that a phrase that one does not quite understand may mean a great deal more than one realizes. From this there is only a little way to go to fall into the habit of setting down one's impressions in all their original vagueness. Fools can always be found to discover a hidden sense in them. There is another form of wilful obscurity that masquerades as aristocratic exclusiveness. The author wraps his meaning in mystery so that the vulgar shall not participate in it. His soul is a secret garden into which the elect may penetrate only after overcoming a number of perilous obstacles. But this kind of obscurity is not only pretentious; it is short-sighted. For time plays it an odd trick. If the sense is meagre time reduces it to a meaningless verbiage that no one thinks of reading. This is the fate that has befallen the lucubrations of those French writers who were seduced by the example of Guillaume Apollinaire. But occasionally it throws a sharp cold light on what had seemed profound and thus discloses the fact that these contortions of language disguised very commonplace notions. There are few of Mallarmé's poems now that are not clear; one cannot fail to notice that his thought singularly lacked originality. Some of his phrases were beautiful; the materials of his verse were the poetic platitudes of his day.

Simplicity is not such an obvious merit as lucidity. I have aimed at it because I have no gift for richness. Within limits I admire richness in others, though I find it difficult to digest in quantity. I can read one page of Ruskin with delight, but twenty only with weariness. The rolling period, the stately epithet, the noun rich in poetic associations, the subordinate clauses that give the sentence weight and magnificence, the grandeur like that of wave following wave in the open sea; there is no doubt that in all this there is something inspiring. Words thus strung together fall on the ear like music. The appeal is sensuous rather than intellectual, and the beauty of the sound leads you easily to conclude that you need not bother about the meaning. But words are tyrannical things, they exist for their meanings, and if you will not pay attention to these, you cannot pay attention at all. Your mind wanders. This kind of writing demands a subject that will suit it. It is surely out of place to write in the grand style of inconsiderable things. No one wrote in this manner with greater success than Sir Thomas Browne, but even he did not always escape this pitfall. In the last chapter of *Hydriotaphia* the matter, which is the destiny of man, wonderfully fits the baroque splendour of the language, and here the Norwich doctor produced a piece of prose that has never been surpassed in our literature; but when he describes the finding of his urns in the same splendid manner the effect (at least to my taste) is less happy. When a modern writer is grandiloquent to tell you whether or no a little trollop shall hop into bed with a commonplace young man you are right to be disgusted.

But if richness needs gifts with which everyone is not endowed, simplicity by no means comes by nature. To achieve it needs rigid discipline. So far as I know ours is the only language in which it has been found necessary to give a name to the piece of prose which is described as the purple patch; it would not have been necessary to do so unless it were characteristic. English prose is elaborate rather than simple. It was not always so. Nothing could be more racy, straightforward and alive than the prose of Shakespeare; but it must be remembered that this was dialogue written to be spoken. We do not know how he would have written if like Corneille he had composed prefaces to his plays. It may be that they would have been as euphuistic as the letters of Queen Elizabeth. But earlier prose, the prose of Sir Thomas More, for instance, is neither ponderous, flowery nor oratorical. It smacks of the English soil. To my mind King James's Bible has been a very harmful influence on English prose. I am not so stupid as to deny its great beauty. It is majestical. But the Bible is an oriental book. Its alien imagery has nothing to do with us. Those hyperboles, those luscious metaphors, are foreign to our genius. I cannot but think that not the least of the misfortunes that the Secession from Rome brought upon the spiritual life of our country is that this work for so long a period became the daily, and with many the only, reading of our people. Those rhythms, that powerful vocabulary, that grandiloquence, became part and parcel of the national sensibility. The plain, honest English speech was overwhelmed with ornament. Blunt Englishmen twisted their tongues to speak like Hebrew prophets. There was evidently something in the English temper to which this was congenial, perhaps a native lack of precision in thought, perhaps a naïve delight in fine words for their own sake, an innate eccentricity and love of embroidery, I do not know; but the fact remains that ever since, English prose has had to struggle against the tendency to luxuriance. When from time to time the spirit of the language has reasserted itself; as it did with Dryden and the writers of Queen Anne, it was only to be submerged once more by the pompositos of Gibbon and Dr. Johnson. When English prose recovered simplicity with Hazlitt, the Shelley of the letters and Charles Lamb at his best, it lost it again with De Quincey, Carlyle, Meredith and Walter Pater. It is obvious that the grand style is more striking than the plain. Indeed many people think that a style that does not attract notice is not style. They will admire Walter Pater's, but will read an essay by Matthew Arnold without giving a moment's attention to the elegance, distinction and sobriety with which he set down what he had to say.

The dictum that the style is the man is well known. It is one of those aphorisms that say too much to mean a great deal. Where is the man in Goethe, in his birdlike lyrics or in his clumsy prose? And Hazlitt? But I suppose that if man has a confused mind he will write in a confused way, if his temper is capricious his prose will be fantastical, and if he has a quick, darting intelligence that is reminded by the matter in hand of a hundred things he will, unless he has great self-control, load his pages with metaphor and simile. There is a great difference between the magniloquence of the Jacobean writers, who were intoxicated with the new wealth that had lately been brought into the language, and the turgidity of Gibbon and Dr. Johnson, who were the victims of bad theories. I can read every word that Dr. Johnson wrote with delight, for he had good sense, charm and wit. No one could have written better if he had not wilfully set himself to write in the grand style. He knew good English when he saw it. No critic has praised Dryden's prose more aptly. He said of him that he appeared to have no art other than that of expressing with clearness what he thought with vigour. And one of his Lives he finished with the words: "Whoever wishes to attain an English style, familiar but not coarse, and elegant but not ostentatious, must give his days and nights to the volumes of Addison." But when he himself sat down to write it was with a very different aim. He mistook the orotund for the dignified. He had not the good breeding to see that simplicity and naturalness are the truest marks of distinction.

For to write good prose is an affair of good manners. It is, unlike verse, a civil art. Poetry is baroque. Baroque is tragic, massive and mystical. It is elemental. It demands depth and insight. I cannot but feel that the prose writers of the baroque period, the authors of King James's Bible, Sir Thomas Browne, Glanville, were poets who had lost their way. Prose is a rococo art. It needs taste rather than power, decorum rather than inspiration and vigour rather than grandeur. Form for the poet is the bit and the bridle without which (unless you are an acrobat) you cannot ride your horse; but for the writer of prose it is the chassis without which your car does not exist. It is not an accident that the best prose was written when rococo with its elegance and moderation, at its birth attained its greatest excellence. For rococo was evolved when baroque had become declamatory and the world, tired of the stupendous, asked for restraint. It was the natural expression of persons who valued a civilized life. Humour, tolerance and horse sense made the great tragic issues that had preoccupied the first half of the seventeenth century seem excessive. The world was a more comfortable place to live in and perhaps for the first time in centuries the cultivated classes could sit back and enjoy their leisure. It has been said that good prose should resemble the conversation of a well-bred man. Conversation is only possible when men's minds are free from pressing anxieties. Their lives must be reasonably secure and they must have no grave concern about their souls. They must attach importance to the refinements of civilization. They must value courtesy, they must pay attention to their persons (and have we not also been told that good prose should be like the clothes of a well-dressed man, appropriate but unobtrusive?), they must fear to bore, they must be neither flippant nor solemn, but always apt; and they must look upon "enthusiasm" with a critical glance. This is a soil very suitable for prose. It is not to be wondered at that it gave a fitting opportunity for the appearance of the best writer of prose that our modern world has seen, Voltaire. The writers of English, perhaps owing to the poetic nature of the language, have seldom reached the excellence that seems to have come so naturally to him. It is in so far as they have approached the ease, sobriety and precision of the great French masters that they are admirable.

Whether you ascribe importance to euphony, the last of the three characteristics that I mentioned, must depend on the sensitiveness of your ear. A great many readers, and many admirable writers, are devoid of this quality. Poets as we know have always made a great use of alliteration. They are persuaded that the repetition of a sound gives an effect of beauty. I do not think it does so in prose. It seems to me that in prose alliteration should be used only for a special reason; when used by accident it falls on the ear very disagreeably. But its accidental use is so common that one can only suppose that the sound of it is not universally offensive. Many writers without distress will put two rhyming words together, join a monstrous long adjective to a monstrous long noun, or between the end of one word and the beginning of another have a conjunction of consonants that almost breaks your jaw. These are trivial and obvious instances. I mention them only to prove that if careful writers can do such things it is only because they have no ear. Words have weight, sound and appearance; it is only considering these that you can write a sentence that is good to look at and good to listen to.

I have read many books on English prose, but have found it hard to profit by them; for the most part they are vague, unduly theoretical, and often scolding. But you cannot say this of Fowler's Dictionary of Modern English Usage. It is a valuable work. I do not think anyone writes so well that he cannot learn much from it. It is lively reading. Fowler liked simplicity, straightforwardness and common sense. He had no patience with pretentiousness. He had a sound feeling that idiom was the backbone of a language and he was all for the racy phrase. He was no slavish admirer of logic and was willing enough to give usage right of way through the exact demesnes of grammar. English grammar is very difficult and few writers have avoided making mistakes in it. So heedful a writer as Henry James, for instance, on occasion wrote so ungrammatically that a schoolmaster, finding such errors in a schoolboy's essay, would be justly indignant. It is necessary to know grammar, and it is better to write grammatically than not, but it is well to remember that grammar is common speech formulated. Usage is the only test. I would prefer a phrase that was easy and unaffected to a phrase that was grammatical. One of the differences between French and English is that in French you can be grammatical with complete naturalness, but in English not invariably. It is a difficulty in writing English that the sound of the living voice dominates the look of the printed word. I have given the matter of style a great deal of thought and have taken great pains. I have written few pages that I feel I could not improve and far too many that I have left with dissatisfaction because, try as I would, I could do no better. I cannot say of myself what Johnson said of Pope: "He never passed a fault unamended by indifference, nor quitted it by despair." I do not write as I want to; I write as I can.

But Fowler had no ear. He did not see that simplicity may sometimes make concessions to euphony. I do not think a far-fetched, an archaic or even an affected word is out of place when it sounds better than the blunt, obvious one or when it gives a sentence a better balance. But, I hasten to add, though I think you may without misgiving make this concession to pleasant sound, I think you should make none to what may obscure your meaning. Anything is better than not to write clearly. There is nothing to be said against lucidity, and against simplicity only the possibility of dryness. This is a risk that is well worth taking when you reflect how much better it is to be bald than to wear a curly wig. But there is in euphony a danger that must be considered. It is very likely to be monotonous. When George Moore began to write, his style was poor; it gave you the impression that he wrote on wrapping paper with a blunt pencil. But he developed gradually a very musical English. He learnt to write sentences that fall away on the ear with a misty languor and it delighted him so much that he could never have enough of it. He did not escape monotony. It is like the sound of water lapping a shingly beach, so soothing that you presently cease to be sensible of it. It is so mellifluous that you hanker for some harshness, for an abrupt dissonance, that will interrupt the silky concord. I do not know how one can guard against this. I suppose the best chance is to have a more lively faculty of boredom than one's readers so that one is wearied before they are. One must always be on the watch for mannerisms and when certain cadences come too easily to the pen ask oneself whether they have not become mechanical. It is very hard to discover the exact point where the idiom one has formed to express oneself has lost its tang. As Dr. Johnson said: "He that has once studiously formed a style, rarely writes afterwards with complete ease." Admirably as I think Matthew Arnold's style was suited to his particular purposes, I must admit that his mannerisms are often irritating. His style was an instrument that he had forged once for all; it was not like the human hand capable of performing a variety of actions.

If you could write lucidly, simply, euphoniously and yet with liveliness you would write perfectly: you would write like Voltaire. And yet we know how fatal the pursuit of liveliness may be: it may result in the tiresome acrobatics of Meredith. Macaulay and Carlyle were in their different ways arresting; but at the heavy cost of naturalness. Their flashy effects distract the mind. They destroy their persuasiveness; you would not believe a man was very intent on ploughing a furrow if he carried a hoop with him and jumped through it at every other step. A good style should show no sign of effort. What is written should seem a happy accident. I think no one in France now writes more admirably than Colette, and such is the ease of her expression that you cannot bring yourself to believe that she takes any trouble over it. I am told that there are pianists who have a natural technique so that they can play in a manner that most executants can achieve only as the result of unremitting toil, and I am willing to believe that there are writers who are equally fortunate. Among them I was much inclined to place Colette. I asked her. I was exceedingly surprised to hear that she wrote everything over and over again. She told me that she would often spend a whole morning working upon a single page. But it does not matter how one gets the effect of the ease. For my part, if I get it all, it is only by strenuous effort. Nature seldom provides me with the word, the turn of phrase, that is appropriate without being far-fetched or commonplace.

6

F. L. Lucas

On the Fascination of Style

In this witty and urbane essay by F. L. Lucas we come across the first commandment of this section: "Thou shalt not puzzle thy reader." All these men seem agreed on that, even to the slightest hitch of puzzlement.

Lucas has much more to say. Note his reasons for mastering language. You have seen some of them before, including the last, the implications of which were developed at length by Orwell. Notice in passing his negative rules, but then go on to his positive suggestions, and what do you find? Honesty, courtesy, clarity, and brevity, for openers. It begins to get monotonous.

When it was suggested to Walt Whitman that one of his works should be bound in vellum, he was outraged—"Pshaw!" he snorted, "—hangings, curtains, finger bowls, chinaware, Matthew Arnold!" And he might have been equally irritated by talk of style; for he boasted of "my barbaric yawp"—he would *not* be literary; his readers should touch not a book but a man. Yet Whitman took the pains to rewrite *Leaves of Grass* four times, and his style is unmistakable. Samuel Butler maintained that writers who bothered about their style became unreadable but he bothered about his own. "Style" has got a bad name by growing associated with precious and superior persons who, like Oscar Wilde, spend a morning putting in a comma, and the afternoon (so he said) taking it out again. But such abuse of "style" is misuse of English. For the word means merely "a way of expressing oneself, in language, manner, or appearance"; or, secondly, "a *good* way of so expressing oneself"—as when one says, "Her behavior never lacked style."

Now there is no crime in expressing oneself (though to try to *im*press oneself on others easily grows revolting or ridiculous). Indeed one cannot help expressing oneself, unless one passes one's life in a cupboard. Even the most rigid Communist, or Organization-man, is compelled by Nature to have a unique voice, unique fingerprints, unique handwriting. Even the signatures of the letters on your breakfast table may reveal more than their writers guess. There are blustering signatures that swish across the page like cornstalks bowed before a tempest. There are cryptic signatures, like a scrabble of lightning across a cloud, suggesting that behind is a lofty divinity whom all must know, or an aloof divinity whom none is worthy to know (though, as this might be highly inconvenient, a docile typist sometimes interprets the mystery in a bracket underneath). There are impetuous squiggles implying that the author is a sort of strenuous Sputnik streaking round the globe every eighty minutes. There are florid signatures, all curlicues and danglements and flamboyance, like the youthful Disraeli (though these seem rather out of fashion). There are humble, humdrum signatures. And there are also, sometimes, signatures that are courteously clear, yet mindful of a certain simple grace and artistic economy—in short, of style.

Since, then, not one of us can put pen to paper, or even open his mouth, without giving something of himself away to shrewd observers, it seems mere common sense to give the matter a little thought. Yet it does

"On the Fascination of Style" from *Holiday*, March 1960. Copyright © 1960 by The Curtis Publishing Co. Reprinted with permission of the Executors of the late F. L. Lucas from *Holiday*.

not seem very common. Ladies may take infinite pains about having style in their clothes, but many of us remain curiously indifferent about having it in our words. How many women would dream of polishing not only their nails but also their tongues? They may play freely on that perilous little organ, but they cannot often be bothered to tune it. And how many men think of improving their talk as well as their golf handicap?

No doubt strong silent men, speaking only in gruff monosyllables, may despise "mere words." No doubt the world does suffer from an endemic plague of verbal dysentery. But that, precisely, is bad style. And consider the amazing power of mere words. Adolf Hitler was a bad artist, bad statesman, bad general, and bad man. But largely because he could tune his rant, with psychological nicety, to the exact wave length of his audi- ences and make millions quarrelsome-drunk all at the same time by his command of windy nonsense, skilled statesmen, soldiers, scientists were blown away like chaff, and he came near to rule the world. If Sir Winston Churchill had been a mere speechifier, we might well have lost the war; yet his speeches did quite a lot to win it.

No man was less of a literary aesthete than Benjamin Franklin; yet this tallow-chandler's son who changed world history, regarded as "a prin- cipal means of my advancement" that pungent style which he acquired partly by working in youth over old *Spectators;* but mainly by being Benja- min Franklin. The squinting demagogue, John Wilkes, as ugly as his many sins, had yet a tongue so winning that he asked only half an hour's start (to counteract his face) against any rival for a woman's favor. "Vote for you," growled a surly elector in his constituency. "I'd sooner vote for the devil!" "But in case your friend should not stand . . . ?" Cleopatra, that ensnarer of world conquerors, owed less to the shape of her nose than to the charm of her tongue. Shakespeare himself has often poor plots and thin ideas; even his mastery of character has been questioned; what does remain unchal- lenged is his verbal magic. Men are often taken, like rabbits, by the ears. And though the tongue has no bones, it can sometimes break millions of them.

"But," the reader may grumble, "I am neither Hitler, Cleopatra, nor Shakespeare. What is all this to me?" Yet we all talk—often too much; we all have to write letters—often too many. We live not by bread alone but also by words. And not always with remarkable efficiency. Strikes, lawsuits, divorces, all sorts of public nuisance and private misery, often come just from the gaggling incompetence with which we express ourselves. Ameri- cans and British get at cross-purposes because they use the same words with different meanings. Men have been hanged on a comma in a statute. And in the valley of Balaclava a mere verbal ambiguity, about *which* guns were to be captured, sent the whole Light Brigade to futile annihilation.

Words can be more powerful, and more treacherous, than we sometimes suspect; communications more difficult than we may think. We are all serving life sentences of solitary confinement within our own bodies; like prisoners, we have as it were, to tap in awkward code to our fellow men in their neighboring cells. Further, when A and B converse, there take part in their dialogue not two characters, as they suppose, but six. For there is A's real self—call it A_1; there is also A's picture of himself—A_2; there is also B's picture of A—A_3. And there are three corresponding personalities of B. With six characters involved even in a simple tête-à-tête, no wonder we fall into muddles and misunderstandings.

Perhaps, then, there are five main reasons for trying to gain some mastery of language:

We have no other way of understanding, informing, misinforming, or persuading one another.

Even alone, we think mainly in words; if our language is muddy, so will our thinking be.

By our handling of words we are often revealed and judged. "Has he written anything?" said Napoleon of a candidate for an appointment. "Let me see his *style*."

Without a feeling for language one remains half-blind and deaf to literature.

Our mother tongue is bettered or worsened by the way each generation uses it. Languages evolve like species. They can degenerate; just as oysters and barnacles have lost their heads. Compare ancient Greek with modern. A heavy responsibility, though often forgotten.

Why and how did I become interested in style? The main answer, I suppose, is that I was born that way. Then I was, till ten, an only child running loose in a house packed with books, and in a world (thank goodness) still undistracted by radio and television. So at three I groaned to my mother, "Oh, I *wish* I could read," and at four I read. Now travel among books is the best travel of all, and the easiest, and the cheapest. (Not that I belittle ordinary travel—which I regard as one of the three main pleasures in life.) One learns to write by reading good books, as one learns to talk by hearing good talkers. And if I have learned anything of writing, it is largely from writers like Montaigne, Dorothy Osborne, Horace Walpole, Johnson, Goldsmith, Montesquieu, Voltaire, Flaubert and Anatole France. Again, I was reared on Greek and Latin, and one can learn much from translating Homer or the Greek Anthology, Horace or Tacitus, if one is thrilled by the originals and tries, however vainly, to recapture some of that thrill in English.

But at Rugby I could *not* write English essays. I believe it stupid to torment boys to write on topics that they know and care nothing about. I used to rush to the school library and cram the subject, like a python swallowing rabbits; then, still replete as a postprandial python, I would tie myself in clumsy knots to embrace those accursed themes. Bacon was wise in saying that reading makes a full man; talking, a ready one; writing, an exact one. But writing from an empty head is futile anguish.

At Cambridge, my head having grown a little fuller, I suddenly found I *could* write—not with enjoyment (it is always tearing oneself in pieces)—but fairly fluently. Then came the War of 1914-18; and though soldiers have other things than pens to handle, they learn painfully to be clear and brief. Then the late Sir Desmond MacCarthy invited me to review for the *New Statesman;* it was a useful apprenticeship, and he was delightful to work for. But I think it was well after a few years to stop; reviewers remain essential, but there are too many books one *cannot* praise, and only the pugnacious enjoy amassing enemies. By then I was an ink-addict—not because writing is much pleasure, but because not to write is pain; just as some smokers do not so much enjoy tobacco as suffer without it. The positive happiness of writing comes, I think, from work when done—decently, one hopes, and not without use—and from the letters of readers which help to reassure, or delude, one that so it is.

But one of my most vivid lessons came, I think, from service in a war department during the Second War. Then, if the matter one sent out was too wordy, the communication channels might choke; yet it if was not absolutely clear, the results might be serious. So I emerged, after six years of it, with more passion than ever for clarity and brevity, more loathing than ever for the obscure and the verbose.

For forty years at Cambridge I have tried to teach young men to write well, and have come to think it impossible. To write really well is a gift inborn; those who have it teach themselves; one can only try to help and hasten the process. After all, the uneducated sometimes express themselves far better than their "betters." In language, as in life, it is possible to be perfectly correct—and yet perfectly tedious, or odious. The illiterate last letter of the doomed Vanzetti was more moving than most professional orators; 18th Century ladies, who should have been spanked for their spelling, could yet write far better letters than most professors of English; and the talk of Synge's Irish peasants seems to me vastly more vivid than the later style of Henry James. Yet Synge averred that his characters owed far less of their eloquence to what he invented for them than to what he had overheard in the cottages of Wicklow and Kerry:

Christy: *It's little you'll think if my love's a poacher's, or an earl's itself, when you'll feel my two hands stretched around you, and I squeezing kisses on your puckered lips, till I'd feel a kind of pity for the Lord God is all ages sitting lonesome in His golden chair.*

Pegeen: *That'll be right fun, Christy Mahon, and any girl would walk her heart out before she'd meet a young man was your like for eloquence, or talk at all.*

Well she might! It's not like that they talk in universities—more's the pity.

But though one cannot teach people to write well, one can sometimes teach them to write rather better. One can give a certain number of hints, which often seem boringly obvious—only experience shows they are not.

One can say: Beware of pronouns—they are devils. Look at even Addison, describing the type of pedant who chatters of style without having any: "Upon enquiry I found my learned friend had dined that day with Mr. Swan, the famous punster; and desiring *him* to give me some account of Mr. Swan's conversation, *he* told me that *he* generally talked in the Paronomasia, that *he* sometimes gave in to the Plocé, but that in *his* humble opinion *he* shone most in the Antanaclasis." What a sluttish muddle of *he* and *him* and *his!* It all needs rewording. Far better repeat a noun, or a name, than puzzle the reader, even for a moment, with ambiguous pronouns. Thou shalt not puzzle thy reader.

Or one can say: Avoid jingles. The B.B.C. news bulletins seem compiled by earless persons, capable of crying round the globe: "The enemy is re*port*ed to have seized this im*port*ant *port,* and reinforcements are hurrying up in sup*port.*" Any fool, once told, can hear such things to be insupportable.

Or one can say: Be sparing with relative clauses. Don't string them together like sausages, or jam them inside one another like Chinese boxes or the receptacles of Buddha's tooth. Or one can say: Don't flaunt jargon, like Addison's Mr. Swan, or the type of modern critic who gurgles more technical terms in a page than Johnson used in all his *Lives* or Sainte-

Beuve in thirty volumes. But dozens of such snippety precepts, though they may sometimes save people from writing badly, will help them little toward writing well. Are there no general rules of a more positive kind, and of more positive use?

Perhaps. There *are* certain basic principles which seem to me observed by many authors I admire, which I think have served me and which may serve others. I am not talking of geniuses, who are a law to themselves (and do not always write a very good style, either); nor of poetry, which has different laws from prose; nor of poetic prose, like Sir Thomas Browne's or DeQuincey's, which is often more akin to poetry; but of the plain prose of ordinary books and documents, letters and talk.

The writer should respect truth and himself; therefore honesty. He should respect his readers; therefore courtesy. These are two of the cornerstones of style. Confucius saw it, twenty-five centuries ago: "The Master said, The gentleman is courteous, but not pliable: common men are pliable, but not courteous."

First, honesty. In literature, as in life, one of the fundamentals is to find, and be, one's true self. One's true self may indeed be unpleasant (though one can try to better it); but a false self, sooner or later, becomes disgusting—just as a nice plain woman, painted to the eyebrows, can become horrid. In writing, in the long run, pretense does not work. As the police put it, anything you say may be used as evidence against you. If handwriting reveals character, writing reveals it still more. You cannot fool *all* your judges *all* the time.

Most style is not honest enough. Easy to say, but hard to practice. A writer may take to long words, as young men to beards—to impress. But long words, like long beards, are often the badge of charlatans. Or a writer may cultivate the obscure, to seem profound. But even carefully muddied puddles are soon fathomed. Or he may cultivate eccentricity, to seem original. But really original people do not have to think about being original—they can no more help it than they can help breathing. They do not need to dye their hair green. The fame of Meredith, Wilde or Bernard Shaw might now shine brighter, had they struggled less to be brilliant; whereas Johnson remains great, not merely because his gifts were formidable but also because, with all his prejudice and passion, he fought no less passionately to "clear his mind of cant."

Secondly, courtesy—respect for the reader. From this follow several other basic principles of style. Clarity is one. For it is boorish to make your reader rack his brains to understand. One should aim at being impossible to misunderstand—though men's capacity for misunderstanding approaches infinity. Hence Molière and Po Chu-i tried their work on their cooks; and Swift his on his menservants—"which, if they did not comprehend, he would alter and amend, until they understood it perfectly." Our bureaucrats and pundits, unfortunately, are less considerate.

Brevity is another basic principle. For it is boorish, also, to waste your reader's time. People who would not dream of stealing a penny of one's money turn not a hair at stealing hours of one's life. But that does not make them less exasperating. Therefore there is no excuse for the sort of writer who takes as long as a marching army corps to pass a given point. Besides, brevity is often more effective; the half can say more than the whole, and to imply things may strike far deeper than to state them at length. And because one is particularly apt to waste words on preambles before coming to the substance, there was sense in the Scots professor who always asked his pupils—"Did ye remember to tear up that fir-r-st page?"

Here are some instances that would only lose by lengthening:

> *It is useless to go to bed to save the light, if the result is twins.* (Chinese proverb)

> *My barn is burnt down—*
> *Nothing hides the moon.* (Complete Japanese poem)

> *Je me regrette.* (Dying words of the gay Vicomtesse d'-Houdetot)

> *I have seen their backs before.* (Wellington, when French marshals turned their backs on him at a reception)

> *Continue until the tanks stop, then get out and walk.* (Patton to the Twelfth Corps, halted for fuel supplies at St. Dizier, 8/30/44)

Or there is the most laconic diplomatic note on record: when Philip of Macedon wrote to the Spartans that, if he came within their borders, he would leave not one stone of their city, they wrote back the one word—"If."

Clarity comes before even brevity. But it is a fallacy that wordiness is necessarily clearer. Metternich when he thought something he had written was obscure would simply go through it crossing out everything irrelevant. What remained, he found, often became clear. Wellington, asked to recommend three names for the post of Commander-in-Chief, India, took a piece of paper and wrote three times—"Napier." Pages could not have been clearer—or as forcible. On the other hand the lectures, and the sentences, of Coleridge became at times bewildering because his mind was often "wiggle-waggle"; just as he could not even walk straight on a path.

But clarity and brevity, though a good beginning, are only a beginning. By themselves, they may remain bare and bleak. When Calvin Coolidge, asked by his wife what the preacher had preached on, replied "Sin," and, asked what the preacher had said, replied, "He was against it," he was brief enough. But one hardly envies Mrs. Coolidge.

An attractive style requires, of course, all kinds of further gifts—such as variety, good humor, good sense, vitality, imagination. Variety means avoiding monotony of rhythm, of language, of mood. One needs to vary one's sentence length (this present article has too many short sentences; but so vast a subject grows here as cramped as a djin in a bottle); to amplify one's vocabulary; to diversify one's tone. There are books that petrify one throughout, with the rigidly pompous solemnity of an owl perched on a leafless tree. But ceaseless facetiousness can be as bad; or perpetual irony. Even the smile of Voltaire can seem at times a fixed grin, a disagreeable wrinkle. Constant peevishness is far worse, as often in Swift; even on the stage too much irritable dialogue may irritate an audience, without its knowing why.

Still more are vitality, energy, imagination gifts that must be inborn before they can be cultivated. But under the head of imagination two common devices may be mentioned that have been the making of many a style—metaphor and simile. Why such magic power should reside in simply saying, or implying, that A is like B remains a little mysterious. But even our unconscious seems to love symbols; again, language often tends to lose itself in clouds of vaporous abstraction, and simile or metaphor can bring it back to concrete solidity; and, again, such imagery can gild the gray flats of prose with sudden sun glints of poetry.

If a foreigner may for a moment be impertinent, I admire the native gift of Americans for imagery as much as I wince at their fondness for slang. (Slang seems to me a kind of linguistic fungus; as poisonous, and as short-lived, as toadstools.) When Matthew Arnold lectured in the United States, he was likened by one newspaper to "an elderly macaw pecking at a trellis of grapes"; he observed, very justly, "How lively journalistic fancy is among the Americans!" General Grant, again, unable to hear him, remarked: "Well, wife, we've paid to see the British lion, but as we can't hear him roar, we'd better go home." By simile and metaphor, these two quotations bring before us the slightly pompous, fastidious, inaudible Arnold as no direct description could have done.

Or consider how language comes alive in the Chinese saying that lending to the feckless is "like pelting a stray dog with dumplings," or in the Arab proverb: "They came to shoe the pasha's horse, and the beetle stretched forth his leg"; in the Greek phrase for a perilous cape—"stepmother of ships"; or the Hebrew adage that "as the climbing up a sandy way is to the feet of the aged, so is a wife full of words to a quiet man"; in Shakespeare's phrase for a little England lost in the world's vastness—"in a great Poole, a Swan's-nest"; or Fuller's libel on tall men—"Ofttimes such who are built four stories high are observed to have little in their cockloft"; in Chateaubriand's "I go yawning my life"; or in Jules Renard's portrait of a cat, "well buttoned in her fur." Or, to take a modern instance, there is Churchill on dealings with Russia: "Trying to maintain good relations with a Communist is like wooing a crocodile. You do not know whether to tickle it under the chin or beat it over the head. When it opens its mouth, you cannot tell whether it is trying to smile or preparing to eat you up." What a miracle human speech can be, and how dull is most that one hears! Would one hold one's hearers, it is far less help, I suspect, to read manuals on style than to cultivate one's own imagination and imagery.

I will end with two remarks by two wise old women of the civilized 18th Century.

The first is from the blind Mme. du Deffand (the friend of Horace Walpole) to that Mlle. de Lespinasse with whom, alas, she was to quarrel so unwisely: "You must make up your mind, my queen, to live with me in the greatest truth and sincerity. You will be charming so long as you let yourself be natural, and remain without pretension and without artifice." The second is from Mme. de Charrière, the Zélide whom Boswell had once loved at Utrecht in vain, to a Swiss girl friend: "Lucinde, my clever Lucinde, while you wait for the Romeos to arrive, you have nothing better to do than become perfect. Have ideas that are clear, and expressions that are simple." ("Ayez des idées nettes et des expressions simples.") More than half the bad writing in the world, I believe, comes from neglecting those two very simple pieces of advice.

In many ways, no doubt, our world grows more and more complex; sputniks cannot be simple; yet how many of our complexities remain futile, how many of our artificialities false. Simplicity too can be subtle—as the straight lines of a Greek temple, like the Parthenon at Athens, are delicately curved, in order to look straighter still.

7

Jacques Barzun and Henry F. Graff

Clear Writing: The Prerequisites

We closed Part One with a noxious list of barbarisms. We closed Part Two with some healthy remedies. We will close Part Three with a list of salutary prescriptions for writing and revising. Always end on a positive note.

You will note that in his discussion Professor Barzun deals with the sentence, rather than the paragraph. Because the sentence is the basic unit of thought in writing, what he has to say about clarity is important. You will find that some of his specific suggestions recall the objections of Joseph Pattison to the qualities of the F paper.

We end with his suggested list of questions to ask yourself when writing and revising. Any number of such lists can be found; and, indeed, you could make up one of your own. But this one is convenient, and not too long or detailed. If you follow it, you too can avoid the F paper— a practical advantage of a healthy style.

As everybody knows, meaning does not come from single words but from words put together in groups—phrases, clauses, sentences. A mysterious bond links these groups of words with our ideas, and this relation leads in turn to the miracle by which ideas pass from one mind to another. The reason for weighing words with care is to make sure that these units of speech correspond truly to one's inner vision; the reason for building sentences with care is to make sure that all the portions of our thought hang together correctly for truth and conveniently for understanding.

Everyone's mind, however eager it may be for information, opposes a certain resistance to the reception of somebody else's ideas. Before one can take in another's intent, the shape, connection, and tendency of one's own ideas have to yield to those same features in the other person's. Accordingly, the writer must somehow induce in that other the willingness to receive the foreign matter. He does so with the aid of a great many devices which, when regularly used, are called the qualities of his speech or writing.

These qualities go by such names as: Clarity, Order, Logic, Ease, Unity, Coherence, Rhythm, Force, Simplicity, Naturalness, Grace, Wit, and Movement. But these are not distinct things; they overlap and can reinforce or obscure one another, being but aspects of the single power called Style. Neither style nor any of its qualities can be aimed at separately. Nor are the pleasing characteristics of a writer's style laid on some preexisting surface the way sheathing and plaster are laid on the rough boards of a half-finished house. Rather, they are the by-product of an intense effort to make words work. By "making them work" we mean here reaching the mind of another and affecting it in such a way as to reproduce there *our* state of mind.

Since you cannot aim directly at style, clarity, precision, and all the rest, what can you do? You can remove the many possible obstacles to understanding, while preserving as much as you can of your spontaneous utterance. All attempts at reproducing a recognized style, whether Biblical, Lincolnesque, or "stark" for modernity, defeat themselves. You cannot be someone other than yourself. The qualities we have listed, and others you can name, should therefore be regarded as so many tests that you apply in the course of revision by self-questioning. You do not, while writing, say to

"Clear Writing: The Prerequisites" abridged from *The Modern Researcher*, Revised Edition, by Jacques Barzun and Henry F. Graff, © 1957 by Jacques Barzun, © 1970 by Harcourt Brace Jovanovich, Inc., and reprinted with their permission.

yourself: "Now I am going to be clear, logical, coherent." You write a sentence and ask, as you go over it: "Can anyone else follow? Perhaps not. Then what is the matter? I see: this does not match that. And here—is this in any way absurd?" Clarity comes when others can follow; coherence when thoughts hang together; logic when their sequence is valid. You achieve these results by changing, cutting, transposing. You may ask: "Is there no way to write so as to avoid all this patching after-the-fact?" There is—and learning how is the subject of this chapter. But note at the outset that any helpful hints will only reduce the amount of rewriting to be done, never remove its necessity.

It is an interesting proof of what has just been said that no satisfactory definition of a sentence has ever been given: there is no specification to which you can build. Yet every educated person recognizes a sentence when he sees one. The mystery of its connection with a train of thought is the point of departure for our effort to make the sentence and the total thought coincide. To say this is to say that notions of correctness or proffers of approved models for sentences will be useless, and even paralyzing, unless they are taken with imagination. Whatever image you may have in mind when you see or hear the word "sentence," that image should not be of something rigid, static, and absolute; a sentence is above all functional, dynamic, and relative. A sentence, perfectly good when taken by itself, may be all wrong when it follows or precedes another. For the thought has to keep moving and its track must be smooth. If you need a structural image of The Sentence, think of it as an organism possessing a skeleton, muscles, and flesh.

Like a skeleton, a sentence is a piece of construction. Traditional grammar in fact speaks of related words as forming "a construction," and calls it awkward or harmonious, allowable or contrary to usage. But do not let the idea of a construction suggest a table or a house; to be sure, a sentence has to stand on its feet, but we liken it to a skeleton because a sentence, like the thought it carries, has to move. Motion is perhaps the fundamental quality of good writing. Motion is what makes writing correspond to thought, which is also a movement from one idea or vision to the next. A reader who knows nothing about the principles of writing may be incapable of analyzing what is wrong as he makes heavy weather through a book. But he feels very keenly whether his mind advances or sticks, goes straight or in circles, marches steadily forward or jerks two steps ahead and three back.

In order to move, the parts of the sentence skeleton must be properly jointed, articulated; the muscles and connective tissue must be strong and inserted at the right places; the burden of ideas must not be too great for the structure. And to cover all this machinery and make it pleasing, the surface must be reasonably varied and polished. Translating this into writers' terms, we say: clauses and phrases must fall into the right pattern of syntax, and the words must be chosen so that the tone and rhythm of the whole are appropriate. A telegraphic message may be exact and well knit, but it lacks grace and sounds unnatural. It moves but does not flow. One cannot imagine reading three hundred pages in telegraphic style. The words omitted in that style and which are restored in ordinary prose are no decoration or added charm; they are simply the rounded contour of the thought, reduced in the telegram to the bare bones.

The return of this image of the skeleton tells us that we have come full circle in our attempt to define at one and the same time what a sentence is and what it does. You may as a result be a little wiser about the virtues to aim at in writing. But you probably think, with reason, that what you need even more than a definition is direct advice, and for this we must look at examples. Yet, we repeat: if you want the examples to be serviceable beyond their immediate instruction, you should study them with the force of our definition behind them.

Let us begin with the schoolbook example: "The wind blew across the desert where the corpse lay and whistled." The sentence moves indeed, and the *information* it contains is not hard to find; but before we quite grasp it we laugh. And this alters the *meaning,* which was not intended to be jocular in the last three words. How to fix it? Our first impulse is to insert a comma after "lay." But reading the result gives an odd impression, as if "and whistled" was a dangling afterthought. Try it aloud and you will hear that a comma pause after "lay" makes "and whistled" sound not simply silly but a trifle puzzling. The only way the sentence sounds rhythmically satisfying is without the pause.

Clearly the diagnosis is that the meaning and the construction are at odds; bad rhythm gives the flaw away, the trouble being that the limb "and whistled" is attached to the wrong part of the body. Since the joke comes from the close link between the corpse and the whistling, we derive from this our first rule of sentence-making: *bring as close together as possible the parts that occur together in the world or go together in your mind.*

Now try to apply the rule to our sentence: "The wind blew across the desert and whistled where the corpse lay." No longer comic, but wrong again, because the new close-linking suggests that the whistling took place only near the corpse. In framing a sentence the need to link and connect implies the need to unlink and detach. Try again: "The wind blew and whistled across the desert where the corpse lay." At last we have the limbs correctly distributed—no front leg is hitched on to the hindquarters. Our sentence passes the test as far as avoiding absurdity and false suggestion goes.

But say it aloud once more and you will notice that it still sounds odd. It leaves the voice up in the air, and with the voice, the meaning. This is because the emphases are off beat. In an ordinary declarative sentence, the two spots of emphasis are the beginning and the end. Hence the two most important elements in the thought must occupy those spots. In our example the main elements obviously are: the whistling wind and the corpse. Whether the corpse lay or stood or leaned is a detail. The last idea sounding in our mind's ear must be "the corpse." Can this be managed? Let us see. "The wind blew and whistled across the desert where lay the corpse." A trifle better, but far from perfect. Why? Because modern English shies away from inversions. Idiomatic turns make a language what it is; to defy idiom is to lose force. In short, to sound natural we must stick to "where the corpse lay."

By this time we are sick and tired of wrestling with these twelve words and we conclude that they cannot be juggled into a proper shape. We are ready to scrap the sentence and go at the idea by a different route when a fresh form occurs to us. "The corpse lay in the desert, across which the wind blew and whistled." This is the best yet. The form is right and if the whole subject were only a little less dramatic we could let it stand. But there is a stiffness about "across which" that suits a description of scenery rather than of lonely death. This impression simply means that we have been made aware of Tone while trying to secure Right Emphasis, Right Linking, and Right Rhythm. These features of the sentence, we repeat, are not separable. On the contrary, a sentence is to be regarded as a compromise among their various demands.

If the Tone of "across which" is unsuitable, what *can* we do with the wretched corpse on our hands? Having twisted and turned it about, all that occurs is to abandon our second construction and try a third: "The corpse lay in the desert, and over it the wind blew and whistled."[1] This is still disappointing: a compound sentence is too weak for this gruesome vision; it separates what eye and ear bring together to the mind. We have dismembered and reconstructed without success. What next?

---

[1] The inveterate verifier is curious about the fact and he asks: *Does* the wind whistle when it blows across an unobstructed waste?

The true solution lies in the so-called periodic sentence, whose form heightens suspense and generally favors rhythm: "Across the desert where the corpse lay, the wind blew and whistled." A peculiarity of the periodic sentence is that its suspensive opening phrase does not monopolize the emphasis we associate with beginnings. The second portion is still emphatic because the forepart rushes down toward it, so to speak, in an effort to complete its own meaning by finding a main subject and verb.

From our experience with a single bad sentence, we can now confirm our first rule of thumb and add to it others for similar use in framing and straightening sentences:

1. Right linking is the prime requisite. Begin by seeing to it that things related are not divided, and that things remote are not falsely joined.

2. Right emphasis comes next. It is what gives momentum to the thought, what makes the sentence move. It starts from a point of superior interest, travels through a valley of detail, and reaches a second point of high interest, which ends the journey by completing or advancing our understanding of the first.

3. When the emphases are right, the rhythm is likely to be right also, for our speaking habits naturally follow our habits of wording and of thought.[2]

4. At any point in the structure, the phrasing must be in keeping with the tenor of the whole. This is a matter partly of diction and partly of construction. The two together produce Tone.

To these four propositions there is an important negative corollary: Although a comma that is missing from a sound sentence should be put in, no putting in of commas will cure a defective sentence. When you are tempted to waste time in this effort, just remember "and whistled."

With these truths in mind, we can refine a little on the art of construction, though with no hope of exhausting the subject of improved sentence-building. We go back to the difficult art of linking. The desire to bring kindred things together often tempts the unwary to use phrases that can be read in two or more ways. Ambiguity sets the reader on the wrong track;

---

[2] This does not mean that in speaking we usually place our words right for emphasis but that we sound them right, and hence the rhythm is natural. One says: "They *are* good— in *my* opinion." To convey the same meaning in print, one must write: "They are, in my opinion, good." Still judging the written word, explain the rather different meanings of: "In my opinion, they are good" and "They, in my opinion, are good."

he must back up and make a fresh start, or perhaps remain in doubt about the right fusion of ideas. When this happens too often, he is understandably aggrieved. Suppose he reads:

> If there is lost motion in the rods and boxes in a boiler of steam generating capacity and a valve distributing power properly when the lever is hooked down, it develops into a pound that is annoying and detrimental to the machinery.

The reader's trouble begins at "steam generating capacity." Should this be "steam-generating," a hyphenated adjective modifying "capacity"? Or should it be "a boiler of steam, generating [power at] capacity"? Below, a similar hesitation arises at "valve distributing power." Doubt is settled by our knowledge that valves distribute power and not the other way round ("valve-distributing power" is nonsense). But we have had to stop and figure this out. The second phrase exactly parallels the first—"steam-generating capacity"—and our retentive ear entices us to give their parallel forms a parallel meaning. Next we are stopped for a further instant at whatever "it" is that "develops into a pound." After talk of steam power, the word "pound" is ambiguous. We see at once that it is not a pound of pressure that is meant but a pound*ing*. Still, we have been jerked to a halt a third time. Finally, another, somewhat different, parallel between the two adjectives in the last part of the sentence tells us that this pounding is "annoying . . . to the machinery."

On the whole, this sentence intended for the instruction of engineers can tell us more about writing than about locomotives. And here is what it tells us: parallelism is so important a device in writing that its use must be kept pure. Do not give parallel forms to disparate ideas, and always carry out the parallels you start with. Do not ever suppose that variation is more elegant. Note the accumulation of horrors in:

> When it came right down to it, he was no more able to spell out a conceptual pattern than, in the last analysis, he felt he could muster up the imagination to face such explosive problems of ethics as his sadly unhappy life had left him no room to size up with detachment.

At the words "he was no more able to," the writer has made a contract with the reader. Those words forecast a "than," to be followed by a second action parallel to the first. The contract here is broken. The "than" duly comes, but its proper adjunct is forgotten while the writer pursues his wandering thought down winding channels. Jargon and rank images ("spell out a pattern," "explosive problems," "room to size up") are mixed with clichés ("in the last analysis"), tautologies ("sadly unhappy"), and the redundancies that spoil the parallel—"he [felt he] could," and the words following "imagination." The cure is to give up the "no more than" construction and make two sentences, one about the conceptual patterns—whatever they may be—and one about the ethical problems of a sadly unhappy life without room.

An observation made in passing when we examined the sentence from the engineer's manual furnishes a second rule of good construction: *the antecedents of pronouns must always be unmistakable.* In the welter of rods, boxes, and valves no one can tell what "it" is that "develops into a pound." It cannot be the engine, which is not even mentioned. The motion, no doubt, develops into a pound, but the only motion mentioned is four lines above and it is *lost* motion. Technically, it is a kind of motion, but in syntax it does not exist. In any event, no less than six nouns in the singular precede "it," and two would be enough to create confusion. By rights, the last in order should be the true antecedent, but that happens to be "lever," which makes nonsense. The "it" is an orphaned relative with no references to show when questioned. . . .

All we have been saying is an extension of our original proposition that "good writing is an intense effort to make words work." The complaints and suggestions about the passages we have examined boil down to the demand that each word—noun, verb, adverb, or any other kind—should contribute something to the sense, and this with economy. If one word can do the work of two, use one. If you absolutely need a phrase, make it short. If the thought is complex and the sentence has to contain several clauses, see to it that each clause expends its energy where none will be wasted, that is, close to the idea it enlarges or qualifies.

A good rule to follow in order to achieve coherence with the least trouble is to stick to your subject, voice, or construction. Do not start with one idea or form and change it in mid-career. . . . "The topic one selects should be clear and precise and when one comes to look for the materials on it, it will be found that the subject itself serves as a guide to their selection." This is no doubt a faithful transcript of the way the thought arose in one mind, but its form is ill adapted to its penetrating another. In a second draft the writer should cling to his grammatical subject and see where it leads him: "The topic selected should be clear and precise—*so that* IT will guide the researcher—*when* HE comes to look for *his* materials." Twenty-three words in place of thirty-five, and a *continuous motion* instead of three hitches—from "the topic" to "when one comes" to an indefinite "it" and back to "the subject" again.

Only remain faithful to your subject and construction, making everything follow the one and fit into the other, and you will be surprised at the ease, speed, and clarity that you will attain. All the thick connective tissue —or clanking chains, rather ("as regards," "as far as . . . is concerned," "in relation to," and the like)—will automatically fall away; associated ideas will be next to next; and your thought will be accessible to the reader who, by definition, is always on the run . . . .

QUESTIONS TO ASK IN WRITING AND REVISING

I a. Has my paper (chapter) a single informing theme, with its proper developments, or is it merely a series of loosely connected ideas and images?

b. Does my beginning begin and does my conclusion conclude? (A beginning should not go back to the Flood, and a conclusion is not the same thing as a summing up.)

c. Is each of my paragraphs a division with a purpose; that is, does it organize a number of sentences into a treatment of one idea and its modifications?

d. Is each sentence contrived to stand on its own feet or is it thrown off balance by the load of qualifiers or the drag of afterthoughts?

e. Have I made proper use of transitional words and phrases to keep all my connections clear? For example, *nevertheless, moreover, even, still, of course* (in its use of minimizing the idea before), *to be sure, admittedly.* (The transitional word or phrase is usually better in the course of the sentence than at the beginning.)

II a. What is the *tone* of my piece? Is it too stiff and too formal, trying for the effect of authority? Is it perhaps too relaxed, too familiar, too facetious? Or is it, as it should be, simple, direct?

b. Are there any passages that I especially prize? If so, am I sure that, in my creative enthusiasm, I am not delighted with something "fancy"?

c. Have I been conscious of the reader and have I consulted his convenience? Or have I, on the contrary, been easy only on myself and used a "private" language?

d. Could I, if called upon to do so, explain the exact meaning and function of every word I have used? For example, *subjective, objective, meaningful, realistic, impact, value.*

180

e. Are my metaphors aids to the reader or merely ways for me to escape my own difficulty?

III a. Is it perfectly clear to which noun or noun-clause my pronouns refer? (The *slightest* ambiguity is fatal.)

b. Have I tried to give an air of judicious reserve by repeating the words *somewhat, rather, perhaps,* and have I used for this purpose the illiterate "to an extent"? Or, conversely, have I overdone the emphatic with *very, invariably, tremendous, extraordinary,* and the like?

c. Have I arbitrarily broken or altered the idiomatic links between certain words, particularly between verbs and their allied prepositions, committing such solecisms as: *disagree . . . to, equally . . . as, prefer . . . than?*

d. Have I imported from sciences and disciplines in which I am interested a vocabulary out of place in civilized writing? What jargon and vogue words have slipped out by force of habit? Examples of jargon are: *integrate, area, parameter, frame of reference, methodology, in terms of, level, approach.*

e. Have I preferred the familiar word to the far-fetched? the concrete to the abstract? the single to the circumlocution? the short to the long?

Four

CASE HISTORIES:
SOME ANALYSES OF STYLE

> For a man to write well there are re-
> quired three necessaries: to read the best
> authors, observe the best speakers, and
> much exercise of his style.
>
> — Ben Jonson, *Timber*

In Part One you were asked to examine some symptoms of bad style in the hopes that you would profit from bad example. In Part Two you were shown evidence that bad style is contagious and can infect the real world, and that others besides writing instructors care about good style. In Part Three you were given some advice on how to improve your style—a sort of handbook of prophylactic suggestions. After all that you might find it interesting and inspirational to examine some healthy specimens. So in the following section you will look at analyses of five classic examples of good style and, for variety's sake—comparison and contrast—a classic hatchet-job analysis of bad style.

In keeping with Ben Jonson's advice above, the examples have been drawn from both authors and speakers. (The third part of his advice is up to you.) Three of the styles analyzed below come from fiction, three of them from nonfiction. Two of them are speeches. Of the nonfiction examples, each has had a profound effect in the real world. Of the fiction examples, two have been very influential in the literature of the twentieth century and the third—James Fenimore Cooper—was highly popular and admired in his time.

The range of emphasis is quite broad. It is hard to imagine two more different styles than the nervous vernacular of Holden Caulfield and the stately formality of the Declaration of Independence. This range underscores an important point: there is no such thing as the *one* good style. It also serves to illustrate a corollary: that style is good which is ideally suited to the situation and the subject matter.

One more thing to keep in mind. We tend to regard such classics of style as having always existed, co-eval with God and suddenly revealed in all their immortal perfection. That is a mistake. All these examples were written by people who sweated and wrestled with words, sentences, and ideas. And they didn't take their present form in a first draft. You may never achieve the eloquence of Lincoln or the incisiveness of Hemingway, but even they did not achieve their mastery without a lot of trial and revision.

Donald P. Costello

The Language of "The Catcher in the Rye"

The Catcher in the Rye *was published in the early
1950's. In spite of the inevitable dating of some of the expressions used by Holden Caulfield, no one who reads the
novel fails to remark on the authenticity of Holden's style
as "an intelligent, educated, Northeastern American adolescent." In this article Mr. Costello isolates and discusses
the particular speech patterns Salinger used to create both
a type and an individual.*

study of the language of J. D. Salinger's *The Catcher in the Rye* can be justified not only on the basis of literary interest, but also on the basis of linguistic significance. Today we study *The Adventures of Huckleberry Finn* (with which many critics have compared *The Catcher in the Rye*) not only as a great work of literary art, but as a valuable study in 1884 dialect. In coming decades, *The Catcher in the Rye* will be studied, I feel, not only as a literary work, but also as an example of teenage vernacular in the 1950s. As such, the book will be a significant historical linguistic record of a type of speech rarely made available in permanent form. Its linguistic importance will increase as the American speech it records becomes less current.

Most critics who looked at *The Catcher in the Rye* at the time of its publication thought that its language was a true and authentic rendering of teenage colloquial speech. Reviewers in the Chicago *Sunday Tribune,* the London *Times Literary Supplement,* the *New Republic,* the New York *Herald Tribune Book Review,* the New York *Times,* the *New Yorker,* and the *Saturday Review of Literature* all specifically mentioned the authenticity of the book's language. Various aspects of its language were also discussed in the reviews published in *America,* the *Atlantic,* the *Catholic World,* the *Christian Science Monitor,* the *Library Journal,* the Manchester *Guardian,* the *Nation,* the *New Statesman and Nation,* the New York *Times Book Review, Newsweek,* the *Spectator,* and *Time.* Of these many reviews, only the writers for the *Catholic World* and the *Christian Science Monitor* denied the authenticity of the book's language, but both of these are religious journals which refused to believe that the "obscenity" was realistic. An examination of the reviews of *The Catcher in the Rye* proves that the language of Holden Caulfield, the book's sixteen-year-old narrator, struck the ear of the contemporary reader as an accurate rendering of the informal speech of an intelligent, educated, Northeastern American adolescent.

In addition to commenting on its authenticity, critics have often remarked—uneasily—the "daring," "obscene," "blasphemous" features of Holden's language. Another commonly noted feature of the book's language has been its comic effect. And yet there has never been an extensive investigation of the language itself. That is what this paper proposes to do.

Even though Holden's language is authentic teenage speech, recording it was certainly not the major intention of Salinger. He was faced with

"The Language of *The Catcher in the Rye*" from *American Speech,* October 1959. Reprinted with permission of the author. Footnotes deleted.

the artistic task of creating an individual character, not with the linguistic task of reproducing the exact speech of teenagers in general. Yet Holden had to speak a recognizable teenage language, and at the same time had to be identifiable as an individual. This difficult task Salinger achieved by giving Holden an extremely trite and typical teenage speech, overlaid with strong personal idiosyncrasies. There are two major speech habits which are Holden's own, which are endlessly repeated throughout the book, and which are, nevertheless, typical enough of teenage speech so that Holden can be both typical and individual in his use of them. It is certainly common for teenagers to end thoughts with a loosely dangling "and all," just as it is common for them to add an insistent "I really did," "It really was." But Holden uses these phrases to such an overpowering degree that they become a clear part of the flavor of the book; they become, more, a part of Holden himself, and actually help to characterize him.

Holden's "and all" and its twins, "or something," "or anything," serve no real, consistent linguistic function. They simply give a sense of looseness of expression and looseness of thought. Often they signify that Holden knows there is more that could be said about the issue at hand, but he is not going to bother going into it:

> ... *how my parents were occupied and all before they had me*
> (5)
> ... *they're* nice *and all (5)*
> *I'm not going to tell you my whole goddam autobiography or anything (5)*
> ... *splendid and clear-thinking and all (6)*

But just as often the use of such expressions is purely arbitrary, with no discernible meaning:

> ... *he's my* brother *and all (5)*
> ... *was in the Revolutionary War and all (6)*
> *It was December and all (7)*
> ... *no gloves or anything (7)*
> ... *right in the pocket and all (7)*

Donald Barr, writing in the *Commonweal,* finds this habit indicative of Holden's tendency to generalize, to find the all in the one:

> *Salinger has an ear not only for idiosyncrasies of diction and syntax, but for mental processes. Holden Caulfield's phrase is "and all"—"She looked so damn* nice, *the way she kept going around and*

around in her blue coat and all"—as if each experience wore a halo. His fallacy is ab uno disce omnes; *he abstracts and generalizes wildly.*

Heiserman and Miller, in the *Western Humanities Review,* comment specifically upon Holden's second most obvious idiosyncrasy: "In a phony world Holden feels compelled to reenforce his sincerity and truthfulness constantly with, 'It really is' or 'It really did.'" S. N. Behrman, in the *New Yorker,* finds a double function of these "perpetual insistences of Holden's." Behrman thinks they "reveal his age, even when he is thinking much older," and, more important, "he is so aware of the danger of slipping into phoniness himself that he has to repeat over and over 'I really mean it,' 'It really does.'" Holden uses this idiosyncrasy of insistence almost every time that he makes an affirmation.

Allied to Holden's habit of insistence is his "if you want to know the truth." Heiserman and Miller are able to find characterization in this habit too:

> *The skepticism inherent in that casual phrase, "if you want to know the truth," suggesting that as a matter of fact in the world of Holden Caulfield very few people do, characterizes this sixteen-year-old "crazy mixed up kid" more sharply and vividly than pages of character "analysis" possibly could.*

Holden uses this phrase only after affirmations, just as he uses "It really does," but usually after the personal ones, where he is consciously being frank:

> *I have no wind, if you want to know the truth. (8)*
> *I don't even think that bastard had a handkerchief, if you want to know the truth. (34)*
> *I'm a pacifist, if you want to know the truth. (44)*
> *She had quite a lot of sex appeal, too, if you really want to know. (53)*
> *I was damn near bawling, I felt so damn happy, if you want to know the truth. (191)*

These personal idiosyncrasies of Holden's speech are in keeping with general teenage language. Yet they are so much a part of Holden and of the flavor of the book that they are much of what makes Holden to be Holden. They are the most memorable feature of the book's language. Although always in character, the rest of Holden's speech is more typical

than individual. The special quality of this language comes from its trite-
ness, its lack of distinctive qualities.

Holden's informal, schoolboy vernacular is particularly typical in its
"vulgarity" and "obscenity." No one familiar with prep-school speech could
seriously contend that Salinger overplayed his hand in this respect. On the
contrary, Holden's restraints help to characterize him as a sensitive youth
who avoids the most strongly forbidden terms, and who never uses vulgarity in a self-conscious or phony way to help him be "one of the boys."
Fuck, for example, is never used as a part of Holden's speech. The word
appears in the novel four times, but only when Holden disapprovingly discusses its wide appearance on walls. The Divine name is used habitually by
Holden only in the comparatively weak *for God's sake, God,* and *goddam.*
The stronger and usually more offense *for Chrissake* or *Jesus* or *Jesus
Christ* are used habitually by Ackley and Stradlater; but Holden uses them
only when he feels the need for a strong expression. He almost never uses
for Chrissake in an unemotional situation. *Goddam* is Holden's favorite adjective. This word is used with no relationship to its original meaning, or to
Holden's attitude toward the word to which it is attached. It simply expresses an emotional feeling toward the object: either favorable, as in
"goddam hunting cap"; or unfavorable, as in "ya goddam moron"; or indifferent, as in "coming in the goddam windows." *Damn* is used interchange-
ably with *goddam;* no differentiation in its meaning is detectable.

Other crude words are also often used in Holden's vocabulary. *Ass*
keeps a fairly restricted meaning as a part of the human anatomy, but it is
used in a variety of ways. It can refer simply to to that specific part of the
body ("I moved my ass a little"), or be a part of a trite expression ("freezing
my ass off"; "in a half-assed way"), or be an expletive ("Game, my ass").
Hell is perhaps the most versatile word in Holden's entire vocabulary; it
serves most of the meanings and constructions which Mencken lists in his
American Speech article on "American Profanity." So far is Holden's use of
hell from its original meaning that he can use the sentence "We had a hell-
uva time" to mean that he and Phoebe had a decidedly pleasant time
downtown shopping for shoes. The most common function of *hell* is as the
second part of a simile, in which a thing can be either "hot as hell" or,
strangely, "cold as hell"; "sad as hell" or "playfull as hell"; "old as hell" or
"pretty as hell." Like all of these words, *hell* has no close relationship to its
original meaning.

Both *bastard* and *sonuvabitch* have also drastically changed in meaning. They no longer, of course, in Holden's vocabulary, have any connection
with the accidents of birth. Unless used in a trite simile, *bastard* is a strong

word, reserved for things and people Holden particularly dislikes, especially "phonies." *Sonuvabitch* has an even stronger meaning to Holden; he uses it only in the deepest anger. When, for example, Holden is furious with Stradlater over his treatment of Jane Gallagher, Holden repeats again and again that he "kept calling him a moron sonuvabitch" (43).

The use of crude language in *The Catcher in the Rye* increases, as we should expect, when Holden is reporting schoolboy dialogue. When he is directly addressing the reader, Holden's use of such language drops off almost entirely. There is also an increase in this language when any of the characters are excited or angry. Thus, when Holden is apprehensive over Stradlater's treatment of Jane, his *goddams* increase suddenly to seven on a single page (p. 39).

Holden's speech is also typical in his use of slang. I have catalogued over a hundred slang terms used by Holden, and every one of these is in widespread use. Although Holden's slang is rich and colorful, it, of course, being slang, often fails at precise communication. Thus, Holden's *crap* is used in seven different ways. It can mean foolishness, as "all that David Copperfield kind of crap," or messy matter, as "I spilled some crap all over my gray flannel," or merely miscellaneous matter, as "I was putting on my galoshes and crap." It can also carry its basic meaning, animal excreta, as "there didn't look like there was anything in the park except dog crap," and it can be used as an adjective meaning anything generally unfavorable, as "The show was on the crappy side." Holden uses the phrases *to be a lot of crap* and *to shoot the crap* and *to chuck the crap* all to mean "to be untrue," but he can also use *to shoot the crap* to mean simply "to chat," with no connotation of untruth, as in "I certainly wouldn't have minded shooting the crap with old Phoebe for a while."

Similarly Holden's slang use of *crazy* is both trite and imprecise. "That drives me crazy" means that he violently dislikes something; yet "to be crazy about" something means just the opposite. In the same way, to be "killed" by something can mean that he was emotionally affected either favorably ("That story just about killed me") or unfavorably ("Then she turned her back on me again. It nearly killed me"). This use of *killed* is one of Holden's favorite slang expressions. Heiserman and Miller are, incidentally, certainly incorrect when they conclude: "Holden always lets us know when he has insight into the absurdity of the endlessly absurd situations which make up the life of a sixteen-year-old by exclaiming, 'It killed me.'" Holden often uses this expression with no connection to the absurd; he even uses it for his beloved Phoebe. The expression simply indicates a high degree of emotion—any kind. It is hazardous to conclude that any of Holden's slang has a precise and consistent meaning or function. These same critics fall into the same error when they conclude that Holden's use of the adjective *old* serves as "a term of endearment." Holden appends this word to almost every character, real or fictional, mentioned in the novel, from the hated "old Maurice" to "old Peter Lorre," to "old Phoebe," and even "old Jesus." The only pattern that can be discovered in Holden's use of this term is that he usually uses it only after he has previously mentioned the character; he then feels free to append the familiar *old*. All we can conclude from Holden's slang is that it is typical teenage slang: versatile yet narrow, expressive yet unimaginative, imprecise, often crude, and always trite.

Holden has many favorite slang expressions which he overuses. In one place, he admits:

> *"Boy!" I said. I also say "Boy!" quite a lot. Partly because I have a lousy vocabulary and partly because I act quite young for my age sometimes. (12)*

But if Holden's slang shows the typically "lousy vocabulary" of even the educated American teenager, this failing becomes even more obvious when we narrow our view to Holden's choice of adjectives and adverbs. The choice is indeed narrow, with a constant repetition of a few favorite words: *lousy, pretty, crumby, terrific, quite, old, stupid*—all used, as is the habit of teenage vernacular, with little regard to specific meaning. Thus, most of the nouns which are called "stupid" could not in any logical framework be called "ignorant," and, as we have seen, *old* before a proper noun has nothing to do with age.

Another respect in which Holden was correct in accusing himself of having a "lousy vocabulary" is discovered in the ease with which he falls into trite figures of speech. We have already seen that Holden's most common simile is the worn and meaningless "as hell"; but his often-repeated "like a madman" and "like a bastard" are just about as unrelated to a literal meaning and are easily as unimaginative. Even Holden's non-habitual figures of speech are usually trite: "sharp as a tack"; "hot as a firecracker"; "laughed like a hyena"; "I know old Jane like a book"; "drove off like a bat out of hell"; "I began to feel like a horse's ass"; "blind as a bat"; "I know Central Park like the back of my hand."

Repetitious and trite as Holden's vocabulary may be, it can, nevertheless, become highly effective. For example, when Holden piles one trite adjective upon another, a strong power of invective is often the result:

> *He was a goddam stupid moron. (42)*
> *Get your dirty stinking moron knees off my chest. (43)*
> *You're a dirty stupid sonuvabitch of a moron. (43)*

And his limited vocabulary can also be used for good comic effect. Holden's constant repetition of identical expressions in countless widely different situations is often hilariously funny.

But all of the humor in Holden's vocabulary does not come from its unimaginative quality. Quite the contrary, some of his figures of speech are entirely original; and these are inspired, dramatically effective, and terribly funny. As always, Salinger's Holden is basically typical, with a strong overlay of the individual:

> *He started handling my exam paper like it was a turd or something. (13)*
> *He put my goddam paper down then and looked at me like he'd just beaten the hell out of me in ping-pong or something. (14)*
> *That guy Morrow was about as sensitive as a goddam toilet seat. (52)*
> *Old Marty was like dragging the Statue of Liberty around the floor. (69)*

Another aspect in which Holden's language is typical is that it shows the general American characteristic of adaptability—apparently strengthened by his teenage lack of restraint. It is very easy for Holden to turn nouns into adjectives, with the simple addition of a -y: "perverty," "Christmasy," "vomity-looking," "whory-looking," "hoodlumy-looking," "show-offy," "flitty-looking," "dumpy-looking," "pimpy," "snobby," "fisty." Like all of English, Holden's language shows a versatile combining ability: "They gave Sally this little blue butt-twitcher of a dress to wear" (117) and "That magazine was some little cheerer upper" (176). Perhaps the most interesting aspect of the adaptability of Holden's language is his ability to use nouns as adverbs: "She sings it very Dixieland and whorehouse, and it doesn't sound at all mushy" (105).

As we have seen, Holden shares, in general, the trite repetitive vocabulary which is the typical lot of his age group. But as there are exceptions in his figures of speech, so are there exceptions in his vocabulary itself, in his word stock. An intelligent, well-read ("I'm quite illiterate, but I read a lot"), and educated boy, Holden possesses, and can use when he wants to, many words which are many a cut above Basic English, including "ostracized," "exhibitionist," "unscrupulous," "conversationalist," "psychic," "bourgeois." Often Holden seems to choose his words consciously, in an effort to communicate to his adult reader clearly and properly, as in such terms as "lose my virginity," "relieve himself," "an alcoholic"; for upon occasion, he also uses the more vulgar terms "to give someone the time," "to take a leak," "booze hound." Much of the humor arises, in fact, from Holden's habit of writing on more than one level at the same time. Thus, we have such phrases as "They give guys the ax quite frequently at Pency" and "It has a very good academic rating, Pency" (7). Both sentences show a colloquial idiom with an overlay of consciously selected words.

Such a conscious choice of words seems to indicate that Salinger, in his attempt to create a realistic character in Holden, wanted to make him aware of his speech, as, indeed, a real teenager would be when communicating to the outside world. Another piece of evidence that Holden is conscious of his speech and, more, realizes a difficulty in communication, is found in his habit of direct repetition: "She likes me a lot. I mean she's quite fond of me" (141), and "She can be very snotty sometimes. She can be quite snotty" (150). Sometimes the repetition is exact: "He was a very nervous guy—I mean he was a very nervous guy" (165), and "I sort, of missed them. I mean I sort of missed them" (169). Sometimes Holden stops specifically to interpret slang terms, as when he wants to communicate the fact that Allie liked Phoebe: "She killed Allie, too. I mean he liked her, too" (64).

There is still more direct evidence that Holden was conscious of his speech. Many of his comments to the reader are concerned with language. He was aware, for example, of the "phony" quality of many words and phrases, such as "grand," "prince," "traveling incognito," "little girls' room," "licorice stick," and "angels." Holden is also conscious, of course, of the existence of "taboo words." He makes a point of mentioning that the girl from Seattle repeatedly asked him to "watch your language, if you don't mind" (67), and that his mother told Phoebe not to say "lousy" (160). When the prostitute says "Like fun you are," Holden comments:

> *It was a funny thing to say. It sounded like a real kid. You'd think a prostitute and all would say "Like hell you are" or "Cut the crap" instead of "Like fun you are." (87)*

In grammar, too, as in vocabulary, Holden possesses a certain self-consciousness. (It is, of course, impossible to imagine a student getting through today's schools without a self-consciousness with regard to grammar rules.) Holden is, in fact, not only aware of the existence of "grammatical errors," but knows the social taboos that accompany them. He is disturbed by a schoolmate who is ashamed of his parents' grammar, and he reports that his former teacher, Mr. Antolini, warned him about picking up "just enough education to hate people who say, 'It's a secret between he and I'" (168).

Holden is a typical enough teenager to violate the grammar rules, even though he knows of their social importance. His most common rule violation is the misuse of *lie* and *lay*, but he also is careless about relative pronouns ("about a traffic cop that falls in love"), the double negative ("I hardly didn't even know I was doing it"), the perfect tenses ("I'd woke him up"), extra words ("like as if all you ever did at Pencey was play polo all the time"), pronoun number ("it's pretty disgusting to watch somebody picking their nose"), and pronoun position ("I and this friend of mine, Mal Brossard"). More remarkable, however, than the instances of grammar rule violations is Holden's relative "correctness." Holden is always intelligible, and is even "correct" in many usually difficult constructions. Grammatically speaking, Holden's language seems to point up the fact that English was the only subject in which he was not failing. It is interesting to note how much more "correct" Holden's speech is than that of Huck Finn. But then Holden is educated, and since the time of Huck there had been sixty-seven years of authoritarian schoolmarms working on the likes of Holden. He has, in fact, been overtaught, so that he uses many "hyper" forms:

> *I used to play tennis with he and Mrs. Antolini quite frequently.*
> *(163)*
>> *She'd give Allie or I a push. (64)*
>> *I and Allie used to take her to the park with us. (64)*
>> *I think I probably woke he and his wife up. (157)*

Now that we have examined several aspects of Holden's vocabulary and grammar, it would be well to look at a few examples of how he puts these elements together into sentences. The structure of Holden's sentences indicates that Salinger thinks of the book more in terms of spoken speech than written speech. Holden's faulty structure is quite common and typical in vocal expression; I doubt if a student who is "good in English" would ever create such sentence structure in writing. A student who showed the self-consciousness of Holden would not *write* so many fragments, such afterthoughts (e.g., "It has a very good academic rating, Pencey" [7]), or such repetitions (e.g., "Where I lived at Pencey, I lived in the Ossenburger Memorial Wing of the new dorms" [18]).

There are other indications that Holden's speech is vocal. In many places Salinger mildly imitates spoken speech. Sentences such as "You could tell old Spencer'd got a big bang out of buying it" (10) and "I'd've killed him" (42) are repeated throughout the book. Yet it is impossible to imagine Holden taking pen in hand and actually writing "Spencer'd" or "I'd've." Sometimes, too, emphasized words, or even parts of words, are italicized, as in "Now *shut up,* Holden. God damn it—I'm *warn*ing ya" (42). This is often done with good effect, imitating quite perfectly the rhythms of speech, as in the typical:

> *I practically sat down on her* lap, *as a matter of fact. Then she* really *started to cry, and the next thing I knew, I was kissing her all over*—any*where*—*her eyes, her* nose, *her forehead, her eyebrows and all, her* ears—*her whole face except her mouth and all. (73)*

The language of *The Catcher in the Rye* is, as we have seen, an authentic artistic rendering of a type of informal, colloquial, teenage American spoken speech. It is strongly typical and trite, yet often somewhat individual; it is crude and slangy and imprecise, imitative yet occasionally imaginative, and affected toward standardization by the strong efforts of schools. But authentic and interesting as this language may be, it must be remembered that it exists, in *The Catcher in the Rye,* as only one part of an artistic achievement. The language was not written for itself, but as a part of a greater whole. Like the great Twain work with which it is often compared, a study of *The Catcher in the Rye* repays both the linguist and the literary critic; for as one critic has said, "In them, 1884 and 1951 speak to us in the idiom and accent of two youthful travelers who have earned their passports to literary immortality."

2

Walker Gibson

Tough Talk: The Rhetoric of Frederic Henry

Ernest Hemingway had probably the greatest impact on the writing style of the twentieth century of any single author. You have probably read A Farewell To Arms, *a passage from which forms the basis for Walker Gibson's analysis of the Hemingway style.*

Notice a trick of Gibson's. In an essay like this, it is always easier to bounce one thing off another than it is to discuss it in isolation. So as a foil Gibson selects a passage from another novel, thus setting up the basic framework of his essay. This is just a more sophisticated and professional use of a rhetorical stategy most writing instructors assign in composition classes, the "comparison and contrast" paper.

> I did not say anything. I was always
> embarrassed by the words . . . .

When a new style swims into our ken, as Hemingway's did in the 1920s, it is new, or was new, in respect to a historical situation. People brought to their reading, just as they still do of course, a set of assumptions about how books ought to be written. No novelist would be interested in a reader who had never read a novel, or who had never experienced, as *he* has experienced, the going literature of the recent past. So Hemingway's assumed reader of the 1920s had an ear tuned to nineteenth-century rhythms and attitudes; it was in their light that Hemingway's style appeared so fresh and exciting. It is still exciting, if not exactly fresh, a generation later, which is testimony enough to the power of a great writer.

But in order to remind ourselves of some of the stylistic expectations against which Hemingway was first read, and to some extent must still be read, it will be useful to contrast the opening of *A Farewell to Arms* (1929) with the opening of a standard sort of American novel of forty years earlier. The opening I have chosen, from W. D. Howells' *A Modern Instance* (1888), has some superficial resemblance in stage setting to Hemingway's opening that may make the contrast in style the more striking. In each case a narrator is introducing us to a scene as well as to himself, and both scenes include a *village* on a *plain*, in the *summer*, with a view of *mountains* and a *river*.

PASSAGE A (HOWELLS)

The village stood on a wide plain, and around it rose the mountains. They were green to their tops in summer, and in the winter white through their serried pines and drifting mists, but at every season serious and beautiful, furrowed with hollow shadows, and taking the light on masses and stretches of iron-grey crag. The river swam through the plain in long curves, and slipped away at last through an unseen pass to the southward, tracing a score of miles in its course over a space that measured but three or four. The plain was very fertile, and its features, if few and of purely utilitarian beauty, had a rich luxuriance, and there was a tropical riot of vegetation when the sun of July beat on those northern fields. They waved with corn and oats to the feet of the mountains, and the potatoes covered a vast acreage with the lines of their intense, coarse green; the meadows were deep with English grass to the banks of the river, that, doubling and returning upon itself, still marked its way with a dense fringe of alders and white birches.

PASSAGE B (HEMINGWAY)

In the late summer of that year we lived in a house in a village that looked across the river and the plain to the mountains. In the bed of the river there were pebbles and boulders, dry and white in the sun, and the water was clear and swiftly moving and blue in the channels. Troops went by the house and down the road and the dust they raised powdered the leaves of the trees. The trunks of the trees too were dusty and the leaves fell early that year and we saw the troops marching along the road and the dust rising and leaves, stirred by the breeze, falling and the soldiers marching and afterward the road bare and white except for the leaves.

The plain was rich with crops; there were many orchards of fruit trees and beyond the plains the mountains were brown and bare. There was fighting in the mountains and at night we could see the flashes from the artillery. In the dark it was like summer lightning, but the nights were cool and there was not the feeling of a storm coming.

Who are these two people talking to us?

The narrator in Passage A (Howells) is concerned with making us see and know the landscape surrounding the village, and he can do this because he can occupy a position where *he* sees and knows this landscape intimately. Let us begin by locating this position, which is expressible in respect to both space and time. Physically, the narrator can speak as from a cloud, a balloon, floating wide-eyed over the plain. He sees large features of the scene—the mountains, the course of the winding river, the fields with their crops. It is a bird's-eye view. He also occupies a favorable position in time. He has been here before, he *knows*. He knows, for example, how the mountains look not only in summer (the *then* of the opening scene), but in winter as well (Sentence A-2). He knows (A-3), even though it is not at present visible, that the river slips away "through an unseen pass" to the southward. This is a speaker whose particular rhetorical personality, which would look very strange in a novel of the second half of the twentieth century, serves to inspire our confidence, partly from its very antiquity. Note that as assumed readers we date the speaker immediately, however vaguely, and date ourselves as well, by ruling out some twentieth-century suspicions and expectations. We are introduced to a familiar kind of traditional gentlemanly voice whose tones we associate with Standard Literature, and whose word we accept absolutely. This man knows what there is to know about this scene. We are in good hands.

The man talking in Passage B speaks to us from an utterly different position. As he thinks back on his experience in the village—and note that it is *his* experience that he thinks back on—the positions he occupies are drastically more limited than those of our airborne observer in A. Everything described in B can be seen (or almost seen) and from one place, the house where *he* lived. The language keeps reminding us of this limitation by returning to the speaker and his companions (*we*) and their vantage point for seeing and feeling. The house "looked across the river"; "we saw the troops"; "we could see the flashes"; "there was not the feeling of a storm coming." The speaker's range is similarly limited in time; all he tells us about is the way things looked during one particular late summer as it became autumn. The other seasons, before he came to live in the village, or after he left, he presumably doesn't know about. We hear the familiar "flatness" of the voice addressing us, the speaker's refusal to say more than he knows from ordinary human experience. He is close-lipped. The simplicity of his style, the apparent simplicity of it, is of course notorious. You would not call this man genial. He behaves rather as if he had known us, the reader, a long time and therefore doesn't have to pay us very much attention. He is more tense, more intense, than A. And after all, we should observe, he is dealing with images of war, and not with a peaceful New England landscape.

So much for one reader's quick first impression of the two personalities addressing us and the positions from which they speak. But I propose a longer look at some grammatical and rhetorical peculiarities of these two speakers, returning often to their personalities and positions to ask how these have been created, and how we may refine our first impressions. How are these impressions justified by the language, if they are? How do details of wording force us to certain conclusions about the man we're being introduced to? If some of what follows seems alarmingly statistical and detailed, I would argue that only by such devices can we begin to understand the effort that went into these two creative acts.

Words, their size. Everybody knows that Hemingway's diction is characterized by short, simple, largely Anglo-Saxon words. Howells' vocabulary is more conventionally extensive. Actually, in the Howells passage, almost three-quarters of the words are monosyllables, while only one word out of twenty is longer than two syllables. It is hardly an elaborate or affected diction. Yet we recognize in Howells that there are particular words, especially the longer words, which for various reasons would be unthinkable in Hemingway. Among them are *beautiful, utilitarian, luxuriance*—and I shall have more to say about them below. For the present, we note that in passage B, the Hemingway passage, over four-fifths of the words (82 per cent) are of one syllable only, an extremely high proportion. What is more remarkable, only two words, or about one in a hundred, are more than two syllables in length. (These two are *afterward* and *artillery*, neither of them very formidable.) The rigorous selection, or limitation, in vocabulary that these figures imply is drastic, and certainly contributes largely to our sense of a laconic, hard-bitten, close-talking fellow. He is literally *curt*.

Modifiers. An important distinction in the way the two speakers choose words has to do with the frequency of their modifiers. What would we expect of a man who knows, who is magically airborne over the landscape, as against a speaker who is laconically reporting the facts of his own limited experience? We would expect that the former would be more free with his modifiers, would be, that is, willing to name the qualities and virtues of things, not just the things themselves. Actually there are about twice as many modifiers in the Howells as in the Hemingway. Some of Howells' adjectives, in particular, have obvious implications of value: *serious, beautiful, rich, utilitarian.* While many others are simply descriptive (if that is possible), such as *green, deep, dense*, every one of the modifiers in B is of the type that purports to avoid value and simply state facts, especially physical facts: *dry, white, blue, dusty, swiftly*, and so on.

Nouns and repetition. A count of nouns in the two passages results in almost identical figures. But because of a great difference in repetition of nouns, there is a difference in the actual repertoire the two writers use. There are 47 appearances of nouns in A, and because repetition is negligible there are 43 different nouns used. In Hemingway I count 46 noun appearances with a remarkable refrain of repetition. Fourteen nouns appear twice or three times; only 32 different nouns are to be found in the passage. The effect of this rather astonishing contrast is worth speculating on. It helps us, again, to understand why we could call the B narrator "close-lipped." He simply doesn't use many words! There is a critical suggestion to the speaker's personality, as if he were saying, I'm not one of your fancy writers, always scrabbling around for elegant variation. I say what I mean.

If I mean the same thing twice, I *say* the same thing twice, and I don't care if it offends the so-called rules of so-called graceful prose.

Imagery, abstract and concrete. It is a commonplace about modern writers, and it may seem to be borne out by our analysis up to this point, that the more recent writers are concerned hardheadedly with things-as-they-are, with precise description rather than with the evaluative blur that we like to think characterizes the older literature. Everybody's passion nowadays for being "concrete" rather than "abstract" represents a fashionable general attitude. But, judging from the present evidence, the commonplace may not be true. Nobody knows, I suspect, how to distinguish concrete words from abstract in any very satisfactory way, but suppose we apply in all innocence this rule of thumb: which of our two speakers tells us more about the scene, supposing we wanted to paint a picture of it? There is no doubt that it is Howells. It is not simply Hemingway's paucity of nouns and modifiers that handicaps him as a scene-painter. It is his very choice of the nouns and modifiers that he does use. Where Hemingway writes *trees*, Howells names them—*alders, birches*. Where Hemingway refers to *crops* and *orchards*, Howells gives us *corn, oats,* and *potatoes*. It is true that Howells includes some words normally thought of as "abstract" (*features, beauty, luxuriance*), while Hemingway gives us plenty of "concrete" nouns, *pebbles* and *boulders, mountains, orchards, soldiers*. But the result is what matters, and in this case the result is that the language creates, in A, a narrator who *cares* about telling us what the landscape looked like, and in B we sense a narrator who cares about something else.

What else does he care about? Why does he, in spite of his superficial and apparent concreteness, tell us so little specifically about the scene? Because the scene, from his position, is not important except as it contributes to his own feelings, his remembered feelings. His recurrences to the act of personal viewing mentioned earlier (*We saw, we could see*) are reminders of the highly personal interest of this speaker. He is not concerned with having us see the landscape, but in having us understand *how he felt*. This is a very different aim; all his devices of grammar and rhetoric are chosen to achieve this aim.

Sentences, their size and structure. Again the short sentence in Hemingway is a commonplace observation, and it no doubt contributes to the curtness we have been noticing. Actually, in these two passages, the difference is only between an average length of 38 words and of 28 words —nothing very spectacular. Much more interesting is the grammatical structure of the sentences of each passage. In A we have both compound and compound-complex sentences, with considerable subordination of clauses. In B we have largely compound sentences made up of coordinate clauses strung together with *and*. (Sentence B-4 is a good example.) When we count up subordinate clauses in the two passages, we discover that in B there are only two, and they are informal and inconspicuous. "The dust they raised," for instance, gives us a modifying clause without the signal *that*, an omission common in oral speech. We are reminded that the narrator knows us, speaks familiarly, doesn't in fact go out of his way for us much. Modifying clauses in A, on the other hand, are crucially different. Here their formal qualities are directed not toward maintaining a pose of familiarity with a reader, but instead toward seriously clarifying for the reader, whom the speaker has only just met, what the landscape looked like. The second half of Sentence A-5, for example, offers us a subordinate clause of some elegance and considerable skill.

> ... the meadows were deep with English grass to the banks of the river, that, doubling and returning upon itself, still marked its way with a dense fringe of alders and white birches.

One may not wish to go so far as to say that the very phrasing here, in its leisurely meandering, doubles and returns upon itself like the river, but one would have to say, at least, that a subordinate clause of this kind, punctuated in this way, would look very odd in Hemingway. You do not talk this way to someone you know easily and intimately.

More spectacular in the Hemingway style, of course, are the successions of coordinate clauses linked by *and*, It is a highly significant grammatical expression, and its significance can be grasped if one tries irreverently to rewrite a coordinate Hemingway sentence in more traditional patterns of subordination. Here is the original sentence B-4, for instance:

> The trunks of the trees too were dusty and the leaves fell early that year and we saw the troops marching along the road and the dust rising and leaves, stirred by the breeze, falling and the soldiers marching and afterward the road bare and white except for the leaves.

Now here is a version attempting to subordinate some of the clauses:

> The leaves fell early that year, which revealed the dusty trunks of trees and the marching troops on the road; when the troops went by, we saw the dust rise, while the leaves fell, stirred by the breeze, but after the soldiers had gone the road was bare and white except for the leaves.

The original B-6 reads this way:

There was fighting in the mountains and at night we could see the flashes from the artillery.

If we subordinate one of these clauses, we must state a relation between them—for example the relation of logical cause:

We knew there was fighting in the mountains, for at night we could see the flashes from the artillery.

Now the damage done to the original, in both cases, is of course catastrophic. In the original B-6, the speaker doesn't say how he knew there was fighting in the mountains. It was just there, ominous, baldly stated. The awareness of the fighting and the seeing of the flashes are all part of a huge complex of personal feeling, and the connections between the various sensations are left (deliberately of course) ambiguous. This is a highly refined example of the leave-it-up-to-the-reader technique that I found so irritating in "Private World" of the preceding chapter.

This is why so many people do not know how to read. They have been taught to turn books into abstractions.

There, as in Hemingway, the logical connection between the two unconnected independent structures was unstated. But there is a difference. In "Private World," the intended connection is plain. What in Hemingway was a suggestive technique for implying several possible connections while stating none, becomes merely a rhetorical gimmick for forcing the reader to supply an obvious meaning. This is what we mean by the Misuse of a Style.

The definite article. I have mentioned a difference in relation with their assumed readers that the two speakers suggest. Whereas the speaker in A keeps his distance, using what we think of as fairly formal discourse, the speaker in B seems to have known the reader before and doesn't trouble himself to explain things as one must for an acquaintance one has just met. A possible cause of this difference between the two speakers can be found in the different ways they use a simple three-letter word—the word *the*. To be statistical again, the incidence of the definite article in the Howells paragraph comes to about 8 per cent; in the Hemingway passage it is about 18 per cent, or almost one word out of every five. It is clearly the Hemingway passage that is unconventional, labeling every other noun with *the*.

What is the effect of such an extraordinary preoccupation?

In the late summer of that year we lived in a house in a village that looked across the river and the plain to the mountains.

One's first naive response to that sentence might be some perfectly pardonable questions. "What year? What river, what plain, what mountains? I don't know what you're talking about." Precisely: the *real* reader doesn't know what the speaker is talking about, but the assumed reader doesn't bother about that. *He* has been placed in a situation where he is expected to assume that he does know what the speaker is talking about. It is as if, for the assumed reader, a conversation had been going on before he opened the book, a conversation that laid the groundwork for all this assumed intimacy. Or it is as if—another analogy—we were suddenly plopped down in a chair listening to a man who has begun telling a story to another man who has just left the room. Curiously the storyteller confuses us with the friend who has just departed, and we find ourselves taking the place of this friend, yoked to the teller as he was. And of course, as always, we can't talk back.

The difference can be realized if again we try an irreverent revision, excising most of the definite articles:

Late in 1915, when I was an officer in the Italian army, my unit lived in a house in a northern Italian village that looked across a river toward some mountains.

In this version, the speaker makes no such assumptions about the common knowledge shared by himself and his assumed reader. Now he names the year and the locale, he defines who "we" are, and his consistent indefinite articles maintain a more distant posture with his reader.

My revision again, naturally, is disastrous. It does more than create distance between reader and speaker. Reading it, one has the impression that the narrator doesn't care much about what he's saying. It starts off like any old war reminiscence. But in Hemingway's version, for many more reasons than I've been able to express here, we feel already the excitement, or what I have to call the intensity, of the narrator. He is deeply involved in his feelings about what he is going to tell us, and perhaps one reason he can give that impression is that he can pretend not to have to worry very much about us, about cueing us in in the conventional way.

The first word of the Howells passage is *The,* but the quickest reading reveals the difference. Here the narrator is describing a scene as if we had never seen it before—as indeed we have not. We need not assume the same kind of intimate relation with the narrator; he keeps us relatively at a distance, and he does not use (as Hemingway does) the first person pronoun. Yet even the Howells narrator launches us somewhat *in medias res,* assuming we will not ask, of his first two words, "What village?" Again the removal of the definite article will show how a speaker can back off even further from his reader, beginning a wholly new relationship with new information: A village stood on a wide plain, and around it rose mountains. One feels, of that sentence, that it should be prefaced by "Once upon a time," and it may be that in telling a fairy story, part of the trick is to assume very little from your reader. Nor is there any effort, in the fairy story, to make the narrator or his tale sound "real." In fact the effort must be just the other way. In the Hemingway kind of story, quite a lot is implied, through intensity of tone, about how seriously, how real, we are to take all this. There is a scale of pretension we could trace, something like this:

> *Fairy story: Here's a little tale of something that (let's pretend) might have happened a long, long time ago in the Land of Nod.*

> *Howells: Here is a story about people behaving much as people in life do behave; I hope you enjoy it.*

> *Hemingway: This is how it really felt to me when it all happened. (Oh yes, if you insist, it's a* story.*)*

My passages can't possibly justify all that. But if there is anything to such a scale, then the Hemingway rhetoric has the effect of including, as part of its fiction, the fiction that all this really happened to a narrator who felt intensely about it, and the reader is maneuvered into a position of sympathy with a person whose principal concern is not with the reader, not with the scene he is describing, but with himself and his own feelings. There is a consequent lift of the voice, a tension in the vocal chords. That is no armchair, relaxed and comfortable, that the Tough Talker occupies.

It will be useful now to summarize the Tough Talker's manner by means of a tentative definition of his personality and rhetoric. In doing so, we remember that our source is only the first 189 words of one Hemingway novel. Nor should we assume that the character described here is absolutely new to literature. What we do have here is an identifiable speaker (Frederic Henry by name), defined in an identifiable rhetoric, some of whose qualities we will be able to recognize in later prose.

A description of a Tough Talker. Frederic Henry is a hard man who has been around in a violent world, and who partially conceals his strong feelings behind a curt manner. He is in fact more concerned with those feelings than he is with the outward scenes he presents, or with cultivating the good wishes of the reader to whom he is introducing himself. He can ignore these traditional services to the reader because he assumes in advance much intimacy and common knowledge. (We are beyond explanations, beyond politenesses.) He presents himself as a believable human character, without omniscience: he knows only what he knows, and is aware of his limitations.

His rhetoric, like his personality, shows its limitations openly: short sentences, "crude" repetitions of words, simple grammatical structures with little subordinating. (I have no use for elegant variation, for the worn-out gentilities of traditional prose.) His tense intimacy with his assumed reader, another man who has been around, is implied by colloquial patterns from oral speech and by a high frequency of the definite article. He lets his reader make logical and other connections between elements. (You know what I mean; I don't have to spell it all out for *you*.) He prefers naming things to describing them, and avoids modification, especially when suggestive of value. All these habits of behavior suggest that he is self-conscious about his language—even about language generally. He is close-lipped, he watches his words.

This suspiciousness about language, only implied in our passage, deserves amplification particularly because it will concern us again later, in other writers. Part of the violent world that the Tough Talker has been around in is the violent verbal world, where words have been so abused that they have lost their lives. In a famous passage later on in *Farewell to Arms* Frederic Henry makes the point explicitly:

> *I did not say anything. I was always embarrassed by the words sacred, glorious, and sacrifice, and the expression in vain. We had heard them, sometimes standing in the rain almost out of earshot, so that only the shouted words came through, and had read them, on proclamations, now for a long time, and I had seen nothing sacred, and the things that were glorious had no glory and the sacrifices were like the stockyards at Chicago if nothing was done with the meat except to bury it. There were many words that you could not stand to hear and finally only the names of places had dignity. Certain numbers were the same way and certain dates and these with the names of the places were all you could say and have them mean*

anything. Abstract words such as glory, honor, courage, or hallow were obscene beside the concrete names of villages, and the numbers of roads, the names of rivers, the numbers of regiments and the dates.

Such a negative attitude toward language, however understandable and right in this novel, becomes deadly in later and less skillful hands. For some members of the Beat Generation all language became meaningless—a conviction peculiarly difficult for a writer to live with. The conviction may have had something to do with the poverty of beat style, and with the early demise of that movement. In any event, a self-conscious anxiety about the very reliability of words has become one of the crosses the modern writer has to bear. Fortunately it can be borne in many ways, from comedy to despair.

Mark Twain

Fenimore Cooper's Literary Offenses

This essay could with some logic have been included in Part One, since it is an exposé of bad writing. But since it is an analysis of a particular writer's style, and since in passing it defines the qualities of good style, it fits just as well here.

If you have ever read any of Cooper's novels you will particularly appreciate this attack. But even if you haven't, you can hardly fail to enjoy the way Twain swings from the heels at Cooper's flaws. Twain was exaggerating to some extent, of course, but underneath the exaggeration you will find a writer who seriously cares about good writing.

> The Pathfinder and The Deerslayer stand at the head of Cooper's novels as artistic creations. There are others of his works which contain parts as perfect as are to be found in these, and scenes even more thrilling. Not one can be compared with either of them as a finished whole.
>
> The defects in both of these tales are comparatively slight. They are pure works of art. *(Prof. Lounsbury)*
>
> The five tales reveal an extraordinary fulness of invention.
>
> . . . One of the very greatest characters in fiction, Natty Bumppo . . .
>
> The craft of the woodsman, the tricks of the trapper, all the delicate art of forest, were familiar to Cooper from his youth up. *(Prof. Brander Matthews)*
>
> Cooper is the greatest artist in the domain of romantic fiction yet produced by America. *(Wilkie Collins)*

J t seems to me that it was far from right for the Professor of English Literature in Yale, the Professor of English Literature in Columbia, and Wilkie Collins to deliver opinions on Cooper's literature without having read some of it. It would have been much more decorous to keep silent and let persons talk who have read Cooper.

Cooper's art has some defects. In one place in *Deerslayer,* and in the restricted space of two-thirds of a page, Cooper has scored 114 offences against literary art out of a possible 115. It breaks the record.

There are nineteen rules governing literary art in the domain of romantic fiction—some say twenty-two. In *Deerslayer* Cooper violated eighteen of them. These eighteen require:

"Fenimore Cooper's Literary Offences" from *Literary Essays* by Mark Twain, Harper and Brothers Publishers, 1899, New York.

1. That a tale shall accomplish something and arrive somewhere. But the *Deerslayer* tale accomplishes nothing and arrives in the air.

2. They require that the episodes of a tale shall be necessary parts of the tale, and shall help to develop it. But as the *Deerslayer* tale is not a tale, and accomplishes nothing and arrives nowhere, the episodes have no rightful place in the work, since there was nothing for them to develop.

3. They require that the personages in a tale shall be alive, except in the case of corpses, and that always the reader shall be able to tell the corpses from the others. But this detail has often been overlooked in the *Deerslayer* tale.

4. They require that the personages in a tale, both dead and alive, shall exhibit a sufficient excuse for being there. But this detail also has been overlooked in the *Deerslayer* tale.

5. They require that when the personages of a tale deal in conversation, the talk shall sound like human talk, and be talk such as human beings would be likely to talk in the given circumstances, and have a discoverable meaning, also a discoverable purpose, and a show of relevancy, and remain in the neighborhood of the subject in hand, and be interesting to the reader, and help out the tale, and stop when the people cannot think of anything more to say. But this requirement has been ignored from the beginning of the *Deerslayer* tale to the end of it.

6. They require that when the author describes the character of a personage in his tale, the conduct and conversation of that personage shall justify said description. But this law gets little or no attention in the *Deerslayer* tale, as Natty Bumppo's case will amply prove.

7. They require that when a personage talks like an illustrated, gilt-edged, tree-calf, hand-tooled, seven-dollar Friendship's Offering in the beginning of a paragraph, he shall not talk like a Negro minstrel in the end of it. But this rule is flung down and danced upon in the *Deerslayer* tale.

8. They require that crass stupidities shall not be played upon the reader as "the craft of the woodsman, the delicate art of the forest," by either the author or the people in the tale. But this rule is persistently violated in the *Deerslayer* tale.

9. They require that the personages of a tale shall confine themselves to possibilities and let miracles alone; or, if they venture a miracle, the author must so plausibly set it forth as to make it look possible and reasonable. But these rules are not respected in the *Deerslayer* tale.

10. They require that the author shall make the reader feel a deep interest in the personages of his tale and in their fate, and that he shall make the reader love the good people in the tale and hate the bad ones. But the reader of the *Deerslayer* tale dislikes the good people in it, is indifferent to the others, and wishes they would all get drowned together.

11. They require that the characters in a tale shall be so clearly defined that the reader can tell beforehand what each will do in a given emergency. But in the *Deerslayer* tale this rule is vacated.

In addition to these large rules there are some little ones. These require that the author shall

12. *Say* what he is proposing to say, not merely come near it.
13. Use the right word, not its second cousin.
14. Eschew surplusage.
15. Not omit necessary details.
16. Avoid slovenliness of form.
17. Use good grammar.
18. Employ a simple and straightforward style.

Even these seven are coldly and persistently violated in the *Deerslayer* tale.

Cooper's gift in the way of invention was not a rich endowment; but such as it was he liked to work it, he was pleased with the effects, and indeed he did some quite sweet things with it. In his little box of stage-properties he kept six or eight cunning devices, tricks, artifices for his savages and woodsmen to deceive and circumvent each other with, and he was never so happy as when he was working these innocent things and seeing them go. A favorite one was to make a moccasined person tread in the tracks of the moccasined enemy, and thus hide his own trail. Cooper wore out barrels and barrels of moccasins in working that trick. Another stage-property that he pulled out of his box pretty frequently was his broken twig. He prized his broken twig above all the rest of his effects, and worked it the hardest. It is a restful chapter in any book of his when somebody doesn't step on a dry twig and alarm all the reds and whites for two hundred yards around. Every time a Cooper person is in peril, and absolute silence is worth four dollars a minute, he is sure to step on a dry twig. There may be a hundred handier things to step on, but that wouldn't satisfy Cooper. Cooper requires him to turn out and find a dry twig; and if he can't do it, go and borrow one. In fact, the Leather Stocking Series ought to have been called the Broken Twig Series.

211

I am sorry there is not room to put in a few dozen instances of the delicate art of the forest, as practised by Natty Bumppo and some of the other Cooperian experts. Perhaps we may venture two or three samples. Cooper was a sailor—a naval officer; yet he gravely tells us how a vessel, driving towards a lee shore in a gale, is steered for a particular spot by her skipper because he knows of an *undertow* there which will hold her back against the gale and save her. For just pure woodcraft, or sailorcraft, or whatever it is, isn't that neat? For several years Cooper was daily in the society of artillery, and he ought to have noticed that when a cannon-ball strikes the ground it either buries itself or skips a hundred feet or so; skips again a hundred feet or so—and so on, till finally it gets tired and rolls. Now in one place he loses some "females"—as he always calls women— in the edge of a wood near a plain at night in a fog, on purpose to give Bumppo a chance to show off the delicate art of the forest before the reader. These mislaid people are hunting for a fort. They hear a cannon-blast, and a cannon-ball presently comes rolling into the wood and stops at their feet. To the females this suggests nothing. The case is very different with the admirable Bumppo. I wish I may never know peace again if he doesn't strike out promptly and *follow the track* of that cannon-ball across the plain through the dense fog and find the fort. Isn't it a daisy? If Cooper had any real knowledge of Nature's ways of doing things, he had a most delicate art in concealing the fact. For instance: one of his acute Indian experts, Chingachgook (pronounced Chicago, I think), has lost the trail of a person he is tracking through the forest. Apparently that trail is hopelessly lost. Neither you nor I could ever have guessed out the way to find it. It was very different with Chicago. Chicago was not stumped for long. He turned a running stream out of its course and there, in the slush in its old bed, were that person's moccasin tracks. The current did not wash them away, as it would have done in all other like cases—no, even the eternal laws of Nature have to vacate when Cooper wants to put up a delicate job of woodcraft on the reader.

We must be a little wary when Brander Matthews tells us that Cooper's books "reveal an extraordinary fulness of invention." As a rule, I am quite willing to accept Brander Matthew's literary judgments and applaud his lucid and graceful phrasing of them, but that particular statement needs to be taken with a few tons of salt. Bless your heart, Cooper hadn't any more invention than a horse, and I don't mean a high-class horse, either, a clothes-horse. It would be very difficult to find a really clever "situation" in Cooper's books, and still more difficult to find one of any kind which he has failed to render absurd by his handling of it. Look at the episodes of "the caves''; and at the celebrated scuffle between Maqua and those others on the table-land a few days later; and at Hurry Harry's queer water-transit from the castle to the ark; and at Deerslayer's half-hour with his first corpse; and at the quarrel between Hurry Harry and Deerslayer later; and at—but choose for yourself; you can't go amiss.

If Cooper had been an observer his inventive faculty would have worked better; not more interestingly, but more rationally, more plausibly. Cooper's proudest creations in the way of "situations" suffer noticeably from the absence of the observer's protecting gift. Cooper's eye was splendidly inaccurate. Cooper seldom saw anything correctly. He saw nearly all things as through a glass eye, darkly. Of course a man who cannot see the commonest little every-day matters accurately is working at a disadvantage when he is constructing a "situation." In the *Deerslayer* tale Cooper has a stream which is fifty feet wide where it flows out of a lake; it presently narrows to twenty as it meanders along for no given reason, and yet when a stream acts like that it ought to be required to explain itself. Fourteen pages later the width of the brook's outlet from the lake has suddenly shrunk thirty feet, and become "the narrowest part of the stream." This shrinkage is not accounted for. The stream has bends in it, a sure indication that it has alluvial banks and cuts them; yet these bends are only thirty and fifty feet long. If Cooper had been a nice and punctilious observer he would have noticed that the bends were oftener nine hundred feet long than short of it.

Cooper made the exit of that stream fifty feet wide, in the first place, for no particular reason; in the second place, he narrowed it to less than twenty to accommodate some Indians. He bends a "sapling" to the form of an arch over this narrow passage, and conceals six Indians in its foliage. They are "laying" for a settler's scow or ark which is coming up the stream on its way to the lake; it is being hauled against the stiff current by a rope whose stationary end is anchored in the lake; its rate of progress cannot be more than a mile an hour. Cooper describes the ark, but pretty obscurely. In the matter of dimensions "it was little more than a modern canal-boat." Let us guess, then, that it was about one hundred and forty feet long. It was of "greater breadth than common." Let us guess, then, that it was about sixteen feet wide. This leviathan had been prowling down bends which were but a third as long as itself, and scraping between banks where it had only two feet of space to spare on each side. We cannot too much admire this miracle. A low-roofed log dwelling occupies "two-thirds of the ark's length" —a dwelling ninety feet long and sixteen feet wide, let us say, a kind of vestibule train. The dwelling has two rooms, each forty-five feet long and sixteen feet wide, let us guess. One of them is the bedroom of the Hutter girls, Judith and Hetty; the other is the parlor in the daytime, at night it is papa's bed-chamber. The ark is arriving at the stream's exit now, whose width has been reduced to less than twenty feet to accommodate the Indi-ans—say to eighteen. There is a foot to spare on each side of the boat. Did the Indians notice that there was going to be a tight squeeze there? Did they notice that they could make money by climbing down out of that arched sapling and just stepping aboard when the ark scraped by? No, oth-er Indians would have noticed these things but Cooper's Indians never no-tice anything. Cooper thinks they are marvelous creatures for noticing but he was almost always in error about his Indians. There was seldom a sane one among them.

The ark is one hundred and forty feet long; the dwelling is ninety feet long. The idea of the Indians is to drop softly and secretly from the arched sapling to the dwelling as the ark creeps along under it at the rate of a mile an hour, and butcher the family. It will take the ark a minute and a half to pass under. It will take the ninety-foot dwelling a minute to pass under. Now, then, what did the six Indians do? It would take you thirty years to guess and even then you would have to give up, I believe. Therefore, I will tell you what the Indians did. Their chief, a person of quite extraordinary intellect for a Cooper Indian, warily watched the canal-boat as it squeezed along under him and when he had got his calculations fined down to ex-actly the right shade, as he judged, he let go and dropped. And *missed the house!* That is actually what he did. He missed the house and landed in the stern of the scow. It was not much of a fall, yet it knocked him silly. He lay there unconscious. If the house had been ninety-seven feet long he would have made the trip. The fault was Cooper's, not his. The error lay in the construction of the house. Cooper was no architect.

There still remained in the roost five Indians. The boat has passed under and is now out of their reach. Let me explain what the five did—you would not be able to reason it out for yourself. No. 1 jumped for the boat but fell in the water astern of it. Then No. 2 jumped for the boat but fell in the water still farther astern of it. Then No. 3 jumped for the boat and fell a good way astern of it. Then No. 4 jumped for the boat and fell in the water *away* astern. Then even No. 5 made a jump for the boat—for he was a Cooper Indian. In the matter of intellect, the difference between a Cooper Indian and the Indian that stands in front of the cigar-shop is not spacious. The scow episode is really a sublime burst of invention but it does not thrill, because the inaccuracy of the details throws a sort of fictitiousness and general improbability over it. This comes of Cooper's inadequacy as an observer.

The reader will find some examples of Cooper's high talent for inaccurate observation in the account of the shooting-match in *The Pathfinder.* "A common wrought nail was driven lightly into the target, its head having been first touched with paint."

The color of the paint is not stated—an important omission, but Cooper deals freely in important omissions. No, after all, it was not an important omission, for this nail-head is *a hundred yards from* the marksmen and could not be seen by them at that distance, no matter what its color might be. How far can the best eyes see a common house-fly? A hundred yards? It is quite impossible. Very well, eyes that cannot see a house-fly that is a hundred yards away cannot see an ordinary nailhead at that distance, for the size of the two objects is the same. It takes a keen eye to see a fly or a nailhead at fifty yards—one hundred and fifty feet. Can the reader do it?

The nail was lightly driven, its head painted, and game called. Then the Cooper miracles began. The bullet of the first marksman chipped an edge of the nail-head; the next man's bullet drove the nail a little way into the target—and removed all the paint. Haven't the miracles gone far enough now? Not to suit Cooper; for the purpose of this whole scheme is to show off his prodigy, Deerslayer-Hawkeye-Long-Rifle-Leather-Stocking-Pathfinder-Bumppo before the ladies.

> *"Be all ready to clench it, boys!"* cried out Pathfinder, stepping *into his friend's tracks the instant they were vacant. "Never mind a new nail; I can see that, though the paint is gone, and what I can see I can hit at a hundred yards, though it were only a mosquito's eye. Be ready to clench!"*
>
> *The rifle cracked, the bullet sped its way, and the head of the nail was buried in the wood, covered by the piece of flattened lead.*

There, you see, is a man who could hunt flies with a rifle, and command a ducal salary in a Wild West show today if we had him back with us.

The recorded feat is certainly surprising just as it stands; but it is not surprising enough for Cooper. Cooper adds a touch. He has made Pathfinder do this miracle with another man's rifle; and not only that, but Pathfinder did not have even the advantage of loading it himself. He had everything against him, and yet he made that impossible shot; and not only made it, but did it with absolute confidence, saying, "Be ready to clench." Now a person like that would have undertaken that same feat with a brick-bat, and with Cooper to help he would have achieved it, too.

Pathfinder showed off handsomely that day before the ladies. His very first feat was a thing which no Wild West show can touch. He was stand-ing with a group of marksmen, observing—a hundred yards from the tar-get, mind; one Jasper raised his rifle and drove the centre of the bull's-eye. Then the Quartermaster fired. The target exhibited no result this time. There was a laugh. "It's a dead miss," said Major Lundie. Pathfinder waited an impressive moment or two; then said, in that calm, indifferent, know-it-all way of his, "No, Major, he has covered Jasper's bullet, as will be seen if any one will take the trouble to examine the target."

Wasn't it remarkable! How *could* he see that little pellet fly through the air and enter that distant bullet-hole? Yet that is what he did; for noth-ing is impossible to a Cooper person. Did any of those people have any deep-seated doubts about this thing? No; for that would imply sanity, and these were all Cooper people.

> *The respect for Pathfinder's skill and for his* quickness and accu-racy of sight [*the italics are mine*] *was so profound and general, that the instant he made this declaration the spectators began to dis-trust their own opinions, and a dozen rushed to the target in order to ascertain the fact. There, sure enough, it was found that the Quarter-master's bullet had gone through the hole made by Jasper's, and that, too, so accurately as to require a minute examination to be cer-tain of the circumstance, which, however, was soon clearly estab-lished by discovering one bullet over the other in the stump against which the target was placed.*

They made a "minute" examination; but never mind, how could they know that there were two bullets in that hole without digging the latest one out? for neither probe nor eyesight could prove the presence of any more than one bullet. Did they dig? No; as we shall see. It is the Pathfin-der's turn now; he steps out before the ladies, takes aim, and fires.

But, alas! here is a disappointment; an incredible, an unimaginable disappointment—for the target's aspect is unchanged; there is nothing there but that same old bullet-hole! "If one dared to hint at such a thing," cried Major Duncan, "I should say that the Pathfinder has also missed the target!" As nobody had missed it yet, the "also" was not necessary; but never mind about that, for the Pathfinder is going to speak.

"No, no, Major," said he, confidently, *"that* would *be a risky dec-*
laration. I didn't load the piece, and can't say what was in it; but if it
was lead, you will find the bullet driving down those of the Quarter-
master and Jasper, else is not my name Pathfinder."

A shout from the target announced the truth of this assertion.

Is the miracle sufficient as it stands? Not for Cooper. The Pathfinder
speaks again, as he "now slowly advances toward the stage occupied by
the females":

"That's not all, boys, that's not all; if you find the target touched
at all, I'll own to a miss. The Quartermaster cut the wood, but you'll
find no wood cut by that last messenger."

The miracle is at last complete. He knew—doubtless *saw*—at the distance of a hundred yards—that his bullet had passed into the hole *without*
fraying the edges. There were now three bullets in that one hole, three bullets embedded processionally in the body of the stump back of the target.
Everybody knew this, somehow or other, and yet nobody had dug any of
them out to make sure. Cooper is not a close observer but he is interesting.
He is certainly always that, no matter what happens. And he is more interesting when he is not noticing what he is about than when he is. This is a
considerable merit.

The conversations in the Cooper books have a curious sound in our
modern ears. To believe that such talk really ever came out of people's
mouths would be to believe that there was a time when time was of no
value to a person who thought he had something to say, when it was the
custom to spread a two-minute remark out to ten, when a man's mouth
was a rolling-mill and busied itself all day long in turning four-foot pigs of
thoughts into thirty-foot bars of conversational railroad iron by attenuation,
when subjects were seldom faithfully stuck to but the talk wandered all
around and arrived nowhere, when conversations consisted mainly of ir-
relevancies with here and there a relevancy, a relevancy with an embar-
rassed look, as not being able to explain how it got there.

Cooper was certainly not a master in the construction of dialogue.
Inaccurate observation defeated him here as it defeated him in so many
other enterprises of his. He even failed to notice that the man who talks
corrupt English six days in the week must and will talk it on the seventh,
and can't help himself. In the *Deerslayer* story he lets Deerslayer talk the
showiest kind of book-talk sometimes and at other times the basest of

base dialects. For instance, when some one asks him if he has a sweet-heart, and if so where she abides, this is his majestic answer:

> *"She's in the forest—hanging from the boughs of the trees, in a soft rain—in the dew on the open grass—the clouds that float about in the blue heavens—the birds that sing in the woods—the sweet springs where I slake my thirst—and in all the other glorious gifts that come from God's Providence!"*

And he preceded that, a little before, with this: "It consarns me as all things that touches a fri'nd consarns a fri'nd." And this is another of his remarks "If I was Injin born, now, I might tell of this, or carry in the scalp and boast of the expl'ite afore the whole tribe; or if my inimy had only been a bear"—and so on.

We cannot imagine such a thing as a veteran Scotch Commander-in-Chief comporting himself in the field like a windy melodramatic actor, but Cooper could. On one occasion Alice and Cora were being chased by the French through a fog in the neighborhood of their father's fort:

> *"Point de quartier aux coquins!" cried an eager pursuer, who seemed to direct the operations of the enemy.*

> *"Stand firm and be ready, my gallant 60ths!" suddenly ex-claimed a voice above them; "wait to see the enemy; fire low, and sweep the glacis."*

> *"Father! father!" exclaimed a piercing cry from out the mist; "it is I! Alice! thy own Elsie! spare, O! save your daughters!"*

> *"Hold!" shouted the former speaker, in the awful tones of pa-rental agony, the sound reaching even to the woods, and rolling back in solemn echo. "Tis she! God has restored me my children! Throw open the sally-port; to the field, 60ths, to the field! pull not a trigger, lest ye kill my lambs! Drive off these dogs of France with your steel!"*

Cooper's word-sense was singularly dull. When a person has a poor ear for music he will flat and sharp right along without knowing it. He keeps near the tune, but it is *not* the tune. When a person has a poor ear for words, the result is a literary flatting and sharping; you perceive what he is intending to say, but you also perceive that he doesn't *say* it. This is Cooper. He was not a word-musician. His ear was satisfied with the *approximate* word. I will furnish some circumstantial evidence in support of this charge. My instances are gathered from half a dozen pages of the tale called *Deerslayer*. He uses "verbal" for "oral"; "precision" for "facility";

"phenomena" for "marvels"; "necessary" for "predetermined"; "unsophisticated" for "primitive"; "preparation" for "expectancy"; "rebuked" for "subdued"; "dependent on" for "resulting from"; "fact" for "condition"; "fact" for "conjecture"; "precaution" for "caution"; "explain" for "determine"; "mortified" for "disappointed"; "meretricious" for "factitious"; "materially" for "considerably"; "decreasing" for "deepening"; "increasing" for "disappearing"; "embedded" for "inclosed"; "treacherous" for "hostile"; "stood" for "stooped"; "softened" for "replaced"; "rejoined" for "remarked"; "situation" for "condition"; "different" for "differing"; "insensible" for "unsentient"; "brevity" for "celerity"; "distrusted" for "suspicious"; "mental imbecility" for "imbecility"; "eyes" for "sight"; "counteracting" for "opposing"; "funeral obsequies" for "obsequies."

There have been some daring people in the world who claimed that Cooper could write English, but they are all dead now—all dead but Lounsbury. I don't remember that Lounsbury makes the claim in so many words, still he makes it, for he says that *Deerslayer* is a "pure work of art." Pure, in that connection, means faultless—faultless in all details—and language is a detail. If Mr. Lounsbury had only compared Cooper's English with the English which he writes himself—but it is plain that he didn't; and so it is likely that he imagines until this day that Cooper's is as clean and compact as his own. Now I feel sure, deep down in my heart, that Cooper wrote about the poorest English that exists in our language, and that the English of *Deerslayer* is the very worst that even Cooper ever wrote.

I may be mistaken, but it does seem to me that *Deerslayer* is not a work of art in any sense; it does seem to me that it is destitute of every detail that goes to the making of a work of art; in truth, it seems to me that *Deerslayer* is just simply a literary *delirium tremens*.

A work of art? It has no invention; it has no order, system, sequence, or result; it has no life-likeness, no thrill, no stir, no seeming of reality; its characters are confusedly drawn, and by their acts and words they prove that they are not the sort of people the author claims that they are; its humor is pathetic; its pathos is funny; its conversations are—oh! indescribable; its love-scenes odious; its English a crime against the language.

Counting these out, what is left is Art. I think we must all admit that.

Carl L. Becker

The Literary Qualities of the Declaration

Thomas Jefferson wrote the Declaration of Independence, revised it at least once, and then submitted it to Congress, which edited it. Carl Becker discusses this process, speculating on the reasons for the various revisions and commenting on the literary, philosophical, and historical considerations that prompted the alterations.

Perhaps nowhere else is the inextricable relationship between thought and style so clearly and fully developed as in this essay. Note also Becker's comments on the relationship between Jefferson's personality and habits of thought and the style of the Declaration. His treatment of Jefferson's limitations and the flatness of the famous, excised "phillipic against Negro slavery" is particularly interesting. Compare the utterances of some "limousine liberals" of today.

$\mathbb{J}$efferson was chosen to draft the Declaration because he was known to possess a "masterly pen." There were perhaps other reasons, but this was the chief one. When he came to Congress in 1775, "he brought with him," says John Adams, "a reputation for literature, science, and a happy talent for composition. Writings of his were handed about remarkable for the peculiar felicity of expression."[1] *Peculiar felicity of expression*—the very words which one would perhaps choose to sum up the distinguishing characteristics of Jefferson's style.

Like many men who write with felicity, Jefferson was no orator. He rarely, if ever, made a speech. "During the whole time I sat with him in Congress," John Adams says, "I never heard him utter three sentences together"—that is, on the floor of Congress; in committees and in conversation he was, on the contrary, "prompt, frank, explicit, and decisive."[2] It might seem that a man who can write effectively should be able to speak effectively. It sometimes happens. But one whose ear is sensitive to the subtler, elusive harmonies of expression, one who in imagination hears the pitch and cadence and rhythm of the thing he wishes to say before he says it, often makes a sad business of public speaking because, painfully aware of the imperfect felicity of what has been uttered, he forgets what he ought to say next. He instinctively wishes to cross out what he has just said, and say it over again in a different way—and this is what he often does, to the confusion of the audience. In writing he can cross out and rewrite at leisure, as often as he likes, until the sound and the sense are perfectly suited —until the thing *composes*. The reader sees only the finished draft.

Not that Jefferson wrote with difficulty, constructing his sentences with slow and painful effort. One who, as an incident to a busy public career, wrote so much and so well, must have written with ease and rapidity. But Jefferson, as the original drafts of his papers show, revised and corrected his writings with care, seeking, yet without wearing his soul threadbare. in the search, for the better word, the happier phrase, the smoother transition. His style has not indeed the achieved perfection, the impeccable surface, of that of a master-craftsman like Flaubert, or Walter Pater; but nei-

---

[1] *Works of John Adams*, II, 514.

[2] *Ibid.*, 511-514.

"The Literary Qualities of the Declaration" from *The Declaration of Independence: A Study in the History of Political Ideas* by Carl Becker. Copyright 1922, 1942 and renewed 1970 by Carl Becker. Reprinted with permission of Alfred A. Knopf, Inc.

ther has it the objectivity, the impersonal frigidity of writing that is perhaps too curiously and deliberately integrated, too consciously made. Having something to say, he says it, with as much art as may be, yet not solely for the art's sake, aiming rather at the ease, the simplicity, the genial urbanity of cultivated conversation. The grace and felicity of his style have a distinctly personal flavor, something Jeffersonian in the implication of the idea, or in the beat and measure of the words. Franklin had equal ease, simplicity, felicity; but no one who knows the writings of Franklin could attribute the Declaration to him. Jefferson communicated an undefinable yet distinctive quality to the Declaration which makes it his.

The Declaration is filled with these felicities of phrase which bear the stamp of Jefferson's mind and temperament: *a decent respect to the opinions of mankind; more disposed to suffer, while evils are sufferable, than to right themselves by abolishing the forms to which they are accustomed; for the sole purpose of fatiguing them into compliance with his measures; sent hither swarms of officers to harrass our people and eat out their substance; hold them as we hold the rest of mankind, enemies in war, in peace friends.* There are some sentences in the Declaration which are more than felicitous. The closing sentence, for example, is perfection itself. Congress amended the sentence by including the phrase, "with a firm reliance upon the protection of divine Providence." It may be that Providence always welcomes the responsibilities thrust upon it in times of war and revolution; but personally, I like the sentence better as Jefferson wrote it. "And for the support of this Declaration we mutually pledge to each other our lives, our fortunes, and our sacred honor." It is true (assuming that men value life more than property, which is doubtful) that the statement violates the rhetorical rule of climax; but it was a sure sense that made Jefferson place "lives" first and "fortunes" second. How much weaker if he had written "our fortunes, our lives, and our sacred honor"! Or suppose him to have used the word "property" instead of "fortunes"! Or suppose him to have omitted "sacred"! Consider the effect of omitting any of the words, such as the last two "ours"—"our lives, fortunes, and sacred honor." No, the sentence can hardly be improved.

There are probably more of these Jeffersonian felicities in the Declaration than in any other writing by him of equal length. Jefferson realized that, if the colonies won their independence, this would prove to be a public document of supreme importance; and the Rough Draft (which may not be the first one) bears ample evidence of his search for the right word, the right phrasing. In the opening sentence, not at all bad as it originally stood, there are four corrections. The first part of the second paragraph seems to have given him much trouble. The Rough Draft reads as follows:

>   *self-evident*
> We hold these truths to be ~~sacred & undeniable;~~ that all men are
>   *they are endowed by their creator with*
> created equal ~~& independent;~~ that ~~from that equal creation they de-~~
> ~~equal rights some of which are~~   *rights; that*   *these*
> ~~rive in rights~~ inherent & inalienable among ~~which~~ are ~~the preservation~~
>
> ~~of~~ life, ~~&~~ liberty, & the pursuit of happiness.

When Jefferson submitted the draft to Adams the only correction which he had made was to write "self-evident" in place of "sacred & undeniable." It is interesting to guess why, on a later reading, the other changes were made. I suspect that he erased "& independent" because, having introduced "self-evident," he did not like the sound of the two phrases both closing with "dent." The phrase "they are endowed by their creator" is obviously much better than "from that equal creation"; but this correction, as he first wrote it, left an awkward wording: "that they are endowed by their creator with equal rights some of which are inherent & inalienable among which are." Too many "which ares"; and besides, why suppose that some rights given by the creator were inherent and some not? Thus we get the form, which is so much stronger, as well as more agreeable to the ear: "that they are endowed by their creator with inherent & inalienable rights." Finally, why say "the preservation of life"? If a man has a right to life, the right to preserve life is manifestly included.

Again, take the close of the last paragraph but one. The Rough Draft gives the following reading:

>   *& to glory*   ~~must~~ *tread*
> The road to ~~glory &~~ happiness is open to us too; we will ~~climb~~ it ~~in a~~
>   *apart from them*
> ~~separately state.~~

The phrase "to happiness & to glory" is better than "to glory & happiness." Placing "glory" before "happiness" might imply that the first aim of the colonists was glory, and that their happiness would come as an incident to the achievement of glory. What needed to be expressed was the idea that the colonists were defending the natural right to happiness, and that the vindication of this inherent human right would confer glory upon them. Did Jefferson, in making the change, reason thus? Probably not. Upon reading it over he doubtless instinctively felt that by placing "happiness" first and repeating the "to" he would take the flatness out of a prosaic phrase. As for the latter part of the sentence, Jefferson evidently first wrote it: "climb it in a separate state." Not liking the word "state," he erased "state" and "in a" and added "-ly" to "separate"; But no, on second thought, that is not much better. "Climb it apart from them"—that would do. So apparently it read when the Declaration was adopted, since "climb" and not "tread" is the reading of all but one of the copies, including the text finally adopted. It may be that Jefferson made the change during the debates in Congress, and then thought better of it, or neglected to get the change incorporated in the final text. There is another correction in the Rough Draft which does not appear in the final form of the Declaration. "Our repeated petitions have been answered only by repeated injury"—so the Declaration reads; but in the Rough Draft the "injury" has been changed to "injuries." This is manifestly better; and as one can hardly suppose Congress would have preferred "injury" to "injuries," it is probable that the change was made after the Declaration was adopted. Jefferson had something of the artist's love of perfection for its own sake, the writer's habit of correcting a manuscript even after it has been published.

Apart from the peculiar felicities of phrasing, what strikes one particularly in reading the Declaration as a whole is the absence of declamation. Everything considered, the Declaration is brief, free of verbiage, a model of clear, concise, and simple statement. In 1856 Rufus Choate referred to it as "that passionate and eloquent manifesto," made up of "glittering and sounding generalities of natural right."[3] Eloquent the Declaration frequently is, in virtue of a certain high seriousness with which Jefferson contrived to invest what was ostensibly a direct and simple statement of fact. Of all words in the language, "passionate" is the one which is least applicable to Jefferson or to his writings. As to "generalities," the Declaration contains relatively few; and if those few are "glittering and sounding" it is in their substance and not in their form that they are so. You may not believe

> *that all men are created equal; that they are endowed by their creator with certain unalienable rights; that among these are life, liberty, and the pursuit of happiness; that to secure these rights governments are instituted among men, deriving their just powers from the con-*

---

[3] Letter to E. W. Farley, Aug. 9, 1856; Brown, S. G. *Life of Rufus Choate,* 324, 326.

> *sent of the governed; that whenever any form of government be-*
> *comes destructive of these ends, it is the right of the people to alter*
> *or to abolish it, and to institute new government, laying its founda-*
> *tions on such principles, and organizing its powers in such form, as to*
> *them shall seem most likely to effect their safety and happiness.*

You may not believe this; but if you do believe it, as Jefferson and his con-
temporaries did, you would find it difficult to say it more concisely; in
words more direct, simple, precise, and appropriate; with less of passionate
declamation, of rhetorical magniloquence, or of verbal ornament. The second paragraph of the Declaration of Independence reminds one of Lincoln's
Gettysburg Address in its unimpassioned simplicity of statement. It glitters
as much, or as little, as that famous document.

Logical sequence and structural unity are not always essential to good
writing; but the rambling and discursive method would scarcely be appropriate to a declaration of independence. Jefferson's declaration, read casually, seems not to possess a high degree of unity. Superficially considered,
it might easily strike one as the result of an uneasy marriage of convenience between an abstract philosophy of government and certain concrete
political grievances. But in truth the Declaration is built up around a single
idea, and its various parts are admirably chosen and skilfully disposed for
the production of a particular effect. The grievances against the king occupy so much space that one is apt to think of them as the main theme. Such
is not the case. The primary purpose of the Declaration was to convince a
candid world that the colonies had a moral and legal right to separate from
Great Britain. This would be difficult to do, however many and serious their
grievances might be, if the candid world was to suppose that the colonies
were politically subordinate to the British government in the ordinary sense.
It is difficult to justify rebellion against established political authority. Accordingly, the idea around which Jefferson built the Declaration was that
the colonists were not rebels against established political authority, but a
free people maintaining long established and imprescriptible rights against
a usurping king. The effect which he wished to produce was to leave a
candid world wondering why the colonies had so long submitted to the
oppressions of this king.

The major premise from which this conclusion is derived is that every
"people" has a natural right to make and unmake its own government; the
minor premise is that the Americans are a "people" in this sense. In establishing themselves in America, the people of the colonies exercised their
natural rights to frame governments suited to their ideas and conditions;

but at the same time they voluntarily retained a union with the people of Great Britain by professing allegiance to the same king. From this allegiance they might at any time have withdrawn; if they had not so withdrawn it was because of the advantages of being associated with the people of Great Britain; if they now proposed to withdraw, it was not because they now any less than formerly desired to maintain the ancient association, but because the king by repeated and deliberate actions had endeavored to usurp an absolute authority over them contrary to every natural right and to long established custom. The minor premise of the argument is easily overlooked because it is not explicitly stated in the Declaration—at least not in its final form. To have stated it explicitly would perhaps have been to bring into too glaring a light certain incongruities between the assumed premise and known historical facts. The rôle of the list of grievances against the king is to make the assumed premise emerge, of its own accord as it were, from a carefully formulated but apparently straightforward statement of concrete historical events. From the point of view of structural unity, the rôle which the list of grievances plays in the Declaration is a subordinate one; its part is to exhibit the historical circumstances under which the colonists, as a "free people," had thrust upon them the high obligation of defending the imprescriptible rights of all men.

Although occupying a subordinate place in the logical structure, the list of grievances is of the highest importance in respect to the total effect which the Declaration aims to produce. From this point of view, the form and substance of these paragraphs constitute not the least masterly part of the Declaration. It is true, books upon rhetoric warn the candidate for literary honors at all hazards to avoid monotony; he ought, they say, to seek a pleasing variety by alternating long and short sentences; and while they consider it correct to develop a single idea in each paragraph, they consider it inadvisable to make more than one paragraph out of a single sentence. These are no doubt good rules, for writing in general; but Jefferson violated them all, perhaps because he was writing something in particular. Of set purpose, throughout this part of the Declaration, he began each charge against the king with "he has": "he has refused his assent"; "he has forbidden his governors"; "he has refused to pass laws"; "he has called together legislative bodies"; "he has refused for a long time." As if fearing that the reader might not after all notice this oft-repeated "he has," Jefferson made it still more conspicuous by beginning a new paragraph with each "he has." To perform thus is not to be "literary" in a genteel sense; but for the particular purpose of drawing an indictment against the king it served very well indeed. Nothing could be more effective than these brief, crisp sentences, each one the bare affirmation of a malevolent act. Keep your mind on the king, Jefferson seems to say; he is the man: *"he has refused"; "he has forbidden"; "he has combined"; "he has incited"; "he has plundered"; "he has abdicated."* I will say he has.

These hard, incisive sentences are all the more effective as an indictment of the king because of the sharp contrast between them and the paragraphs, immediately preceding and following, in which Jefferson touches upon the sad state of the colonists. In these paragraphs there is something in the carefully chosen words, something in the falling cadence of the sentences, that conveys a mournful, almost a funereal, sense of evils apprehended and long forefended but now unhappily realized. Consider the phrases which give tone and pitch to the first two paragraphs: "when in the course of human events"; "decent respect to the opinions of mankind"; "all experience hath shewn"; "suffer while evils are sufferable"; "forms to which they are accustomed"; "patient sufferance of these colonies"; "no solitary fact to contradict the uniform tenor of the rest." Such phrases skilfully disposed have this result, that the opening passages of the Declaration give one the sense of fateful things impending, of hopes defeated and injuries sustained with unavailing fortitude. The contrast in manner is accentuated by the fact that whereas the king is represented as exclusively aggressive, the colonists are represented as essentially submissive. In this drama the king alone acts—he conspires, incites, plunders; the colonists have the passive part, never lifting a hand to burn stamps or destroy tea; they suffer while evils are sufferable. It is a high literary merit of the Declaration that by subtle contrasts Jefferson contrives to conjure up for us a vision of the virtuous and long-suffering colonists standing like martyrs to receive on their defenseless heads the ceaseless blows of the tyrant's hand.

Like many men with a sense for style, Jefferson, although much given to polishing and correcting his own manuscripts, did not always welcome changes which others might make. Congress discussed his draft for three successive days. What uncomplimentary remarks the members may have made is not known; but it is known that in the end certain paragraphs were greatly changed and others omitted altogether. These "depredations"—so he speaks of them—Jefferson did not enjoy: but we may easily console ourselves for his discomfiture since it moved the humane Franklin to tell him a story. Writing in 1818, Jefferson says:

> *I was sitting by Dr. Franklin, who perceived that I was not insensible to these mutilations. "I have made it a rule," said he, "whenever in my power, to avoid becoming the draughtsman of papers to be*

reviewed by a public body. I took my lesson from an incident which I will relate to you. When I was a journeyman printer, one of my companions, an apprentice Hatter, having served out his time, was about to open shop for himself. His first concern was to have a handsome signboard, with a proper inscription. He composed it in these words: 'John Thompson, Hatter, makes and sells hats for ready money,' with a figure of a hat subjoined. But he thought he would submit it to his friends for their amendments. The first he shewed it to thought the word 'hatter' tautologous, because followed by the words 'makes hats' which shew he was a hatter. It was struck out. The next observed that the word 'makes' might as well be omitted, because his customers would not care who made the hats. If good and to their mind, they would buy, by whomsoever made. He struck it out. A third said he thought the words 'for ready money' were useless as it was not the custom of the place to sell on credit. Every one who purchased expected to pay. They were parted with, and the inscription now stood 'John Thompson sells hats.' 'Sells hats' says his next friend? 'Why nobody will expect you to give them away. What then is the use of that word?' It was stricken out, and 'hats' followed it, the rather, as there was one painted on the board. So his inscription was reduced ultimately to 'John Thompson' with the figure of a hat subjoined." [4]

Jefferson's colleagues were not so ruthless as the friends of John Thompson; and on the whole it must be said that Congress left the Declaration better than it found it. The few verbal changes that were made improved the phraseology, I am inclined to think, in every case. Where Jefferson wrote: "He has erected a multitude of new offices by a self-assumed power, and sent hither swarms of officers to harrass our people and eat out their substance," Congress cut out the phrase, "by a self-assumed power." Again, Jefferson's sentence, "He has abdicated government here, withdrawing his governors, and declaring us out of his allegiance and protection," Congress changed to read, "He has abdicated government here by declaring us out of his protection and waging war against us." Is not the phraseology of Congress, in both cases, more incisive, and does it not thus add something to that very effect which Jefferson himself wished to produce?

Aside from merely verbal changes, Congress rewrote the final paragraph, cut out the greater part of the paragraph next to the last, and omit-

---

[4] *Writings of Thomas Jefferson* (Ford ed.), X, 120.

ted altogether the last of Jefferson's charges against the king. The final paragraph as it stands is certainly much stronger than in its original form. The Declaration was greatly strengthened by using, for the renunciation of allegiance, the very phraseology of the resolution of July 2, by which Congress had officially decreed that independence which it was the function of the Declaration to justify. It was no doubt for this reason mainly that Congress rewrote the paragraph; but the revision had in addition the merit of giving to the final paragraph, what such a paragraph especially needed, greater directness and assurance. In its final form, the Declaration closes with the air of accepting the issue with confident decision.

In cutting out the greater part of the next to the last paragraph, Congress omitted, among other things, the sentence in which Jefferson formulated, not directly indeed but by allusion, that theory of the constitutional relation of the colonies to Great Britain which is elsewhere taken for granted: "We have reminded them [our British brethren] ... that in constituting indeed our several forms of government, we had adopted one common king; thereby laying a foundation for perpetual league and amity with them; but that submission to their parliament was no part of our constitution, nor ever in idea, if history may be credited." Perhaps the Declaration would have been strengthened by including an explicit formulation of this theory. But if the theory was to be expressly formulated at all, Jefferson was unfortunate both in the form and in the order of the statement. Unfortunate in the form, which is allusive, and in the last phrase ambiguous— "Nor ever in idea, if history may be credited." Unfortunate in the order, because, if the theory was to be expressly formulated at all, its formulation should manifestly have preceded the list of charges against the king. In general, this paragraph, as originally written, leaves one with the feeling that the author, not quite aware that he is done, is beginning over again. In the form adopted, it is an admirable brief prelude to the closing paragraph.

The last of Jefferson's charges against the king was what John Adams called the "vehement philippic against negro slavery."[5]

> *He has waged cruel war against human nature itself, violating its most sacred rights of life and liberty in the persons of a distant people who never offended him, captivating and carrying them into slavery in another hemisphere, or to incur miserable death in their transportation thither. This piratical warfare, the opprobrium of* infidel *powers, is the warfare of the* Christian *king of Great Britain. Deter-*

---

[5] *Works of John Adams*, II, 514.

mined to keep open a market where MEN should be bought and sold,
he has prostituted his negative for suppressing every legislative at-
tempt to prohibit or to restrain this execrable commerce; and that
this assemblage of horrors might want no fact of distinguished die,
he is now exciting these very people to rise in arms among us, and to
purchase that liberty of which he deprived them, by murdering the
people upon whom he also obtruded them; thus paying off former
crimes committed against the liberties of one people, with crimes
which he urges them to commit against the lives of another.

Congress omitted this passage altogether. I am glad it did. One does
not expect a declaration of independence to represent historical events
with the objectivity and exactitude of a scientific treatise; but here the dis-
crepancy between the fact and the representation is too flagrant. Especially, in view of the subsequent history of the slave trade, and of slavery
itself, without which there would have been no slave trade, these charges
against the king lose whatever plausibility, slight enough at best, they may
have had at the time. But I have quoted this passage in full once more, not
on account of its substance but on account of its form, which is interesting, and peculiarly significant in its bearing upon Jefferson's qualities and
limitations as a writer. John Adams thought it one of the best parts of the
Declaration. It is possible that Jefferson thought so too. He evidently gave
much attention to the wording of it. But to me, even assuming the charges
against the king to be true, it is the part of the Declaration in which Jefferson conspicuously failed to achieve literary excellence.

The reason is, I think, that in this passage Jefferson attempted something which he was temperamentally unfitted to achieve. The passage was
to have been the climax of the charges against the king; on its own showing of facts it imputes to him the most inhuman acts, the basest motives;
its purpose, one supposes, is to stir the reader's emotions, to make him feel
a righteous indignation at the king's acts, a profound contempt for the man
and his motives. Well, the passage is clear, precise, carefully balanced. It
employs the most tremendous words—"murder," "piratical warfare,"
"prostituted," "miserable death." But in spite of every effort, the passage
somehow leaves us cold; it remains, like all of Jefferson's writing, calm and
quiescent; it lacks warmth; it fails to lift us out of our equanimity. There is
in it even (something rare indeed in Jefferson's writings) a sense of labored
effort, of deliberate striving for an effect that does not come.

This curious effect, or lack of effect, is partly due to the fact that the
king's base actions are presented to us in abstract terms. We are not per-
mitted to see George III. George III does not repeal a statute of South Car-

olina in order that Sambo may be sold at the port of Charleston. No, the Christian king wages "cruel war against human nature," he prostitutes "his negative for the suppression of every legislative attempt to prohibit or to restrain this execrable commerce." We have never a glimpse of poor dumb Negroes gasping for breath in the foul hold of a transport ship, or driven with whips like cattle to labor in a fetid rice swamp; what we see is human nature, and the "violation of its most sacred rights in the persons of a distant people." The thin vision of things in the abstract rarely reaches the sympathies. Few things are less moving than to gaze upon the concept of miserable death, and it is possible to contemplate "an assemblage of horrors that wants no fact of distinguished die" without much righteous indignation.

Yet the real reason lies deeper. It is of course quite possible to invest a generalized statement with an emotional quality. Consider the famous passage from Lincoln's second Inaugural:

> Fondly do we hope—fervently do we pray—that this mighty scourge of war may speedily pass away. Yet, if God wills that it continue until all the wealth piled by the bondman's two hundred and fifty years of unrequited toil shall be sunk, and until every drop of blood drawn with the lash shall be paid by another drawn by the sword, as was said three thousand years ago, so still it must be said, "the judgments of the Lord are true and righteous altogether."

Compare this with Jefferson's

> And that this assemblage of horrors might want no fact of distinguished die, he is now exciting these very people to rise in arms against us, and to purchase that liberty of which he deprived them, by murdering the people upon whom he also obtruded them; thus paying off former crimes committed against the liberties of one people, with crimes which he urges them to commit against the lives of another.

Making every allowance for difference in subject and in occasion, these passages differ as light differs from darkness. There is a quality of deep feeling about the first, an indefinable something which is profoundly moving; and this something, which informs and enriches much of Lincoln's writing, is rarely, almost never present in the writing of Jefferson.

This something, which Jefferson lacked but which Lincoln possessed in full measure, may perhaps for want of a better term be called a profoundly emotional apprehension of experience. One might say that Jefferson felt with the mind, as some people think with the heart. He had enthusiasm, but it was enthusiasm engendered by an irrepressible intellectual curiosity. He was ardent, but his ardors were cool, giving forth light without heat. One never feels with Jefferson, as one does with Washington, that his restraint is the effect of a powerful will persistently holding down a profoundly passionate nature. One has every confidence that Jefferson will never lose control of himself, will never give way to purifying rage, relieving his overwrought feelings by an outburst of divine swearing. All his ideas and sentiments seem of easy birth, flowing felicitously from an alert and expeditious brain rather than slowly and painfully welling up from the obscure depths of his nature. "I looked for gravity," says Maclay, giving his first impressions of Jefferson, "but a laxity of manner seemed shed about him. He spoke almost without ceasing; but even his discourse partook of his personal demeanor. It was loose and rambling; and yet he scattered information wherever he went, and some even brilliant sentiments sparkled from him."

Jefferson's writing is much like that—a ceaseless flow, sparkling, often brilliant, a kind of easy improvisation. There are in his writings few of those ominous overtones charged with emotion, and implying more than is expressed. Sometimes, indeed, by virtue of a certain facility, a certain complacent optimism, by virtue of saying disputed things in such a pleasant way, his words imply even less than they mean. When, for example, Jefferson says "the tree of Liberty must be refreshed from time to time with the blood of patriots and tyrants," so far from making us shudder, he contrives to throw about this unlovely picture a kind of arcadian charm. You will hardly think of Jefferson, with lifted hand and vibrant voice, in the heat of emotion striking off the tremendous sentence, "Give me liberty or give me death!" I can imagine him saying, "Manly spirit bids us to choose to die freemen rather than to live slaves." The words would scarcely lift us out of our seats, however we might applaud the orator for his peculiar felicity of expression.

Felicity of expression—certainly Jefferson had that; but one wonders whether he did not perhaps have too much of it. This sustained felicity gives one at times a certain feeling of insecurity, as of resting one's weight on something fragile. Jefferson's placidity, the complacent optimism of his sentiments and ideas, carry him at times perilously near the fatuous. One would like more evidence that the iron had some time or other entered his soul, more evidence of his having profoundly reflected upon the enigma of existence, of having more deeply felt its tragic import, of having won his convictions and his optimisms and his felicities at the expense of some painful travail of the spirit. What saved Jefferson from futility was of course his clear, alert intelligence, his insatiable curiosity, his rarely failing candor, his loyalty to ideas, his humane sympathies. Yet we feel that his convictions, his sympathies, his ideas are essentially of the intellect, somehow curiously abstracted from reality, a consciously woven drapery laid over the surface of a nature essentially aristocratic, essentially fastidious, instinctively shrinking from close contact with men and things as they are.

Not without reason was Jefferson most at home in Paris. By the qualities of his mind and temperament he really belonged to the philosophical school, to the Encyclopaedists, those generous souls who loved mankind by virtue of not knowing too much about men, who worshipped reason with unreasoning faith, who made a religion of Nature while cultivating a studied aversion for "enthusiasm," and strong religious emotion. Like them, Jefferson, in his earlier years especially, impresses one as being a radical by profession. We often feel that he defends certain practices and ideas, that he denounces certain customs or institutions, not so much from independent reflection or deep-seated conviction on the particular matter in hand as because in general these are the things that a philosopher and a man of virtue ought naturally to defend or denounce. It belonged to the eighteenth-century philosopher, as a matter of course, to apostrophize Nature, to defend Liberty, to denounce Tyranny, perchance to shed tears at the thought of a virtuous action. It was always in character for him to feel the degradation of Human Nature when confronted with the idea of Negro Slavery.

This academic accent, as of ideas and sentiments belonging to a system, of ideas uncriticized and sentiments no more than conventionally felt, is what gives a labored and perfunctory effect to Jefferson's famous "philippic against Negro slavery." Adams described it better than he knew. It is indeed a philippic; it is indeed vehement; but it is not moving. It is such a piece as would be expected of a *"philosophe"* on such an occasion. We remain calm in reading it because Jefferson, one cannot but think, remained calm in writing it. For want of phrases charged with deep feeling, he resorts to italics, vainly endeavoring to stir the reader by capitalizing and underlining the words that need to be stressed—a futile device, which serves only to accentuate the sense of artifice and effort, and, in the case of "the *Christian* king of Great Britain," introduces the wholly incongruous note of snarling sarcasm, reminding us for all the world of Shylock's "these be the *Christian* husbands." Jefferson apprehended the injustice of slavery; but one is inclined to ask how deeply he felt it.

It may be said that Jefferson touches the emotions as little in other parts of the Declaration as in the philippic on slavery. That is in great measure true; but in the other parts of the Declaration, which have to do for the most part with an exposition of the constitutional rights of the colonies, or with a categorical statement of the king's violations of these rights, the appeal is more properly to the mind than to the heart; and it was in appealing to the reader's mind, of course, that Jefferson was at his best. Taking the Declaration as a whole, this is indeed its conspicuous quality: it states clearly, reasons lucidly, exposes felicitously; its high virtue is in this, that it makes a strong bid for the reader's assent. But it was beyond the power of Jefferson to impregnate the Declaration with qualities that would give to the reader's assent the moving force of profound conviction. With all its precision, its concise rapidity, its clarity, its subtle implications and engaging felicities, one misses a certain unsophisticated directness, a certain sense of impregnable solidity and massive strength, a certain effect of passion restrained and deep convictions held in reserve, which would have given to it that accent of perfect sincerity and that emotional content which belong to the grand manner.

The Declaration has not the grand manner—that passion under control which lifts prose to the level of true poetry. Yet it has, what is the next best thing, a quality which saves it from falling to the prosaic. It has elevation. I have said that Franklin had, equally with Jefferson, clarity, simplicity, precision, felicity. If Franklin had written the Declaration it would have had all of these qualities; but Franklin would have communicated to it something homely and intimate and confidential, some smell of homespun, some air of the tavern or the print shop. Franklin could not, I think, have written this sentence:

> *When in the course of human events it becomes necessary for one people to dissolve the political bands which have connected them with another, and to assume among the powers of the earth the separate and equal station to which the laws of nature and of nature's god entitle them, a decent respect to the opinions of mankind requires that they should declare the causes which impel them to the separation.*

Or this one:

> *Prudence indeed will dictate that governments long established should not be changed for light and transient causes; and accordingly all experience hath shewn that mankind are more disposed to suffer,*

> *while evils are sufferable, than to right themselves by abolishing the forms to which they are accustomed.*

Or this:

> *And for the support of this declaration we mutually pledge to each other our lives, our fortunes, and our sacred honor.*

These sentences may not be quite in the grand manner; but they have a high seriousness, a kind of lofty pathos which at least lift the Declaration to the level of a great occasion. These qualities Jefferson was able to communicate to his writing by virtue of possessing a nature exquisitely sensitive, and a mind finely tempered; they illustrate, in its subtler forms, what John Adams called his "peculiar felicity of expression."

5

Gilbert Highet

The Gettysburg Address

The Gettysburg Address is the most familiar piece of prose in America. If there's one thing you can count on everyone knowing, it's the opening sentence and other assorted phrases. You have been told from the time you first studied history in school that it is the most noble, eloquent, and moving document in American history. Everyone parrots this opinion, but it is highly doubtful if very many people can say why it is so. For instance, did you ever notice the metaphor of birth that underlies the first sentence?

In this essay, Gilbert Highet analyzes the rhetorical structure and techniques of the Address, taking it apart to see how it works. It is a humbling lesson in how unobservant most of us are.

These five words stand at the entrance to the best-known monument of American prose, one of the finest utterances in the entire language, and surely one of the greatest speeches in all history. Greatness is like granite: it is molded in fire, and it lasts for many centuries.

Fourscore and seven years ago . . . It is strange to think that President Lincoln was looking back to the 4th of July 1776, and that he and his speech are now further removed from us than he himself was from George Washington and the Declaration of Independence. Fourscore and seven years before the Gettysburg Address, a small group of patriots signed the Declaration. Fourscore and seven years after the Gettysburg Address, it was the year 1950,[1] and that date is already receding rapidly into our troubled, adventurous, and valiant past.

Inadequately prepared and at first scarcely realized in its full importance, the dedication of the graveyard at Gettysburg was one of the supreme moments of American history. The battle itself had been a turning point of the war. On the 4th of July 1863, General Meade repelled Lee's invasion of Pennsylvania. Although he did not follow up his victory, he had broken one of the most formidable aggressive enterprises of the Confederate armies. Losses were heavy on both sides. Thousands of dead were left on the field, and thousands of wounded died in the hot days following the battle. At first, their burial was more or less haphazard; but thoughtful men gradually came to feel that an adequate burying place and memorial were required. These were established by an interstate commission that autumn, and the finest speaker in the North was invited to dedicate them. This was the scholar and statesman Edward Everett of Harvard. He made a good speech—which is still extant: not at all academic, it is full of close strategic analysis and deep historical understanding.

Lincoln was not invited to speak, at first. Although people knew him as an effective debater, they were not sure whether he was capable of making a serious speech on such a solemn occasion. But one of the impressive things about Lincoln's career is that he constantly strove to *grow*.

---

[1]   In November 1950 the Chinese had just entered the war in Korea.

"The Gettysburg Address" from *A Clerk of Oxenford* by Gilbert Highet. Copyright © 1954 by Gilbert Highet. Reprinted with permission of Oxford University Press, Inc.

He was anxious to appear on that occasion and to say something worthy of it. (Also, it has been suggested, he was anxious to remove the impression that he did not know how to behave properly—an impression which had been strengthened by a shocking story about his clowning on the battlefield of Antietam the previous year.) Therefore when he was invited he took considerable care with his speech. He drafted rather more than half of it in the White House before leaving, finished it in the hotel at Gettysburg the night before the ceremony (not in the train, as sometimes reported), and wrote out a fair copy next morning.

There are many accounts of the day itself, 19 November 1863. There are many descriptions of Lincoln, all showing the same curious blend of grandeur and awkwardness, or lack of dignity, or—it would be best to call it humility. In the procession he rode horseback: a tall lean man in a high plug hat, straddling a short horse, with his feet too near the ground. He arrived before the chief speaker, and had to wait patiently for half an hour or more. His own speech came right at the end of a long and exhausting ceremony, lasted less than three minutes, and made little impression on the audience. In part this was because they were tired, in part because (as eyewitnesses said) he ended almost before they knew he had begun, and in part because he did not speak the Address, but read it, very slowly, in a thin high voice, with a marked Kentucky accent, pronouncing "to" as "toe" and dropping his final R's.

Some people of course were alert enough to be impressed. Everett congratulated him at once. But most of the newspapers paid little attention to the speech, and some sneered at it. The *Patriot and Union* of Harrisburg wrote, "We pass over the silly remarks of the President; for the credit of the nation we are willing ... that they shall no more be repeated or thought of"; and the London *Times* said, "The ceremony was rendered ludicrous by some of the sallies of that poor President Lincoln," calling his remarks "dull and commonplace." The first commendation of the Address came in a single sentence of the Chicago *Tribune*, and the first discriminating and detailed praise of it appeared in the Springfield *Republican*, the Providence *Journal*, and the Philadelphia *Bulletin*. However, three weeks after the ceremony and then again the following spring, the editor of *Harper's Weekly* published a sincere and thorough eulogy of the Address, and soon it was attaining recognition as a masterpiece.

At the time, Lincoln could not care much about the reception of his words. He was exhausted and ill. In the train back to Washington, he lay down with a wet towel on his head. He had caught smallpox. At that moment he was incubating it, and he was stricken down soon after he re-entered the White House. Fortunately it was a mild attack, and it evoked one of his best jokes: he told his visitors, "At last I have something I can give to everybody."

He had more than that to give to everybody. He was a unique person, far greater than most people realize until they read his life with care. The wisdom of his policy, the sources of his statesmanship—these were things too complex to be discussed in a brief essay. But we can say something about the Gettysburg Address as a work of art.

A work of art. Yes: for Lincoln was a literary artist, trained both by others and by himself. The textbooks he used as a boy were full of difficult exercises and skillful devices in formal rhetoric, stressing the qualities he practiced in his own speaking: antithesis, parallelism, and verbal harmony. Then he read and reread many admirable models of thought and expression: the King James Bible, the essays of Bacon, the best plays of Shakespeare. His favorites were *Hamlet, Lear, Macbeth, Richard III,* and *Henry VIII,* which he had read dozens of times. He loved reading aloud, too, and spent hours reading poetry to his friends. (He told his partner Herndon that he preferred getting the sense of any document by reading it aloud.) Therefore his serious speeches are important parts of the long and noble classical tradition of oratory which begins in Greece, runs through Rome to the modern world, and is still capable (if we do not neglect it) of producing masterpieces.

The first proof of this is that the Gettysburg Address is full of quotations—or rather of adaptations—which give it strength. It is partly religious, partly (in the highest sense) political: therefore it is interwoven with memories of the Bible and memories of American history. The first and the last words are Biblical cadences. Normally Lincoln did not say "fourscore" when he meant eighty; but on this solemn occasion he recalled the important dates in the Bible—such as the age of Abram when his first son was born to him, and he was "fourscore and six years old." [2] Similarly he did not say there was a chance that democracy might die out: he recalled the somber phrasing of the Book of Job—where Bildad speaks of the destruction of one who shall vanish without a trace, and says that "his branch shall be cut off; his remembrance shall perish from the earth." [3] Then again, the famous description of our State as "government of the people, by the people, for the people" was adumbrated by Daniel Webster in 1830 (he

---

[2] Gen. 16.16; cf. Exod. 7.7.

[3] Job 18.16-17; cf. Jer. 10.11, Micah 7.2.

spoke of "the people's government, made for the people, made by the people, and answerable to the people") and then elaborated in 1854 by the abolitionist Theodore Parker (as "government of all the people, by all the people, for all the people"). There is good reason to think that Lincoln took the important phrase "under God" (which he interpolated at the last moment) from Weems, the biographer of Washington; and we know that it had been used at least once by Washington himself.

Analyzing the Address further, we find that it is based on a highly imaginative theme, or group of themes. The subject is—how can we put it so as not to disfigure it?—the subject is the kinship of life and death, that mysterious linkage which we see sometimes as the physical succession of birth and death in our world, sometimes as the contrast, which is perhaps a unity, between death and immortality. The first sentence is concerned with birth:

Our fathers brought forth *a* new *nation,* conceived *in liberty.*

The final phrase but one expresses the hope that

this nation, under God, shall have a new birth *of freedom.*

And the last phrase of all speaks of continuing life as the triumph over death. Again and again throughout the speech, this mystical contrast and kinship reappear: "those who *gave their lives* that that nation might *live,"* "the brave men *living* and *dead,"* and so in the central assertion that the dead have already consecrated their own burial place, while "it is for us, the *living,* rather to be dedicated . . . to the great task remaining," The Gettysburg Address is a prose poem; it belongs to the same world as the great elegies, and the adagios of Beethoven.

Its structure, however, is that of a skillfully contrived speech. The oratorical pattern is perfectly clear, Lincoln describes the occasion, dedicates the ground, and then draws a larger conclusion by calling on his hearers to dedicate themselves to the preservation of the Union. But within that, we can trace his constant use of at least two important rhetorical devices.

The first of these is *antithesis:* opposition, contrast. The speech is full of it. Listen:

The world will little note		*what* we say *here*
	nor long remember	
but	*it can never* forget	*what* they did *here.*

And so in nearly every sentence: "brave men, *living* and *dead*"; "to *add* or *detract*." There is the antithesis of the Founding Fathers and the men of Lincoln's own time:

> *Our* fathers brought forth *a new nation* ...
> *now* we *are testing whether that nation* ... *can* long endure.

And there is the more terrible antithesis of those who have already died and those who still live to do their duty. Now, antithesis is the figure of contrast and conflict. Lincoln was speaking in the midst of a great civil war.

The other important pattern is different. It is technically called *tricolon* —the division of an idea into three harmonious parts, usually of increasing power. The most famous phrase of the Address is a tricolon:

> *government of the people*
> *by the people*
> *and for the people.*

The most solemn sentence is a tricolon:

> *we cannot dedicate*
> *we cannot consecrate*
> *we cannot hallow   this ground.*

And above all, the last sentence (which has sometimes been criticized as too complex) is essentially two parallel phrases, with a tricolon growing out of the second and then producing another tricolon: a trunk, three branches, and a cluster of flowers. Lincoln says that it is for his hearers to be dedicated to the great task remaining before them. Then he goes on,

> *that from these honored dead*

—apparently he means "in such a way that from these honored dead"—

> *we take increased devotion to that cause.*

Next, he restates this more briefly:

> *that we here highly resolve* ...

And now the actual resolution follows, in three parts of growing intensity:

> *that these dead shall not have died in vain*
> *that this nation, under God, shall have a new birth*
> > *of freedom*

and that (one more tricolon)

> *government of the people*
> > *by the people*
>
> *and   for the people*
>
> *shall not perish from the earth.*

Now, the tricolon is the figure which, through division, emphasizes basic harmony and unity. Lincoln used antithesis because he was speaking to a people at war. He used the tricolon because he was hoping, planning, praying for peace.

No one thinks that when he was drafting the Gettysburg Address, Lincoln deliberately looked up these quotations and consciously chose these particular patterns of thought. No, he chose the theme. From its development and from the emotional tone of the entire occasion, all the rest followed, or grew—by that marvelous process of choice and rejection which is essential to artistic creation. It does not spoil such a work of art to analyze it as closely as we have done; it is altogether fitting and proper that we should do this: for it helps us to penetrate more deeply into the rich meaning of the Gettysburg Address, and it allows us the very rare privilege of watching the workings of a great man's mind.

6

Burnham Carter, Jr.

President Kennedy's Inaugural Address

When President Kennedy delivered his inaugural address, and in the middle of it asked, "Will you join in that historic effort?" many of the audience spontaneouly cried "Yes!" Such a response, on such a formal occasion as a Presidential Inauguration, especially on a freezing day outside in the wind,, is evidence of the power and appeal of Mr. Kennedy's words.

In this essay, Mr. Carter, like Gilbert Highet with the Gettysburg Address, describes the stylistic devices by which President Kennedy achieved that effect. He makes an important point: just because you can identify certain conscious rhetorical techniques in a work doesn't necessarily mean you are questioning the author's sincerity.

After John Fitzgerald Kennedy had delivered his Inaugural Address on January 20, 1961, many hailed it as "a great speech" (*Life*) or as "distinguished for its style and brevity as well as for its meaty content" (the *New York Times*). A few commentators denigrated it as mere "mood music" for a new administration (the *Reporter*). In the last year I have asked several groups of students to study it as a piece of rhetoric. On each occasion the class has enjoyed working with a piece of contemporary prose by a man of eminence, and they are pleased to discover so much to discuss about Mr. Kennedy's word choice, figurative language, phrase-making, and variety of appeals.

Alliteration offers an easy start: "Civility is not a sign of weakness, and sincerity is always subject to proof" is a fine instance, although the smoothness of the phrasing will lead some to overlook the host of *s*'s. When the President says he hopes to enlarge the area in which the UN's "writ may run," many will not see the economy and force of this example until they try a paraphrase, such as "until its decisions may have the force of law." Along the same lines, an alert reader will enjoy an internal rhyme like "the steady spread of the deadly atom."

In considering connotations, one notices right away that Mr. Kennedy uses the word *pledge* seven times in a row (the last two with slight variations, to avoid monotony). *Promise* would never do here, for "promises, promises, always promises" has become a cant phrase for us. The reasons for his choice are clear when we remember the happy contexts in which we use *pledge:* swearing allegiance to the flag, making a gift to the church or other charity, drinking a friend's health, and even in the marriage ceremony ("and thereto I plight thee my troth"). The final use of this key word shows a nice distinction. To Soviet Russia Mr. Kennedy offers "not a *pledge* but a *request*," for one's enemy does not deserve the same promise of support as do one's allies. *Request* will suffice. Lest he seem petulant, he dignifies the U.S.S.R. as "those nations who would make themselves our *adversary*," a designation that recalls the high seriousness of Milton's virtue that "sallies out and seeks her *adversary*," or the word's use in the Sermon on the Mount and elsewhere in Scripture.

The address is full of richly connotative words. Consider the force of "*unleashed* powers of destruction" as opposed, say, to *released*, or the re-

---

furbishing of the tired phrases *balance of power* and *iron curtain* with fresh variants, "balance of *terror*" and "iron *tyranny.*" With such changes the President calls upon an echo in the reader's mind yet avoids the cliché.

It is as a phrasemaker that Mr. Kennedy has made his strongest mark in both his formal and informal speeches. The two best known epigrams in the Inaugural Address are "Let us never negotiate out of fear, but let us never fear to negotiate" and "Ask not what your country can do for you, but what you can do for your country." These inversions sound deceptively easy and inevitable, as do all such concise and pointed expressions. The writer uses few and simple words; he changes the order or alters the wording only slightly; and the result is memorable because it is short, witty and precise. In his September 25th speech to the UN, the President employs a similar reversal when he asserts, "Mankind must put an end to war, or war will put an end to mankind."

Mr. Kennedy is fond of paradox; witness the following two examples: "Only when our arms are sufficient beyond doubt can we be certain beyond doubt that they will never be employed" (from the Inaugural Address), and terror will always fail as a policy weapon because "men are not afraid to die for a life worth living" (from the UN address). The first of these points up the inescapable irony of any massive defensive effort. The triple walls of Carcassonne were a major reason why it was rarely attacked and, after 1240, never taken; similarly the United States is to spend billions for defense to make sure, hopefully, that none of it will ever be used. How absurd, and yet how true—that is the calculated effect of paradox. The second example relies on the ancient and honorable concept of dying in order that another might live better, of giving up one's life to "save" it. In each instance the writer must produce a statement that is self-contradictory on the surface but in a larger sense correct.

Wit of this sort is risky. It demands attention, and listeners to political speeches are notoriously slack. It depends on the reader's catching on to the allusion, irony, or contradiction quickly, and often the writer receives only incomplete comprehension, as Dean Swift learned with *A Modest Proposal.* In his Inaugural Address Mr. Kennedy requests that new nations remember that "in the past, those who foolishly sought power by riding the tiger end up inside." Whether the allusion is to a folk saying of the sort Mr. Khrushchev favors, or to the old limerick of the lady from Niger,* Mr. Ken-

---

* There once was a lady from Niger
Who smiled as she rode on a tiger.
They came back from the ride
With the lady inside
And the smile on the face of the tiger.

nedy's witty analogy may miss the listeners who have never heard of it or annoy others who distrust all cleverness. Those who know the allusion or have a taste for the wry epigram, however, will enjoy this touch of the sardonic. That the President himself savors a bit of sarcasm is evident from the following dinner party parody he gave of his own famous address:

> We observe tonight not a celebration of freedom but a victory of party, for we have sworn to pay off the same party debt our forebears ran up nearly a year and three months ago. Our deficit will not be paid off in the next hundred days, nor will it be paid off in the first one thousand days, nor in the life of this Administration. Nor, perhaps, even in our lifetime on this planet. But let us begin—remembering that generosity is not a sign of weakness and that ambassadors are always subject to Senate confirmation. For if the Democratic party cannot be helped by the many who are poor, it cannot be saved by the few who are rich. So let us begin. (The New York Times magazine, Feb. 25, 1962, p. 70)

Not all of Mr. Kennedy's care for phrasing is for elegance. Much of it is for clarity and emphasis, especially the repetitions, which are of course intentional and not (like many of our own) the result of inattention or an impoverished vocabulary. The President uses them to give order and balance to a series of thoughts, as in the five paragraphs beginning "To those old allies . . . , to those new states," etc. Such repetition of a minor word in the construction allows the listener to rest as he follows the steps in the speaker's program. Later Mr. Kennedy's four repetitions of "let both sides" stress the mutual responsibility of the U.S.A. and the U.S.S.R., and at the same time organize his proposals so that the millions in his audience can follow him easily.

Parallelism and antithesis are major devices in the President's style. He describes the new generation of Americans as "born in this country, tempered by war, disciplined by a hard and bitter peace, proud of our ancient heritage . . ." Studied parallelism should hardly become an earmark of every writer's style—such a return to euphuism would be appalling—but it is important for him to recognize it when he sees it and to be able to use it himself when the occasion demands. The same is true for Mr. Kennedy's fondness for antithesis. His opening sentence, "we observe today not a victory of party but a celebration of freedom," employs the same careful contrast as "I come to bury Caesar, not to praise him." Throughout the Inaugural Address one finds not because, not because, but because, or "not as a call to bear arms . . . , not as a call to battle . . . , but a call to bear the burden . . ." In part this device is definition of an idea by elimination, but it also offers a welcome simplicity of argument. "If a free society cannot help the many who are poor, it cannot save the few who are rich," regardless of its position, is a good example of a phrasing that is tidy, balanced, and easy on the ear. A sentence that seems to say so much in so little is always likely to be persuasive. Mr. Kennedy's poet laureate, Robert Frost, has a similar penchant for gnomic utterances, as in "We dance around in a ring and suppose,/ But the secret sits in the middle and knows," or "I never dared be radical when young/ For fear it would make me conservative when old." As a final example of Mr. Kennedy's balanced style, the conclusion of his address to the UN is notable:

> *Together we shall save our planet or together we shall perish in its flames. Save it we can and save it we must, and then shall we earn the eternal thanks of mankind and, as peacemakers, the eternal blessings of God.*

Here the repetition in the first sentence allows the contrast of *save* versus *perish* to shine forth, just as the repetition of *save it we* stresses the double obligation of *can* and *must*. Seldom do most of us think to reverse the order of subject and verb, as the President effectively does here.

President Kennedy relies on metaphor throughout his address. "The bonds of mass misery . . . , the chains of poverty . . . , a beachhead of cooperation [pushing back] the jungles of suspicion . . ." We need to ask, "Is this comparison correct?" and then "How effective do I find it?" In his third paragraph Mr. Kennedy says that "the torch has been passed to a new generation of Americans." As a symbol of freedom, of any light we use to hold back the dark, be it physical or spiritual, *torch* has a traditional value. To some it may even be a cliché, however honored by the wind and weather of time, like the Statue of Liberty. Perhaps the listener will recall Olympic runners bringing the divine flame from Mt. Olympus to the meeting of the competitors. *Torch* is surely correct enough here, for the parallel is clear; whether or not it is wholly successful depends on the degree of literary sophistication of the audience.

A similar reliance on a traditional symbol occurs in the President's peroration, when he announces that "now the trumpet summons us again," for bugles have been used in times of crisis since the days of Charlemagne or even Joshua. A more direct metaphor occurs later in the reference to the four "common enemies of mankind: tyranny, poverty, disease, and war itself." With the trumpet having already established a Biblical context, it is not much of a leap to associate these four adversaries with a similar quartet, the four horsemen of the Apocalypse: conquest, slaughter, famine, and death. Unfortunately, mention of "the four horsemen" in a Midwestern classroom is liable to produce only "Miller, Crowley, Layden, and Stuhldreher," the lethal backfield of Notre Dame in the twenties.

Lastly, the various appeals of the Inaugural Address are designed to call upon all the ideals of the listener. The opening paragraph urges a new unity, a closing of ranks after the campaign, by reference to the common tradition of Presidents taking office in the last 171 years. Mr. Kennedy speaks of "our forebears ... nearly a century and three quarters ago," just as Mr. Lincoln cited "our forefathers ... four score and seven years ago." Unity established, the President speaks of Americans as *tempered, disciplined* and *proud*, as men willing to *pay any price, bear any burden, meet any hardship, support any friend, oppose any foe*. Such an appeal to stoicism and courage insures an optimistic attitude toward the obligations which he will list next. Finally, for over two thirds of the speech Mr. Kennedy speaks only of *we*, from the opening words, "We observe today," to "But let us begin." Only when his sense of our unified strength has been well established does he switch to "in *your* hands" and "will *you* join in that historic effort?" By way of encouragement he speaks briefly of his own attitude: "*I* do not shrink from this responsibility—*I* welcome it." Then quickly he returns to "the devotion which *we* bring to this endeavor," and the final, overriding emphasis is on *our* reward, *our* deeds and *our* work.

The last paragraph of the Inaugural Address illustrates almost all the rhetorical techniques noted so far: the alliteration, the simple yet precise wording, the inverted sentences, the intentional repetitions, the sense of community and tradition. All are here, plus another, as yet unmentioned element. The subject matter of this address is foreign policy, but the aim is not only to reassure other nations of our plans but to encourage Americans to implement them. Many a speaker makes his cause a crusade, for "if God be on our side, who can be against us?" A religious motif runs through this speech, from the reference to "Almighty God" and "the hand of God," to the quotations from Isaiah 58:6 and Romans 12:12, the allusion to Armageddon in "mankind's final war," that trumpet call, and "the faith, the devotion" stressed in the final paragraphs and especially in the last sentence:

> With a good conscience our only sure reward, with history the final judge of our deeds, let us go forth to lead the land we love, asking His blessing and His help, but knowing that here on earth God's work must truly be our own.

Few will miss the echo here of Lincoln's "With malice toward none, with charity toward all," and the phrase "God's work must truly be our own" has a Puritan ring. Such company is highly honorific.

As these religious and historical allusions are ticked off, a danger arises that threatens the integrity of the entire speech. The familiarity of a religious or idealistic appeal may lead to the superficial conclusion that a successful speech is pure semantics. The easily cynical will sneer that political speeches are all "hokum," "political propaganda," or "Fourth of July oratory." A careful analysis of this address, however, ought not to persuade the writer that now he has the inside story, that now, like Mr. Barnum, he can fool some of the people some of the time. Instead, he should see in this address a craftsman at work, but not let his sophomoric glee at discovering how words are used lead him to scoff at the idealism present, however familiar its form. Such a reader should be asked to look at his own last piece of writing. Can he, like Mr. Kennedy, vary his sentence length from 80 words to 4, yet average a mature 26? Can he successfully echo his opening stand in his conclusion, as the President does with "Let us go forth"? And would he be willing to submit a statement of his beliefs to the scrutiny of the entire world? Few of us risk as much in a lifetime of speaking and writing as much as does the President in a single day.

The 1961 Inaugural Address offers an appealing entry into the world of word choice, sentence construction, and emotional appeals. And as we watch a young, successful and highly literate man like Mr. Kennedy work successfully to convince others, perhaps we will become more concerned with our own ability to express ourselves. The Inaugural Address forms a good exercise in close reading, and the student will find in it more to write about than he has time for. A cynical few will demur at parts of the speech as old bromides, but by far the majority will conclude, as Dr. Johnson did with Gray's *Elegy,* that here we meet "images which find a mirror in every mind, and sentiments to which every bosom returns an echo."

Appendices

The Gettysburg Address

When, in the Course of human events, it becomes necessary for one people to dissolve the political bands which have connected them with another, and to assume, among the Powers of the earth, the separate and equal station to which the Laws of Nature and of Nature's God entitle them, a decent respect to the opinions of mankind requires that they should declare the causes which impel them to the separation.

We hold these truths to be self-evident, that all men are created equal, that they are endowed by their Creator with certain unalienable Rights, that among these, are Life, Liberty, and the pursuit of Happiness. That, to secure these rights, Governments are instituted among Men, deriving their just Powers from the consent of the governed. That, whenever any form of Government becomes destructive of these ends, it is the Right of the People to alter or to abolish it, and to institute new Government, laying its foundation on such Principles, and organizing its Powers in such form, as to them shall seem most likely to effect their Safety and Happiness. Prudence, indeed, will dictate that Governments long established should not be changed for light and transient causes; and, accordingly, all experience hath shewn, that mankind are more disposed to suffer, while evils are sufferable, than to right themselves by abolishing the forms to which they are accustomed. But, when a long train of abuses and usurpations, pursuing invariably the same Object, evinces a design to reduce them under absolute Despotism, it is their right, it is their duty, to throw off such Government, and to provide new Guards for their future Security. Such has been the patient sufferance of these Colonies; and such is now the necessity which constrains them to alter their former Systems of Government. The history of the present King of Great Britain is a history of repeated injuries and usurpations, all having in direct object the establishment of an absolute Tyranny over these States. To prove this, let Facts be submitted to a candid world.

He has refused his Assent to Laws the most wholesome and necessary for the public good.

He has forbidden his Governors to pass Laws of immediate and pressing importance, unless suspended in their operation till his Assent should be obtained; and when so suspended, he has utterly neglected to attend to them.

He has refused to pass other Laws for the accommodation of large districts of People, unless those People would relinquish the right of Representation in the legislature; a right inestimable to them and formidable to tyrants only.

He has called together legislative bodies at places unusual, uncomfortable, and distant from the depository of their Public Records, for the sole Purpose of fatiguing them into compliance with his measures.

He has dissolved Representative Houses repeatedly, for opposing, with manly firmness, his invasions on the rights of the People.

He has refused for a long time, after such dissolutions, to cause others to be elected; whereby the Legislative Powers, incapable of Annihilation, have returned to the People at large for their exercise; the State remaining in the mean time exposed to all the dangers of invasion from without, and convulsions within.

He has endeavoured to prevent the Population of these States; for that purpose obstructing the Laws for Naturalization of Foreigners; refusing to pass others to encourage their migrations hither, and raising the conditions of new Appropriations of Lands.

He has obstructed the Administration of Justice, by refusing his Assent to Laws for establishing Judiciary Powers.

He has made Judges dependent on his Will alone, for the tenure of their offices, and the amount and payment of their salaries.

He has erected a multitude of New Offices, and sent hither swarms of Officers to harrass our People, and eat out their substance.

He has kept among us, in times of Peace, Standing Armies, without the Consent of our legislatures.

He has affected to render the Military independent of and superior to the Civil Power.

He has combined with others to subject us to a jurisdiction foreign to our constitution, and unacknowledged by our laws; giving his Assent to their Acts of pretended Legislation:

For quartering large bodies of armed troops among us:

For protecting them, by a mock Trial, from Punishment for any Murders which they should commit on the Inhabitants of these States:

For cutting off our Trade with all parts of the world:

For imposing Taxes on us without our Consent:

For depriving us, in many cases, of the benefits of Trial by Jury:

For transporting us beyond Seas to be tried for pretended offences:

For abolishing the free System of English Laws in a neighbouring province, establishing therein an Arbitrary government, and enlarging its Boundaries, so as to render it at once an example and fit instrument for introducing the same absolute rule into these Colonies:

For taking away our Charters, abolishing our most valuable Laws, and altering fundamentally the Forms of our Governments:

For suspending our own Legislatures, and declaring themselves invested with Power to legislate for us in all cases whatsoever.

He has abdicated Government here, by declaring us out of his protection, and waging War against us.

He has plundered our seas, ravaged our Coasts, burnt our towns, and destroyed the Lives of our People.

He is at this time transporting large Armies of foreign Mercenaries to compleat the works of death, desolation and tyranny, already begun with circumstances of Cruelty and perfidy scarcely paralleled in the most barbarous ages, and totally unworthy the Head of a civilized nation.

He has constrained our fellow Citizens, taken Captive on the high Seas, to bear Arms against their Country, to become the executioners of their friends and Brethren, or to fall themselves by their Hands.

He has excited domestic insurrections amongst us, and has endeavoured to bring on the inhabitants of our frontiers, the merciless Indian Savages, whose known rule of warfare, is an undistinguished destruction of all ages, sexes and conditions.

In every stage of these Oppressions, We have Petitioned for Redress, in the most humble terms: Our repeated Petitions, have been answered only by repeated injury. A Prince, whose character is thus marked by every act which may define a Tyrant, is unfit to be the ruler of a free People.

Nor have We been wanting in attentions to our British brethren. We have warned them from time to time of attempts by their legislature to extend an unwarrantable jurisdiction over us. We have reminded them of the circumstances of our emigration and settlement here. We have appealed to their native justice and magnanimity, and we have conjured them by the ties of our common kindred, to disavow these usurpations, which, would inevitably interrupt our connexions and correspondence. They too have been deaf to the voice of justice and consanguinity. We must, therefore, acquiesce in the necessity, which denounces our Separation, and hold them, as we hold the rest of mankind, Enemies in war, in Peace Friends.

WE, THEREFORE, the Representatives of the UNITED STATES OF AMERICA, in GENERAL CONGRESS assembled, appealing to the Supreme Judge of the World for the rectitude of our intentions, DO, in the Name, and by Authority of the good People of these Colonies, solemnly PUBLISH and DECLARE, That these United Colonies are, and of Right, ought to be FREE AND INDEPENDENT STATES; that they are Absolved from all Allegiance to the British Crown, and that all political connexion between them and the State of Great Britain, is and ought to be totally dissolved; and that, as FREE and INDEPENDENT STATES, they have full Power to levy War, conclude Peace, contract Alliances, establish Commerce, and to do all other Acts and Things which INDEPENDENT STATES may of right do. AND for the support of this Declaration, with a firm reliance on the protection of divine Providence, we mutually pledge to each other our Lives, our Fortunes, and our sacred Honour.

Abraham Lincoln

The Declaration of Independence

Four score and seven years ago our fathers brought forth on this continent, a new nation, conceived in liberty, and dedicated to the proposition that all men are created equal.

Now we are engaged in a great civil war, testing whether that nation, or any nation so conceived and so dedicated, can long endure. We are met on a great battlefield of that war. We have come to dedicate a portion of that field, as a final resting place for those who here gave their lives that that nation might live. It is altogether fitting and proper that we should do this.

But, in a larger sense, we cannot dedicate—we cannot consecrate—we cannot hallow—this ground. The brave men, living and dead, who struggled here, have consecrated it, far above our poor power to add or detract. The world will little note, nor long remember what we say here, but it can never forget what they did here. It is for us the living, rather, to be dedicated here to the unfinished work which they who fought here have thus far so nobly advanced. It is rather for us to be here dedicated to the great task remaining before us—that from these honored dead we take increased devotion—that we here highly resolve that these dead shall not have died in vain—that this nation, under God, shall have a new birth of freedom—and that government of the people, by the people, for the people, shall not perish from the earth.

John F. Kennedy

Inaugural Address

Mr. Chief Justice, President Eisenhower, Vice President Nixon, President Truman, reverend clergy, fellow citizens, we observe today not a victory of party, but a celebration of freedom —symbolizing an end, as well as a beginning—signifying renewal, as well as change. For I have sworn before you and Almighty God the same solemn oath our forebears prescribed nearly a century and three quarters ago.

The world is very different now. For man holds in his mortal hands the power to abolish all forms of human poverty and all forms of human life. And yet the same revolutionary beliefs for which our forebears fought are still at issue around the globe—the belief that the rights of man come not from the generosity of the state, but from the hand of God.

We dare not forget today that we are the heirs of that first revolution. Let the word go forth from this time and place, to friend and foe alike, that the torch has been passed to a new generation of Americans—born in this century, tempered by war, disciplined by a hard and bitter peace, proud of our ancient heritage—and unwilling to witness or permit the slow undoing of those human rights to which this Nation has always been committed, and to which we are committed today at home and around the world.

Let every nation know, whether it wishes us well or ill, that we shall pay any price, bear any burden, meet any hardship, support any friend, oppose any foe, in order to assure the survival and the success of liberty.

This much we pledge—and more.

To those old allies whose cultural and spiritual origins we share, we pledge the loyalty of faithful friends. United, there is little we cannot do in a host of cooperative ventures. Divided, there is little we can do—for we dare not meet a powerful challenge at odds and split asunder.

To those new States whom we welcome to the ranks of the free, we pledge our words that one form of colonial control shall not have passed away merely to be replaced by a far greater iron tyranny. We shall not always expect to find them supporting our view. But we shall always hope to find them strongly supporting their own freedom—and to remember that, in the past, those who foolishly sought power by riding the back of the tiger ended up inside.

"Inaugural Address" by John F. Kennedy from *To Turn the Tide* by John F. Kennedy (Harper & Row, Publishers, 1962).

To those peoples in the huts and villages across the globe struggling to break the bonds of mass misery, we pledge our best efforts to help them help themselves, for whatever period is required—not because the Communists may be doing it, not because we seek their votes, but because it is right. If a free society cannot help the many who are poor, it cannot save the few who are rich.

To our sister republics south of our border, we offer a special pledge—to convert our good words into good deeds, in a new alliance for progress, to assist free men and free governments in casting off the chains of poverty. But this peaceful revolution of hope cannot become the prey of hostile powers. Let all our neighbors know that we shall join with them to oppose aggression or subversion anywhere in the Americas. And let every other power know that this hemisphere intends to remain the master of its own house.

To that world assembly of sovereign states, the United Nations, our last best hope in an age where the instruments of war have far outpaced the instruments of peace, we renew our pledge of support—to prevent it from becoming merely a forum for invective—to strengthen its shield of the new and the weak—and to enlarge the area in which its writ may run.

Finally, to those nations who would make themselves our adversary, we offer not a pledge but a request: that both sides begin anew the quest for peace, before the dark powers of destruction unleashed by science engulf all humanity in planned or accidental self-destruction.

We dare not tempt them with weakness. For only when our arms are sufficient beyond doubt can we be certain beyond doubt that they will never be employed.

But neither can two great and powerful groups of nations take comfort from our present course—both sides overburdened by the cost of modern weapons, both rightly alarmed by the steady spread of the deadly atom, yet both racing to alter that uncertain balance of terror that stays the hand of mankind's final war.

So let us begin anew—remembering on both sides that civility is not a sign of weakness, and sincerity is always subject to proof. *Let us never negotiate out of fear. But let us never fear to negotiate.*

Let both sides explore what problems unite us instead of laboring those problems which divide us.

Let both sides, for the first time, formulate serious and precise proposals for the inspection and control of arms—and bring the absolute power to destroy other nations under the absolute control of all nations.

Let both sides seek to invoke the wonders of science instead of its terrors. Together let us explore the stars, conquer the deserts, eradicate disease, tap the ocean depths, and encourage the arts and commerce.

Let both sides unite to heed in all corners of the earth the command of Isaiah—to "undo the heavy burdens and to let the oppressed go free."

And if a beachhead of cooperation may push back the jungle of suspicion, let both sides join in creating a new endeavor, not a new balance of power, but a new world of law, where the strong are just and the weak secure and the peace preserved.

All this will not be finished in the first 100 days. Nor will it be finished in the first 1,000 days, nor in the life of this administration, nor even perhaps in our lifetime on this planet. But let us begin.

In your hands, my fellow citizens, more than in mine, will rest the final success or failure of our course. Since this country was founded, each generation of Americans has been summoned to give testimony to its national loyalty. The graves of young Americans who answered the call to service are found around the globe.

Now the trumpet summons us again—not as a call to bear arms, though arms we need; not as a call to battle, though embattled we are; but a call to bear the burden of a long twilight struggle, year in, and year out, "rejoicing in hope, patient in tribulation"—a struggle against the common enemies of man: tyranny, poverty, disease, and war itself.

Can we forge against these enemies a grand and global alliance, North and South, East and West, that can assure a more fruitful life for all mankind? Will you join in that historic effort?

In the long history of the world, only a few generations have been granted the role of defending freedom in its hour of maximum danger. I do not shrink from this responsibility—I welcome it. I do not believe that any of us would exchange places with any other people or any other generation. The energy, the faith, the devotion which we bring to this endeavor will light our country and all who serve it—and the glow from that fire can truly light the world.

And so, my fellow Americans, ask not what your country can do for you: Ask what you can do for your country.

My fellow citizens of the world: Ask not what America will do for you, but what together we can do for the freedom of man.

Finally, whether you are citizens of America or citizens of the world, ask of us the same high standards of strength and sacrifice which we ask of you. With a good conscience our only sure reward, with history the final judge of our deeds, let us go forth to lead the land we love, asking His blessing and His help, but knowing that here on earth God's work must truly be our own.

A 2
B 3
C 4
D 5
E 6
F 7
G 8
H 9
I 0
J 1